Financial Mail
on Sun

Complete Guide
to the Financial
Markets

*Financial Mail
on Sunday*

Complete Guide
to the Financial
Markets

Dan Atkinson

RANDOM HOUSE
BUSINESS BOOKS

Published by Business Books in 2002

1 3 5 7 9 10 8 6 4 2

Copyright © 2001 by Dan Atkinson

Dan Atkinson has asserted his right under the Copyright, Designs and Patents Act, 1988 to be identified as the author of this work

First published by Business Books in 2002.

Business Books
The Random House Group Limited
20 Vauxhall Bridge Road, London, SW1V 2SA

Random House Australia (Pty) Limited
20 Alfred Street, Milsons Point, Sydney,
New South Wales 2061, Australia

Random House New Zealand Limited
18 Poland Road, Glenfield
Auckland 10, New Zealand

Random House (Pty) Limited
Endulini, 5a Jubilee Road, Parktown 2193, South Africa

The Random House Group Limited Reg. No. 954009

www.randomhouse.co.uk

A CIP catalogue record for this book
is available from the British Library

Papers used by Random House
are natural, recyclable products made from wood grown in sustainable forests. The manufacturing processes conform to the environmental regulations of the country of origin

ISBN 0 7126 8092 6

Typeset in Sabon by MATS, Southend-on-Sea, Essex
Printed and bound in Great Britain by
Mackays of Chatham PLC, Chatham, Kent

Dedication

For Sarah

Acknowledgements:

Of the very many people who gave advice and assistance. I should like to thank especially Duncan McKenzie, director of economics at International Financial Services London, for his patience and courtesy, and Ben Laurance, editor of Financial Mail on Sunday, for his scrutiny of the manuscript and his wise and friendly counsel thereon.

Contents

1

A view of the City: A personal introduction

Always give the same performance and, if possible, always wear the same suit

**Attributed to John Le Mesurier,
British actor, 1912–83**

WHEN the search was on for someone to write this book, it was inevitable, somehow, that those behind the project should turn to me. I had worked in the City. I had lived in the City for thirteen years. I was even educated courtesy of the City Corporation, at a school previously based in the City. My father had worked in the City. My brother had worked in the City. My stepmother had worked in the City. I even have a cousin by marriage working in the City.

Impressive, isn't it?

Well, no not really. In fact, this roster of City connections is misleading: any book about the City drawn from my family history would concentrate on, respectively, the newspaper business (in its Fleet Street days), the library service, the doings of a small firm of solicitors of the type you don't see advising multi-billion pound takeover bids, the College of Arms and the Bar.

In other words, all of the people above, while indeed plying their trades within the Square Mile, had no connection whatever with the financial services industry, for which 'the City' has served as a synonym for more than a century.

Nor, in fact, does a surprisingly large number of the City's huge daytime workforce. The Rector of St Bartholomew the Great, the meat porters of Smithfield Market, the judges at Old Bailey – all work in the City, but are not, in the hackneyed phrase, 'something in the City'. By the same token, not all of 'the City' is any more to be found inside the Square Mile. Whether Canary Wharf to the east or the thriving financial services centres of Leeds and Edinburgh to the north, 'City' business is increasingly conducted outside the City of London.

At the risk of hate mail from all points of the compass, I intend to use 'the City' in its widest sense throughout this book. After all, 'the City' is too useful a piece of shorthand to be discarded lightly – seven short letters do the work of dozens. However, the ease of using this beautifully concise piece of shorthand brings with it the responsibility of definition. What do we mean by the City?

Here, the confusion is long-standing, with large swathes of the population using the term as a catch-all phrase for commercial and industrial management in its entirety. Thus the striking engine driver, quizzed by journalists, will denounce his own paltry wages in comparison to the riches available to the 'businessmen I take up to the City every day'. He is not alone. To millions of people, if you are in a senior business position and you commute to London, by road or rail, then you are 'something in the City'.

The 1986 Guinness scandal did involve some City institutions. But Ernest Saunders, its chief villain (or victim, depending on your viewpoint) was an industrial manager with no City background, and the only connection Guinness itself enjoyed with the 'city' was with its original home, the city of Dublin. Nevertheless, Guinness was reported *ad nauseam* as 'a City scandal'.

Let's turn to the dictionary. Chambers' tells us: '(with "the" and often with cap[ital letter]) the centre of British financial affairs, most banks etc. being in the City of London'.

That is a bit more like it. The City is 'about' banking and finance, that is to say the processes of taking on money and lending it out, of creating vehicles in which money can be moved from those who have it to those who need it, with – it is hoped – both parties gaining from the transaction. There is currently an 'unemployment bond' being put together by philanthropic City types to raise a seven-figure sum to be lent to a selected project, tackling joblessness in deprived areas. The bond's backers will forgo their interest on the bond, thus the project is lent only the lesser sum that would have been left after interest is taken into account and interest is not charged. The balance of the bond is lent, interest-free, to a second, smaller project. By forgoing interest, the backers are effectively making a loss – all in a good cause.

At the risk of disillusioning you early on in the book, I have to tell you that this type of transaction is not common in the City.

So, on one level, the City is about moving money around from one place to another. On the basis of this unglamorous activity, the City makes – or rather, allows to be made, by its apologists in the media and Westminster – ludicrously inflated claims about its importance to the national well-being. During my sixteen years as a financial journalist, I have heard it claimed, variously, that the City / the financial services industry accounts for 10 per cent of the British economy, for nearly all Britain's net overseas earnings, for 20 per cent of all jobs, and is solely responsible for our ability to import more goods than we export. At times, it has been suggested that only the City prevents a general collapse into Haitian standards of living and sub-Saharan levels of national debt.

So what is the truth? We turn to an outfit called International Financial Services London. This is a lobby group set up specifically to plug the concerns and contribution of the City. Until the late-1990s, it took its name from so-called 'invisible' exports (services, rather than 'visible' goods), and called itself British Invisibles. This sounded too much like a bad 1960s science-fiction television programme, so now it is International Financial Services London.

Fortunately, for our purposes, IFSL is – despite its remit – absolutely straight, and its statistical and research service is excellent. What is more, it is free for all to read on the internet (www.ifsl.org.uk); giving away valuable material for nothing is another uncommon practice in the Square Mile. So, let us take a look at that contribution, courtesy of this fine organisation: 'The financial sector makes a substantial contribution to the UK economy equivalent to 5.8 per cent of gross domestic product . . . more than a third of this is generated by companies located in the City of London.'

Now, 5.8 per cent is not to be sniffed at. It is about two and a half times the contribution of agriculture, for example. On the other hand, it is only about a quarter of the contribution made by manufacturing industry. And it has fallen a little as well, from 6.1 per cent in 1998.

How about the City as a huge job spinner? Financial services on its broadest definition – in other words, taking in every building society branch and insurance brokerage – employed fewer than one million people in the UK in September 2000 – 996,000. That's just over three per cent of a workforce of 29 million. And that figure has fallen, as well, as bank branches have closed and financial service companies have 'consolidated' (i.e. merged with each other and sacked surplus workers). In 1989, the recent peak, financial services employed 1,051,000 people. The slump of the early 1990s cut that to 973,000 in 1993, while recovery took it back to 1,014,000 in 1999. Clearly, the figure goes up and down, and the 2000 total may well increase in years to come. But it hardly suggests a triumphant onward march for a financial services sector sweeping all outmoded industries before it and creating exciting new job opportunities for all.

The City itself has done rather better in job terms in recent years, suggesting the number of 'Chiefs' and sub-chiefs is increasing while the 'Indians' are given their cards and told their branch is 'no longer viable'. As a percentage of total financial services employment, the City of London accounted for 11.7 per cent in

1991; by 1998 that was up to 13.8 per cent.

So what about those 'invisibles'?

In 2000, Britain imported more goods ('visible' trade) than she exported to the tune of £28.8 billion. But she exported more invisibles than she imported, to the tune of £12.6 billion. Of course, that doesn't balance out the deficit on visibles, thus Britain clocked up a £16.1 billion current account deficit in 2000.

Let's break down those invisibles. The smallest share is 'transfers' to and from international organisations such as the European Union. Here, we ran a small deficit – £3.8 billion.

Then comes 'income'. This is much more promising. Here Britain recorded a £5.5 billion surplus. It includes returns on direct investments overseas (such as a British investment in a US car factory), on 'portfolio investment' (i.e. British investors buying shares in foreign companies), other investments and return on overseas 'reserve assets' – that is, securities and other assets held in reserve by British banks, insurance companies and so forth.

The smallest category is 'compensation of employees', in other words remittances home of salaries earned abroad by British subjects. This showed a £183 million surplus, small and insignificant enough almost to count as a 'rounding error' in the vast depths of Britain's current account numbers.

Direct investment is much chunkier – an £11 billion surplus. But how much of this is down to the City? Not a lot, according to IFSL. Four-fifths of direct overseas investments is accounted for by 'private non-financial corporations', which is the jargon term for business, commerce and industry – the players in the real economy.

Portfolio investment, where the City dominates, managed a modest £383 million surplus, with reserve assets chipping in another £985 million.

On 'other investment' – anything that fits none of the other categories – Britain turned in a turkey of a performance, running a £7 billion deficit. Let us be generous and assume none of this loss was due to the financial services industry. Even so, the figures hardly bear out the idea of the City bravely holding the line against a current-account collapse. The real economy earnings on direct investment – £8.8 billion – more than make up for the 'other investment' losses. Financial services' £2.2 billion share of direct investment earnings, plus the £383 million earned on portfolio investment and £985 million on reserve assets, wouldn't come close, totalling just £3.6 billion.

Of course, there's more to the City than simply sitting on overseas investments. Larger by far is the portion of Britain's trade in services that is covered by the umbrella term 'financial'. Overall, in 2000, this earned Britain £10.3 billion, unchanged on the year before and up from £8.9 billion in 1998.

Using rather different figures, which combine earnings from both investments overseas and trade in services, and which are calculated on a different basis, the contributions of the different sectors broke down this way in 1999:

The banks have netted £14 billion from the rest of the world against £9 billion two years earlier. Insurance companies netted a further £7 billion, up from £6 billion in 1997. And pension funds lifted their contribution to the balance of payments from £1.7 billion in 1997 to £2.8 billion in 1999.

Earnings, like shares, can of course go down as well as up. In the volatile heart of the City, securities dealing made just £1.9 billion for Britain in 1999, against £2.7 billion in 1997. There were also decreases in unit trust earnings, from £851 million to £785 million and in investment trust earnings, from £342 million to £219 million. Futures and options dealing took a knock as well, from £150 million net earnings to £143 million.

To return to where we were, the City is primarily a machine for moving money about. That is not an overly-glamorous task, and its importance to the national economy is, as we have seen, considerable but far from critical. Nor is the City uniformly efficient in this rather mundane core task. True, large sums of money held by City institutions or important clients can be flashed across the globe in the time it takes an electrical impulse to zip down a wire. But it is a different story when it comes to the transmission of small amounts of money held by ordinary people and small and medium-sized businesses. By 2000, the sluggishness of the payments clearing system – chiefly cheque clearing – had provoked a national outcry, and the eleven banks running Britain's payments systems responded with a pledge of same-day clearing of cheques (in contrast to the current minimum of three days) by the middle of 2001. Of course, same-day clearing had long been available to important corporate clients, but, the banks pledged, it would soon be available to all. Truly, the twenty-first century had dawned in banking.

I am writing this in the middle of 2001 and same-day cheque clearing for all has not yet arrived. Nor is it going to. On 11 August, Richard Tyson-Davies, external affairs chief for the clearing system APACS, told BBC Radio 4's *Inside Money* that the banks had shelved their promised same-day system. 'It is on the back-burner,' he told a reporter. Continuing the culinary metaphor, he added: 'It hasn't been taken off the cooker'. The cost of the system had been too great, he said. Asked if this meant the banks had dropped same-day clearing to save money, he replied: 'True'.

Of course, the cost to the banks of same-day clearing is more than just the expense of setting up an all-singing all-dancing payments system capable of handling the millions of cheques written by the hoi polloi. During the three days the money is unavailable for the use of either the payer or the payee, it is, happily, available for the use of the banking system. Banks make considerable money, perhaps £800,000 a day from the 'float' – the £4 billion in transit from one customer to another at any one time – lending it out on the overnight market, either to each other or to other major corporate borrowers. In light of this, it is hardly surprising that, as *Inside Money* discovered, the delay is not in the payments system as such – the existing payments machinery can settle a cheque in nine hours – but either side of the system, in the banks themselves.

This is the first essential fact to be grasped about the collection of businesses and institutions that make up the City – they are far, far better at making money for themselves than for their customers. So biased in this direction are their internal systems that, when those systems fail, they invariably fail on the side of the institution, not the customer.

My time as a financial journalist has been routinely punctuated by announcements from financial services companies of all types, regretting a 'breakdown in controls' that has resulted in a notifiable (i.e. large) loss. This 'breakdown' is usually described as having been spotted during a routine inspection by auditors or supervisors, leading one to wonder how many other 'breakdowns' have gone unnoticed. Because the one common factor is that these breakdowns always but always result in losses to clients, not to the institution. I am not talking about fraud here, but about a casual disregard for the client's interests. You can bet that any 'breakdown' that threatened the institution's own profits would be noticed and put right without any hanging around for a routine audit or regulatory inspection.

Of course, there is a rather more elevated view of the City than simply as a place where money is moved around and occasionally 'clipped' to provide the generous remuneration without which the money-movers are unable to perform their tasks. In this view, the City is not about money at all, but about risk.

Some aspects of the City are self-evidently about judging and pricing risk. Insurance is one, venture capital another. Indeed, venture capital used to be called 'risk capital', but this sounded a little risky, whereas 'venture capital' had dashing overtones of Sir Walter Raleigh. But risk is not confined to patches of the Square Mile; it is the thread that connects all its disparate activities. The City is a market in risk. Its personnel evaluate risk and put a price on it. They package it up and trade it. In doing so, they actually help the world to manage risk. They make the world a safer place.

At least, that is what you will be told.

For the investor, obviously, risk is ever-present, for the small, private investor. Swiss-American speculator Max Gunther, writing in 1985, noted:

> People who offer to counsel you in money management almost always call themselves 'investment' advisers, not speculation advisers. It sounds more serious and impressive that way . . . But they are all dealing with speculation . . . They just don't like to say it.
>
> There is even a class of securities that financial experts like

to call 'investment-grade'. That makes them sound very dignified, awe-inspiring and super-safe. An adviser, talking about such a security in appropriately solemn tones, can convince a novice that this is the long-sought high-paying investment without risk.[1]

Citing a few choice examples of investment grade securities that took a dive and stayed in the doldrums for years afterwards – IBM, General Motors, Radio Corporation of America – Gunther demolishes the whole notion.

And what goes for the small investor must surely go for the large investor too? Quite right, although large investors – whether banks or pension funds – tend to be better informed than smaller investors and to be able to spot trouble more quickly. But a great deal of activity in the City has nothing whatever to do with investment as such, and everything to do with pushing someone else (the client) into the line of fire while taking a fee for doing so.

Straightforward stockbroking is the most obvious example of this. The broker takes a commission for buying and selling securities on behalf of a client. Investment banks, by contrast, run their own trading books, attempting to make a 'turn' on the difference between buying a security and selling it. Surely this involves risk?

Yes it does, although the investment banks go to great lengths to minimise the risk, using powerful computers to keep their books in balance. On occasion, disreputable traders working for investment banks have taken the principle of protecting the bank's positions at all costs to an extreme (and illegal) extent, with so-called 'rat trading', in which profitable positions in the market are booked, after the event, to the bank's in-house trading profits and loss-making trades are booked to clients who have, unwisely, given the bank discretion to manage their portfolios.

Rat trading is rare. Yet major City institutions make great efforts to take as few risks as possible. This risk-aversion can have ironic consequences. In the so-called 'derivatives' markets, products

1. Max Gunther; *The Zurich Axioms*; Souvenir Press; 1985.

are sold explicitly on the basis that they reduce risk. For example, a bank has a basket of shares that it hopes will hold its present value of £100 for another six months and fears the shares in the basket may fall, cutting into the £100 total. The derivatives market will sell the bank a contract in which the bank sells the shares now for £100, with delivery delayed for six months. Should the shares rise in the next six months, the bank will forgo the extra profit, but should they fall, the bank's position is protected, as it is able to collect £100 in six months' time.

Ironically, such attempts to eliminate risk may have precisely the opposite effect, because derivatives markets can take on an unpredictable life of their own. In the 1987 worldwide stock market crash, derivative products – that had been bought precisely to insure against any fall in US share prices – fell very heavily as the stock market plunged, because those who held the products were selling them now to lock in the value of the real shares they held.

Should exchange prices fail to recover, they would have sold at the old, higher prices now.

Unfortunately, mass-selling of the derivative products sent prices on the derivatives exchanges plunging well below the prices of the real shares on which the derivative contracts were based. Speculators seeking a quick profit thus sold the real shares on the Stock Exchange and bought contracts in those same shares at a lower price on the derivatives exchange, further depressing share prices, and triggering more selling of contracts taken to protect the value of those shares . . . and so on.

It would be tempting to conclude that, far from bravely making a market in risk, shouldering the problems of the world, and helping ordinary people and businesses to lay off many of the hazards in their financial lives, the City is frantically passing the parcel of risk from one institution to another, with none keen to hold the fizzing bomb for any length of time. And there is doubtless more than a little truth in this.

But the real question at the heart of the City is whether it is essentially based on risk or prudence. Put another way, is the City fundamentally a system of prices (which, reflecting risk, go up and down) or a system of fees (which, being fixed, are safe and predictable). The immediate answer is that it is both: some parts of the financial-services industry are fee-earning, others are price-making, and others still combine the two.

However, the creative tension that drives the financial-services industry is the pursuit of the rewards that come from risk-taking with the security that comes from fee-earning. There is nothing disreputable in this. Were you to be offered odds of 100-1 on Christmas in Britain falling in December in the year 2003, would you not take the bet with both hands? Indeed, the entire business community is, in a sense, driven by the desire not to embrace the competitive ethos but to escape from it – to earn the profits due to a victor in a free-enterprise economy while doing everything possible to ensure that any real-life competitors are few and far between, and preferably hobbled by the sort of Government regulation against which businessmen rail in public. The economist John Kenneth Galbraith has poked fun at senior business executives who complain about relentlessly tough conditions in 'the market', which is, says Professor Galbraith, 'a place most of them have never been'.

This dynamic – the search for maximum reward with minimum risk – is often translated into a phrase that you will hear many times in the City, which is that 'markets are driven by two things only – fear and greed'. That isn't a bad aphorism as far as it goes; it does, after all, summarise quite pithily the risk / reward tension that we have discussed. Unfortunately, 'fear'n'greed' has been elevated to the status of a Unified Theory of Everything in the City – a status it does not deserve. Because alongside fear and greed is an equally powerful motive force in the City – optimism. You will have heard vague talk from time to time about 'bulls and bears' – those who act on the belief that the market they are investing in will rise, and those acting on the belief that it will fall. You may assume there is some sort of rough balance between the two; that they represent the yin and yang of the City.

Nothing could be further from the truth.

When it comes to a bull population, the City is like the Royal

Agricultural Show. And when it comes to a bear population, the City is like . . . the Royal Agricultural Show. Just look at the tons of analysis put out by investment banks and brokers, advising clients on which shares to sell, which to hold and which to buy. Even in a falling stock market, the number of 'sell' recommendations can be as little as 10 per cent of the total. Much the same goes for other securities as well. Even away from exchange-based business, the City's relentless optimism holds sway, from the colossal over-the-counter purchases of debt issued by such international titans as Argentina, to the ballooning amounts of consumer credit advanced by the clearing banks and other financial institutions to consumers with no obvious means of repayment.

In part, this is self-interest of the most fundamentally Darwinian kind. Ultimately, an everlasting bull market is a theoretical possibility, while a long-running bear market would conclude with the extinction of all securities trading and financial business in general. More to the point, a bull market is both generous and forgiving; mediocre traders can produce respectable results when asset values are rising, and the benign tide of asset inflation will lift even disastrous speculations off the rocks. Career opportunities are plentiful, bonuses are generous, and a virtuous circle of profit is set in motion.

A bear market throws this process into a disastrous reverse thrust. Who, having decided on a career in the City, is going to prefer the latter to the former? It would be as if a newly-qualified barrister specialising in matrimonial law were immediately to make a large donation to Relate. The difference between the Bar and the City is that the Bar is unable directly to influence the buoyancy of its own market (other than by asking its many members in Parliament to pass ever-more complex legislation, a service those members seem happy to provide anyway), whereas the City in total – both the 'sell side', the investment banks and others, and the 'buy side', the large fund managers – is in a powerful position at least to encourage asset values on their upward march.

But self-interest is only a part of it. More fundamental still is a total climate-change in the City during the past quarter-century – a

shift from fearing the future to a firm conviction that the best is yet
to come.

In the mid-1970s, for example, the outlook for the City as a
whole was grim to say the least. Between 1 January and 31
December 1974, the FT Index collapsed from 344 points to 163, a
plunge that made Black Monday on 19 October 1987 look like a
mild correction in values (as, indeed, it proved to be). In contrast to
1987, nobody in power in 1974 seemed much interested in lending
a helping hand as brokers haemorrhaged money and investment
groups such as Slater Walker slid into insolvency. On the contrary,
the newly-elected Labour government's powerful left-wing was
committed both to wholesale nationalisation of major industrial
companies (thus shrinking the share base of the Stock Exchange),
and to taking control of banking and financial services. For the left,
the crash was stark evidence of the 'crisis of capitalism', and many
in the City agreed, although they blamed Labour's victory in the 28
February election for sparking that crisis.

Were a young radical of those days to have taken lunch in the
City and to have suggested to his host that the days of the Square
Mile and of the capitalist system as a whole were numbered, he may
well have found that host in gloomy agreement. But had he gone on
to ask why the host's firm had no women partners, or childcare
facilities, or any senior employees other than those hired on the tried
and trusted basis of 'family and firsts', (those with first-class degrees)
the same host would have looked at him as if he were stark raving
mad.

Today, of course, the mirror-image prevails. There is no quicker
way for an outsider to gain an oddball reputation than to hint that,
for example, giving the Bank of England power over interest rates
may not prove to be the masterstroke it is currently proclaimed.
Strange glances can be instantly provoked by the suggestion that deregulation of financial services, or the abolition of exchange controls,
may have been serious strategic errors. In the mid-1990s, one
journalist was being lunched by the boss of a merchant bank keen to
promote the bank's intention of becoming a big player in the so-
called private finance initiative, the scheme to bring private-sector

money and expertise to the running of certain public services. When the journalist suggested that public services may be best run by public servants, the lunch was terminated more or less on the spot.

But mention equal opportunities, or family-friendly working practices, and the same audience will put on a show of political correctness that would have shamed Ken Livingstone's Greater London Council in the early 1980s.

When the City thought it was going to lose its livelihood, it clung ferociously to all the things that did not really matter: the white-tie dinners, the gentlemen's-club atmosphere and the general public-school ethos. Now its central function is secure, it can cheerfully abandon these fripperies and concentrate on the task in hand: profit.

In the process, it must be said, the 'City type' has mutated to the point of disappearance. This, rather than computer screens or 'dress-down Friday', is the largest visible change of the last two decades, the real symptom of the shift from pessimism to optimism. Not that there was ever one 'City type', but rather that the fine gradations among the different types – clearly noticeable up to the mid-1980s – have largely vanished.

Traditionally, a merchant banker 'cut' (snubbed) a stock-broker, and a stockbroker cut a stockjobber – what we would now call a share trader. All three cut clearing bankers – generally regarded as provincial grammar school boys in polyester shirts – except when they wanted their money, which was quite a lot of the time. Across the City in the Lloyd's insurance market, the distinctions were based less on hostility and more on an ethos of 'different strokes for different folks'. Thus the brokers (who acted for clients seeking insurance cover) projected an image of top-class salesmanship and the underwriters (who wrote the actual policies) were cast in the role of creative genius / madman. Both breeds despised the personnel of the mainstream insurance companies for their caution and their inability to have a good time.

Everyone regarded commodities traders as 'nutters' or 'spivs'; bond dealers were boring; foreign-currency traders were forever teetering on the edge of 'burn-out' (and so were mentally unstable and unlikely to prove good company for very long), and everybody but everybody despised 'licensed dealers'. These unfortunates were a sort of second-class type of stockbroker licensed by the Department of Trade and Industry, and were widely believed to be no better than crooks and thieves, although this was not always the case.

Technology and greatly altered institutional structures have gone a long way to erasing these caste distinctions, particularly in the stock market and the general field of corporate finance. But perhaps the biggest change is that the old labels have ceased to apply.

Up until the mid-1980s, a merchant banker was defined as a senior employee of a member of the Accepting Houses Committee, membership of the committee being what defined an institution as a merchant bank. A stockbroker or jobber was an individual member of the London Stock Exchange (all firms then being partnerships). To trade commodities required membership of a number of (sometimes tiny) commodities exchanges. A banker was a person considered 'fit and proper' to be so by the Bank of England.

Today, individuals are licensed by one body, the Financial Services Authority (FSA), and they are licensed to *do* things rather than to *be* things. These 'authorised activities' are many and various, and carefully calibrated to take account of the experience and qualifications of the person concerned. Nevertheless, they are grouped into a number of broad categories, of which the most important are:

- **Management and control**
  Management of part or all of a financial services business and control of other people is a key authorised activity and authorisation is probably the most prestigious of the FSA's 'tickets'. The downside is that, should anything go wrong on the manager's watch, the FSA disciplinary machine will be correspondingly harsher in its attitude.

- **Trading on an exchange**
  This ticket is the essential accessory for anyone wishing to ape

the characters in films such as *Wall Street, Limit Down* and *Trading Places*. Without authorisation, you won't get anywhere near a market place.

- **Advising clients**

  Every investment salesman needs a ticket in this category, whether they be pitching a huge equity placing to the manager of a multi-billion pound investment fund or plugging Scottish Widows savings plans to, well, a Scottish widow. Corporate finance advisers – merchant bankers, in traditional usage – will almost certainly need this ticket, unless they are styled as management consultants and claim to be offering advice solely on business management rather than financial and investment matters. Also caught in this net are the City's analysts, the in-house economists and other financial wizards who cast a critical eye over the latest trade figures, Marks & Spencer profits and Japanese stock market returns and issue the abovementioned 'buy' and (occasional) 'sell' notices and other pieces of research. The only way out is to consult only on broad economic matters and never to recommend any particular security. Actually, that is not quite true. There is a category of people who can offer specific advice without being authorised – financial journalists.

- **Handling client money**

  This is the 'hot' ticket, covering a very sensitive area of financial services. Throughout the 1990s, cases of misappropriation of client funds plagued the 'retail' sector of the financial services industry – the mis-named 'insurance brokers' and others who specialise in the savings and investments of ordinary people. Often the person concerned had held an 'advice only' licence from the regulator, but had talked the clients into handing over their funds nevertheless. The most common fraud in this area was 'teeming and lading', or what the Americans call a 'Ponzi scheme'. Investment returns due to existing clients were paid out of the initial payment of new clients. For as long as fresh investors could be lined up, the scheme could run on. The original investments, of course, had been either stolen or lost in fruitless speculation.

Managers of large funds, it goes without saying, need this ticket.

More than anything, it is this type of 'functional' authorisation that has blurred the old distinctions. If someone is an authorised controller or manager, working for, let us say, Dresdner Kleinwort Wasserstein, in charge of the paperclip department, no-one is going to object should he wish to describe himself as a merchant banker. There are those who say the old distinctions have been replaced by new ones, and there is something in this. Perhaps the biggest divide is between those who are 'customer facing' and those who are not – in particular the difference between securities traders on the one hand and securities salesmen and corporate financiers on the other. Traders spend much of their time dealing with other traders, with the result that the general ethos is rather more rugged – sometimes coarse – than that governing the outlook of salesmen and corporate financiers, who are forever on their way to meeting an actual or potential client. The trader / salesman distinction can be overdone, however, fuelled by *Wall Street* style mythology. People have switched between the roles and will continue to do so. Similarly, the suggestion that there is a huge difference between the manners and mores of the 'sell' side (chiefly investment banks) and the 'buy' side (chiefly pension funds) is an exaggeration – former 'sellers' have carved out successful careers as 'buyers' and there has been traffic in the other direction.

The distinction between trading and corporate finance is more evident, not least because many corporate financiers have come up through the ranks of accountancy, only later shifting over to investment banking. The aggression needed in a good trader must, at the very least, be sublimated in corporate finance, where the three most important considerations are held to be the client, then the client and finally the client.

Yet foreign ownership, and the concentration under one corporate roof of a host of services formerly provided by members of a variety of self-contained closed shops, is not only rubbing out the old differences; it is bringing to the City a new breed of people who scarcely consider themselves 'City types' of any description, old or new. They prefer to think in terms of the elite 'symbolic-analyst' workers identified in 1991 by President Bill Clinton's future Labour Secretary Robert Reich as the top dogs in the new world order. These have been defined as knowledge workers who are problem identifiers, solvers and brokers. In the words of Professor Ian Angell of the London School of Economics, these people 'create and manipulate cyphers in a way that adds value'.

This is the sort of language that the new breed likes to hear; they may not be acquainted with the writings of Mr Reich or Professor Angell, but they would agree with every word. They see the City institutions, already vastly bigger after two decades of mergers and takeovers, converging inexorably into a handful of 'professional services firms' – giant banks-cum-brokerages-cum-fund managers-cum accountants / consultants – who will pay, at the top level, truly spectacular rewards.

We are a long way down this road already. In 1980, the head of a big-four clearing bank earned about ten times the salary of a skilled Ford worker at Dagenham. By 2000, that ratio had widened to about 250 times.

As for the convergence, that will be apparent as you read some of the later chapters in this book. How do you discuss derivatives in one chapter, while having a separate chapter on commodities? The commodities market is dominated by derivatives. So is the corporate bond market, which has a section all of its own. Then there are the 'old professions', law and accountancy, increasingly mixing it with upstart investment bankers. And so on. Today's City really does fit together in a way that yesterday's never did. It fits together also into what has become – for the first time since 1913 – a single international capital market, and is rapidly becoming a single international market for investment products and general financial services. Thirty years ago, the City's chief link-point with the outside world was the foreign exchange market, which transmitted, in rather jerky signals, external investment opinion about Britain.

Today the barriers are down and every transaction is, potentially, a foreign transaction. Rules for the conduct of business used to be laid down behind closed doors at the Stock Exchange or some other self-regulatory body. Now they are more likely to have originated with the European Union, the Bank for International Settlements in Basle or the Group of Seven financial stability forum.

Above all, the City's investment banks and securities houses are now very largely foreign owned. This is the end point of a process that began two decades ago whereby the City itself was thrown to the mercy of the market forces that it had long prescribed for every other industry.

The City gent, then, is certainly dead, and the City type is seriously endangered. Yet the City is, in many ways, more profitable and more significant on the world stage than ever before.

This is a paradox of the modern City. As we shall discover, it is far from being the only one.

2

A Place Apart: 'The fabled City'

And finally, between the rich West
End and the poor East End, like a
jewel wedged between a marble slab
and an earthen floor, lay the fabled
'City', the oldest London of all

Susan Howatch,
The High Flyer **(Little Brown, 1999)**

IT is thought London's name derives from the ancient British word 'Londo', meaning 'a wild place'. To the City's critics, that description holds good today. Founded by the Romans in about 50 AD, it became the capital of Roman Britain after the rebellion of Queen Boadicea in 61 AD.

Edward the Confessor established rival Westminster as a political seat, but it was not until the reign of William the Conqueror from 1066 to 1087 that the division between the traders of the City and the court up the river became explicit. This was a little hard on the City merchants, who had done their best to ingratiate themselves with the new king. To this day, references in official circles are never to 'William the Conqueror' but to the more neutral 'William the Norman'.

It did them no good. Conqueror or Norman (or even Norman Conqueror), William I distrusted the City and preferred to keep his court uncontaminated at Westminster and his treasury even further away, in Winchester, still the nation's official capital.

This division between the two cities at the heart of London persisted down the centuries, with the result that the Square Mile has long seemed a place apart. Today, while appearing on the map as just one of London's twenty-two boroughs, the City's powers and system of election are very different from those of its fellow authorities in the greater metropolitan area. Every year, the City's twenty-five wards elect 112 Common Councilmen. They form the main body of the corporation, and work in tandem with the twenty-five Aldermen, one for each ward, of whom at any one time one will be Lord Mayor.

The franchise, covering both individuals and business partnerships, has been much criticised both by those who believe the business vote is undemocratic and by those who find the partnership criterion anachronistic, excluding as it does the giant limited companies that dominate the modern City. Proposals for reform are under discussion at the time of writing, with the Corporation suggesting a widening of the business franchise to include limited companies. Critics in the governing Labour Party retort that this would merely entrench the undemocratic nature of the City voting system, claiming a business vote has no place in the twenty-first century. The Corporation bats back this criticism by asking whether anyone seriously suggests the future of this priceless asset should be entrusted to a few hundred people living in the Barbican estate.

Whatever the outcome, it will be a long time before the City becomes just another London borough.

But the sense of the City as a place apart extends well beyond its unique local government arrangements. Down the centuries, kings, queens and governments, in their attempts to access the nation's wealth, have regularly found themselves effectively negotiating with a nebulous yet unmistakable power. Rulers in other countries, accustomed to treating society's treasure as their own, would have been appalled by such a state of affairs, yet it can be argued that such a rudimentary balance of power has proved a cornerstone of the rule of law in Britain. Furthermore, this clear delineation has greatly helped the development of sophisticated debt markets, helping to make the City a hub of technical expertise in raising money and trading securities.

And if the City is something of a state within a state, and then it has, usually, been happy to tolerate the same privilege when enjoyed by others. Those who delight in political curios will cherish the unique self-governing status of, for example, the Inner and Middle Temple just off Fleet Street, whose lawyerly inhabitants have reserved to themselves such powers as the issuing of parking tickets. Similarly, the ancient and peculiar rights of the Dean and Chapter of St Paul's Cathedral over neighbouring Paternoster Square have proved something of a headache for developers anxious to unlock the potential of the site, or further vandalise the heart of the City, depending upon your point of view.

The political significance of the City did not, over the centuries, disappear entirely as commercial interests took over. Apart from anything else, the presence within its boundaries of vital state institutions such as the Central Criminal Court at Old Bailey, the Guildhall and the Mansion House, ensured a high political profile. But with state power moving up river to Westminster, and with the Port of London, and its associated trading opportunities close at hand, the City's direction was clear from the Middle Ages onwards. It is not so much that the City, in the words of Alexandre Ledru-Rollin, 'has never raised its eyes or its heart above its masts and cargoes'. Rather, it has had to establish a role for itself in the absence of the obvious function of serving as the nation's capital city and political seat.

That said, it was not until the late nineteenth century that 'the City' became a synonym for the nation's chief commercial, financial and legal district. Indeed, it was not finally until the heavy bombing of World War Two flattened much of what remained of ordinary working-class housing in the Square Mile that the contemporary notion of the City as a lightly populated centre full of offices and trading floors took root.

In Dickens' time, the City's commercial importance was undoubted and yet it remained simultaneously a centre of slum housing and very high rates of street crime. And one hundred years before Dickens, both Whitecross and Redcross streets, the first still with us, the second now buried somewhere beneath the Barbican, were notorious no-go areas for respectable citizens. Worse still, the so-called 'rents' on the fringes of the City, such as Greenhill Rents near Smithfield Market and Chichester Rents off Chancery Lane, were especially feared. Under the archaic eighteenth-century legal system, they were, as Church land, places in which criminals could claim permanent sanctuary. This is particularly ironic in the case of Chichester Rents, given that during the 1990s it was the site of an Old Bailey satellite court established especially to deal with large-scale fraud trials.

Lawlessness abated during the Victorian era, although the City was far from being the smoothly purring machine of the post-war period. The paradox, whereby the City was simultaneously a place in which poor people lived, and to which rich people travelled from fashionable west London in order to raise or make money, gave the City its unique late-Victorian character. This was enriched by the addition of a third social group – the striving middle-classes, who would staff the banks, brokerages and insurance companies of the Square Mile. Here was the world of Pooter, hero of *The Diary of a Nobody*, by George Grossman (1892), and of his ill-starred son Lupin, the would-be speculator sometimes hailed as history's first yuppie.

Even between the wars, the City of TS Eliot – a poet whose many great accomplishments included the ability to make both the Square Mile and the Church of England seem romantic – contains characters other than the 'hollow men' who serviced its institutions and lunched at the Cannon Street Hotel. In Lower Thames Street, for example, the narrator of *The Waste Land* comes across fishermen drinking in a pub to the sound of mandolins.

While the last of the dockers hung on into the 1960s, something of the working-class City survived. But with docking moving down river to Tilbury, with the mighty production industry of Fleet Street migrating in the same direction and with e-mail and secure electronic transmission heralding the demise of the Square Mile's messenger boys (none of whom ever seemed to be under the age of fifty), the City has lost most of its blue-collar ballast.

Some would say that in doing so it has lost much of its old charm. The hard-headed would respond that the City is not a museum and that no sacrifices are too great to ensure 'London's position as an international financial centre'.

Those words are placed in inverted commas because, as the newcomer will soon discover, it is not possible to spend very long in the City without hearing them. One could say without too much exaggeration that they make up something of a mantra for those in senior positions across the Square Mile. Their constant repetition is a symptom of a certain insecurity, but at the same time an affirmation of what life – or at least life in the City – is all about. 'London's position as an international financial centre' is to the City bigwig what 'Britain punching above her weight in world affairs' is to the Foreign Office mandarin – an unquestioned good, a tremendous thing in its own right.

Indeed, the outside observer may be forgiven for believing this dominance stretches back centuries, during which time London's international status has been largely unchallenged. Only recently, he may believe, has it regrettably been necessary to share some of this status with Wall Street and, more recently, Tokyo.

Nothing could be further from the truth. In the late Middle Ages, London was outshone by far by the banking centres of Italy such as Florence and Venice. In the late sixteenth and early seventeenth century, Amsterdam seemed set fair to emerge as the financial hub of the post-medieval world. Smaller centres such as Hamburg and Sweden offered real competition.

The root of London's status as a financial centre is inextricably intertwined with its position as a trading port. In 1566, the Royal Exchange was created as a clearing house for business amongst merchants both British and foreign. This institution (it would be misleading to use the word 'building' given it has twice been replaced) has been central to the development of the City. At different times, it has housed the Stock Exchange, the East India

Company, Lloyd's of London and the London International Financial Futures Exchange.

Yet in its early days, the exchange was little more than a market place for the sale of physical commodities such as cloth, wine and spices. For the development of finance as an activity in its own right, the City had to await the growth of the coffee houses in the seventeenth century. The first of these, founded by Daniel Edwards, started something of a craze. The establishment later to be hailed as the precursor of the Stock Exchange – Jonathan's coffee house – was founded in 1698 just a few short years after the opening of Lloyd's coffee house in 1687, from which developed the eponymous insurance market.

The story of the three centuries since then has been the story not only of the tail wagging the dog in terms of finance coming to dominate shipping and trading, but of that tail becoming immensely larger and more important than its erstwhile master. Even developments that ought to have proved catastrophic for the fledgling City – such as the notorious South Sea Bubble and the costly drain on national resources represented by the Napoleonic wars – ultimately proved grist to the mill in the creation of a technically complex and outward-looking financial market place.

Yet challengers were always present, chief among them the French, who were as keen to outpace Britain financially as they were to overhaul her industrial performance and imperial reach. The sub-plot of all the grand schemes for reforming French banking, public finance and currency during the hundred years from Napoleon to the Panama Canal investment scandal, was the replacement of London by Paris as universal financial pivot point. Emile Zola encapsulates this in his novel *Money* (1896) with politics and finance stirred into a heady brew as the anti-hero plots the creation of a gigantic bank. At one and the same time, he hopes, the bank will dish 'the Jew Gundermann' (Baron James de Rothschild), make France the greatest financial power in Europe, establish French hegemony over the Near East, put the Pope on a throne in Jerusalem and, naturally, net the anti-hero a very large fortune.

More recently, and rather more seriously, the City has faced three potentially terminal crises. The first, in the immediate aftermath of World War Two, related directly to Britain's shattered financial position. An apparently lethal cocktail of exchange control, devaluation and the nationalisation of large chunks of the equity base of the stock market's trading operations, threatened to push the Square Mile to the margins of national life.

The second major trauma was linked to chronic weakness in Britain's position overseas. Continuing balance of payments deficits, along with rising inflation at home and around the world, led in the late 1960s to a frenzy of speculation in the City, with hot money pouring out of sterling and into gold. In November 1967 sterling was devalued. The following year the gold market in London had to be closed, a move that threatened the City's position as the pivot of world bullion trading.

A mere six years later the third crisis struck, although there are those who would argue that the stock market crash of February 1974 and the soaring inflation that accompanied it were merely the final boiling over of the witches' brew that had started to bubble at the end of the 1960s. The crisis of the mid-1970s hit everyone: while the future of City firms was in doubt as business slumped, the government itself found it nearly impossible to find buyers for its own gilt-edged stock.

Give or take the odd price crash – of which Black Monday on 19 October 1987 is the best known – the City has, on the surface, never looked back from the dark days three decades ago. At the turn of the Millennium, turnover in shares and other investments had boomed, share price indices reached record highs, and salaries and bonuses paid to the cream of City workers dwarfed the sort of money that could be expected even by senior partners in days gone by.

What explains this remarkable recovery? For the City's top brass, the miracle cure can be summed up in one word: change.

It is not simply that life in the Square Mile has altered out of all recognition since the late 1960s, although it undoubtedly has. It is not even that a powerful faction within the City's boundaries has actively promoted and encouraged such change, although this, too, is beyond question. Rather, it is the case that change has become the City's standard operating procedure. The key figures who have pushed through some of the colossal shifts in practice and structure during the past two decades could hardly, with the greatest respect, have been described as young Turks.

Of course, to critics it is notable that the City is happy to change absolutely everything – other than the economic and financial system under which we live. As we saw in the preface, the City's new mood of confidence over the past twenty years has banished all such talk from polite company.

Indeed, the newly-emboldened City has been expanding down river; fears in the 1980s that the huge Docklands development would usurp the City by supplying modern spacious accommodation for banks and brokerages proved unfounded. This had less to do with the exodus itself – which did happen to a considerable extent – but rather with the failure of Docklands to develop any character or centre of its own. Whereas in the 1980s the 'threat' had been couched in cultural as much as commercial terms, the non-appearance of the much-vaunted 'Water City' environment made Docklands rather more of an annexe of the Square Mile and rather less of a rival centre.

Few will be surprised if, early in the current century, the City Fathers are able to persuade a review commission on local government that the Square Mile ought to become rather less square and considerably more than a mile, with a deft redrawing of its boundaries in an easterly direction.

The turning point in the City's affairs – in the official history, at least – came in 1986, the year before Black Monday, with the series of reforms centred on the Stock Exchange that came to be known as Big Bang. In combination with another series of radical changes affecting financial institutions outside the exchange – in particular, a new *laissez-faire* attitude to mergers between banks, to cross-border competition from Europe, to incursions by different sorts of institutions on each other's business, and to the transformation of mutual building societies and insurers into profit-making limited companies – the Big Bang reforms were to set in train an unstoppable series of changes.

By the turn of the century, even diehards who had opposed

new-fangled technology, the destruction of the tried and tested partnership system in broking (the business of buying and selling shares on behalf of clients) and market-making (the business of trading shares on one's own book), the arrival of huge quantities of foreign capital (and with it foreign control) and, perhaps above all, the surrender of the City's cherished independence and self-regulation; even they could look back and agree that all had, after all, been for the best.

But curiously, while this may indeed be the best of times for the City, it is simultaneously quite possibly if not the worst then at least the most troubling time of the last two hundred years. Quite simply, the enormous changes wrought in the Square Mile in the name of international competitiveness were, by the turn of the twenty-first century, beginning to look increasingly like a devil's bargain.

Come the year 2001, there was not a single British-owned major investment bank left in the City. In a quarter of London where, as we have seen, optimism is not only infectious but a virtual job requirement, this was hailed by one and all as posing no problem whatsoever. Ownership, they decreed, was irrelevant; what mattered was that banks and other institutions should wish to base themselves in the City to take advantage of the local skills base, the friendly legal and tax structure, and the favourable position in the middle of the world's time zones.

A few sceptics worried about a 'Wimbledon effect', with Great Britain laying on the courts, the strawberries and the crowds – all for the benefit of foreign players. In fact, the fate threatening the Square Mile could be viewed rather closer to home than the venerable tennis-club on the fringes of south London. Half a mile from the City's western boundary lies Covent Garden, once a vital market place for the trading of fruit and vegetables and now a tourist trap full of expensive eateries and street-corner theatricals.

With its beautiful churches, historic monuments and charming alleyways, the City could slip comfortably into a post-financial role supplying museums, restaurants and places of interest for the up-market tourist. It could be promoted as the 'old town' of London, which, indeed, it is.

High-speed communications technology, combined with aggressive competition from other centres in Europe, threaten to erode the City's advantages. And such erosion, once started, is both terrifyingly swift and very difficult to stop. Nobody over the age of thirty-five will need reminding of the fate of Britain's motor car, motor-cycle and shipbuilding industries; all world-beaters into the 1960s. Nor will that same age group forget how, within a few short years of childhood, the words 'made in England' were transformed from a guarantee of quality into something of a joke.

Furthermore, the City has in recent memory already lost one of its major industries. Until the late-1980s it was able to boast, alongside finance and law, the print media as a jewel in its crown. The disappearance of Fleet Street put an end to that as national newspapers headed for points east and west. Of course, the press was never central to the City's activities. Nevertheless the nature of its leaving ought to give pause for thought. The exodus was driven by a mixture of hard-headed commercial sense and technical change. It was in no sense the City's 'fault'. But the newspapers did leave, all the same.

Could the same thing really happen on a large scale to the City's chief 'industry'? Probably not in the extreme form suggested. There will always be law firms and accountancy practices who prefer the relative calm of the City to the hubbub of the West End. And some of the more discreet stockbrokers and private banks will linger. So will a few life offices, along possibly with one or two of the more recherché commodity markets.

But the City would effectively have ceased to exist. The livery companies would still hold the odd dinner and the Lord Mayor would doubtless stage his parade once a year. City police officers would continue to walk the beat and City councilmen would pore over planning applications.

However, the notion of 'London's position as an international financial centre' would have quietly expired. Such a Square Mile would have about as much connection with the great currents of world finance as modern-day Ealing has with the global film business.

To many, all this cannot come a moment too soon. Its sternest critics claim the City has quite simply pulled the British economy out of shape for most of the past hundred years. By forcing politicians to tailor economic policy to suit City requirements – in particular, by pursuing high interest rates and a strong pound at all costs – the financiers of the Square Mile have ensured British industry is permanently trying to compete with the brakes slammed on hard. Anyone seriously interested, they say, in the revival of British manufacturing and engineering would greet the demise of the City with unalloyed joy.

We shall examine these claims later in the book. For now, it is sufficient simply to note that there is nothing particularly secure about London's current position on the world's financial stage. For the financiers of the Square Mile, as for the rest of us, there is, ultimately, no abiding city.

3

Paper Tiger: Stocks and shares in London

HANCOCK: All right, come on, how does it work?

JAMES: Well, you only own investing shares, now that entitles you to put money into the firm. I own all the voting shares, which entitles me to take money out.

From *Hancock's Half Hour*, BBC Radio, 24 November 1959

A giant jumble sale: how the stock market trades second-hand goods

At the heart of the equity market – the stock market, to most of us – there is a riddle. The very first thing that the interested observer is told by a friendly official spokesperson is that the function of the equity market is to raise capital for industry and commerce. Without the stock market, new companies would be starved of funds. Scientific inventions would languish in potting sheds. New medicines, new means of transport, developments in food, technology and fashion – without equity finance, none would see the light of day.

Don't take it on trust. Here is the London Stock Exchange website on the subject: 'We provide the markets and means of raising capital for UK and international companies'. Equally respectable is the judgment of *The Economist* periodical's *Guide to Financial Markets*: 'Raising capital remains the main function of equity markets'.

Herein lies the riddle. Because our interested, open-minded observer cannot help noticing one thing. Which is quite simply this: raising capital for business is not the main function of the equity market.

In June 2001, total turnover on the London Stock Exchange main market was £151,985 million. Of that, less than 1 per cent – £1,080 million – was accounted for by new issues. A further £112 million was taken up by the issue of new shares by companies already listed on the market – so-called 'rights issues'. Then 'other issues', including 'placings' of shares in the market, accounted for another £269.5 million. That gives us a grand total of £1,461.5 million in money raised for business, commerce and industry. In other words, a shade over 0.96 per cent of total turnover.

Which leaves our fresh-faced newcomer wondering what exactly is the purpose of the remaining 99 per cent of activity on the London main market? If just £1,461.5 million is going to fund business, whatever happened to the remaining £150,523.5 million? After all, £150 billion is a fair sum to go missing in one month. It is equivalent to about half the annual budget of HM Government.

The simple answer is that the vast majority of trading on the London market, or any other major exchange, is 'secondary trading'. And perhaps the pithiest description of secondary trading occurs in the novel *The Bonfire of the Vanities* by Tom Wolfe. Judy McCoy is explaining to her daughter what daddy does for a living. In fact, he trades bonds rather than equities, but the principle holds good for both. Daddy's current market play involves French government stock. She explains:

'Pierce & Pierce [the trading house] doesn't issue them for the French government and doesn't buy them from the French government but from whoever has already bought them from the French government. So Pierce & Pierce's transactions have nothing to do with anything France hopes to build or develop or . . . achieve. It's all been done long before Pierce & Pierce enters the picture. So they're just sort of . . . Slices of cake. Golden cake. And Pierce & Pierce collects millions of marvellous' – she shrugged – 'golden crumbs'.

Secondary trading, quite simply, involves buying and selling securities issued long ago, either from the people who originally bought them or, more likely, from people who bought them from the people who bought them from the people who originally bought them.

As John Maynard Keynes said: '[The] daily revaluations of the Stock Exchange . . . are primarily made to facilitate transfers of old investments between one individual and another'.

Could this go on indefinitely? In the very long term, no. Over time, the existing share base is eroded because shares are taken out of circulation through takeovers, bankruptcies, management Buy-outs and mergers. Any stock market will ultimately need an infusion of fresh shares to keep the game going.

But in the short term – certainly. Equity traders can happily deal in existing shares without ever having to worry whether any new ones are in the pipeline. As our figures show, the vast majority of equity turnover represents the transfer of old shares. Each of those transfers involves no transmission of wealth whatever to the issuing company. A once and for all transmission took place the day the shares were listed on the market.

It is true that the day-to-day price remains important for the issuing company. Apart from anything else, that price affects the amount of capital that could be raised by an issue of new shares. And it is more than likely that the management and even some of the employees of the issuing company are themselves shareholders, with a portion of their personal savings committed to the company's paper worth.

Nevertheless, it is stretching it a bit to describe the raising of capital for business as the main function of a stock market. In reality, a Stock Exchange is four markets in one. In descending order of importance, they are:

- a market in the right to a slice of a company's income.
  Shares carry the entitlement to a distribution of the company's profits, assuming there are any. These are called dividends and are usually payable twice a year, the initial payment at the six-month stage described as the 'interim dividend', followed by the 'final dividend' at the year end. Together they make up the 'total dividend'. As the market's view of a company's earning potential changes, so does the share price. In contrast to interest payments on a loan, with most shares there is nothing fixed or guaranteed regarding the dividend. In its role as a market in income rights, a stock market allows its participants to form views on the likely size of a company's income and to bid against each other for a share in that income. The size of this total income pot is colossal: in 1999, UK companies paid out £100 billion in dividends, equivalent to 11 per cent of gross domestic product.

- a market in the right to a slice in the increased capital value of a company.

This aspect of the market displays the City's famous, or infamous, 'short termism'. Buying shares for income tends to be a longer term commitment than buying them in the hope that the share price itself will rise substantially above the cost price. Of course they may not rise at all, but then they may not pay any income either, should things go badly wrong. Such is the high adventure of business. Nevertheless, an investor convinced that shares in a particular company are about to take off is unlikely to be over-concerned about that company's income-generating potential.

- a market in corporate control.
  The very word 'equity' means just what it says; in the Chambers' Dictionary definition, 'an equitable right'. A holder of ordinary shares owns the issuing company in strict proportion to the percentage of the total number of shares that she holds. This ownership is 'equitable' because the investor has forgone the security that comes from simply lending money to the business concerned, and, in return, is given a stake in its ownership. For the vast majority of issuing companies for the vast majority of the time, this market in corporate control is largely theoretical. It becomes much more important in certain circumstances. The obvious case is a takeover bid for the company, in which the shareholders' role as owners comes to the fore. After all, it is they who will decide the company's fate. Another circumstance would be a so-called 'shareholder revolt', in which some or all of the shareholders are so dissatisfied with the management's performance that they seek to have the board removed and replaced with new appointees. This market in corporate control is, in practice, closely related to the second of our markets – that in capital appreciation. Little is as certain to make a company's share price shoot upwards than the suggestion that it is the subject of a takeover bid. Similarly, there are few more depressing influences upon a share price than news that the board and the shareholders are at loggerheads.

- a market in the raising of new capital for business.

At last! Right at the bottom of the list we find the alleged chief function of the equity market, that noble pursuit of finding funds for struggling inventors, self-made businessmen and the tycoons of tomorrow. As we have seen, raising new money for business activity is far and away the least important activity on the stock market, although it has long been the sole justification for the whole business of equity trading. Way back in 1959, John Benn, then chairman of a life assurance company, wrote: 'Many people think of the Stock Exchange as a sort of casino, and of course there are speculators in the Throgmorton Street, although their role is not very significant in relation to the total business transacted. But taking risks in putting money to work plays an important role in the City of London, and without this necessary and adventurous factor a great amount of economic activity would not take place'. Actually, what is 'not very significant' is the stock market's role in raising money for business. The vast majority of finance for industry and commerce does not come from the equity market

True, figures from Britain's official data bureau, National Statistics, suggest, when translated on to a graph, that shares and other equity finance take the lion's share of the sources of funds for industrial and commercial companies. Nearly £100 billion of share and equity finance was outstanding at the end of 1999 against just £40 billion in loans and about the same in bonds. But this is misleading on several fronts. Treating equity as a liability puts it on a par with the classical rolling overdraft facility. As we have seen, equities are sold once and for all raising a once and for all sum of money. Furthermore, figures from the Bank for International Settlements suggest total outstanding bonds issued by UK companies other than financial institutions stood at $149 billion in June 2000, which translates into something closer to £100 billion than £40 billion. We take a much closer look at bonds later in this chapter.

Finally, a great deal of seed capital for businesses is not captured by the official data. It includes informal intra-family loans and bank finance raised on an individual-customer basis by sole traders. One anecdote illuminates this latter phenomenon. During the early-1990s, a businessman became aware during the recession of an opportunity to buy cheaply a company making medical videos. The company was sound, but was part of a larger group, which was experiencing great difficulties. The man's bank simply would not advance him the £10,000 needed; burnt by the recession, it was making no business loans at that time. Only later did it dawn on the dejected businessman that the credit limit on his gold card, issued by the very same bank, was £10,000. He put the company, as they say, on plastic.

The concentration of apologists for the equity market upon 'raising finance for business' is rather curious. It is reminiscent of those army recruiting advertisements in the 1960s that stressed foreign travel, skiing and social life and made no mention whatever of military combat. The apologists may be on stronger ground were they to make rather more of the market's role as what the legendary US investor Warren Buffett described as 'a reference point'. True, Buffett did go on to say that this reference point was useful only 'to see if anybody is offering to do anything foolish'. Nevertheless, Keynes put it more elegantly:

> [Stock market prices] inevitably assert a decisive influence on the rate of current investment. For there is no sense in building up a new enterprise at a cost greater than that at which a similar existing asset can be purchased whilst there is any inducement to spend on a new project what may seem an extravagant sum, if it can be floated off on the Stock Exchange at an immediate profit.

US economist James Tobin concurs. His 'Q' theory states that, over time, the capital value of all companies on any stock market cannot exceed the value at current prices of all the assets of those companies. Thus the state of play on a stock market can be a valuable tool in assessing the viability of a business project. Not that such assessments will necessarily deter the project managers. Analysts at now defunct Yamaichi Securities in London calculated in 1995 that Eurotunnel, the cross-Channel train operator, had doubled the capacity to take people across the English Channel but had done so at forty times the replacement cost of all the assets of all the existing ferry companies. In light of this, Eurotunnel's long history of refinancings and debt moratoria can hardly have come as a surprise.

Not that the dealers on the London stock market, or on any other exchange, are in business to provide useful statistics for venture capitalists, any more than they are in business primarily to raise capital for industry and commerce. As we saw above, their fundamental role is to trade in three different types of entitlements: to income, to capital gain and to corporate control. So different are these entitlements from one another that attempts have been made over the years to issue different securities for each entitlement. Perhaps the most long-lasting and successful, both in London and, with variations, in New York is the 'preference share', or 'A share', which pays its holder dividends ahead of the ordinary shareholders but which carries no voting rights, and so is effectively a share relating only to the company's income. Less popular, particularly with the Stock Exchange authorities, have been shares conferring special voting rights – in effect, a special entitlement to corporate control. Over the years, these have been issued by companies as diverse as Reuters, the international news agency, and the Savoy Hotel. British and other governments have issued perhaps the most powerful of all 'control' shares: the so-called 'golden shares' in a privatised industry. Here, one single share can block all the other shares on matters of control of the business. This single share is held by the government concerned, and is not for sale.

In Britain, the hub of this colossal trade in entitlements is the London Stock Exchange. It is no longer strictly accurate to describe share trading as taking place 'on' the exchange, as the old trading floor has long since closed. Nevertheless, contrary to excitable predictions the 1980s, a regulated market place remained essential for the conduct of large-scale 'multilateral' trading – trading in which each party need neither know nor care who is on the other side of the deal. And, contrary to a further slew of excitable predictions in the 1990s, the original London Stock Exchange has not been ousted from its central position – not yet at least – by upstart newcomers offering hot technology and ultra-low costs. By value, something like 99 per cent of all share trading takes place on the exchange's main list. UK companies whose shares are quoted on the main list have a total capital value – that is to say, the value of all their shares – of £1,500 billion, as of September 2001. By contrast, the exchange's own mini-market for smaller companies, the Alternative Investment Market, or AIM, boasts a total capitalisation of £13 billion.

We shall look later at the exchange's chief competitors in London. Suffice to say for now that the exchange remains overwhelmingly dominant.

On the face of it, the exchange's ability to survive and thrive is quite remarkable. This is not so much because of the tough competition or technical challenges that it has faced, or was expected to face. Rather, it is that to even the most sympathetic outside observer, the management of this market place for several decades has being quite simply abominable. Behind the scenes, to be fair, it was a different story, as we shall see later. But to witness the top brass of the exchange in action since at least 1970 is to marvel that there is any share trading left in London at all.

Thirty years ago, the exchange was still arguing about whether or not to admit women to membership, a mere half-century or so after agreeing to admit such obviously inferior professions as medicine and the law. Women were allowed in, finally, in 1973, but even then the exchange insisted it was not bowing to 'fashion' but merely that – through its union that year with provincial exchanges such as Birmingham – female stockbrokers from those exchanges were now members.

With that triumph for modernity out of the way, the exchange was able to get down to the serious business of nearly bankrupting itself over a new computerised settlement system, Talisman. Costs ran completely out of control and the exchange came within an ace of cancelling the whole project. As if to show how deeply the lessons had been read, marked, learned and inwardly digested, the exchange made exactly the same mistakes with the successor to Talisman, Taurus. Begun in 1981, Taurus was supposed to be in operation by the end of the 1980s. It wasn't. Four years late, Taurus was finally cancelled in March 1993 at a total cost approaching half a billion pounds. The exchange suffered the ultimate ignominy of having the Bank of England – fresh from its own recent glories, such as the 1991 collapse of Bank of Credit and Commerce International – step in and take control of Taurus's successor, Crest.

Meanwhile, the exchange had clocked up new triumphs. Incapable of managing its own affairs, the exchange decided in the early-1990s to try its hand at running everybody else's instead. Codes on 'corporate governance' proliferated, with the exchange making it clear that any company wishing to be listed and failing to sign up to these guidelines would be required to explain why. The codes, however, were not uniformly imposed. When the exchange's AIM market was launched in June 1995, it soon emerged that one of the flagship flotations was a company falsely claiming support for its projects from, among others, Buckingham Palace and President Mandela of South Africa.

As these sideshows rumbled on, the exchange itself was creaking badly. Big Bang, it emerged, had been less of an earthquake and rather more a typically British attempt to change everything while keeping it exactly the same. In particular, the salesmen and market-makers were really just brokers and jobbers in disguise. Worse, the computerised price displays, available to all, were virtually meaningless. Market-makers preferred to deal on anonymous 'inter-dealer broker' screens, whose prices were not available for inspection by the great unwashed. The whole system was looking increasingly antiquated and out of step with other financial centres.

After much huffing and puffing, and the ousting in early 1996 of chief executive Michael Lawrence, the exchange switched partly from a system of competing quotes from market-makers to one that based trading in the biggest shares upon an electronic order-book.

We shall look at this in more detail later, but for now it is enough to say that this new system, SETS, was not without its problems.

Just as it seemed things couldn't get any worse, they did.

In the early summer of 2000, chairman Donald Cruikshank announced plans for a merger with Germany's Deutsche Börse. The new entity was to be called iX, which sounded like a short-handed cricket team. Nor did the deal itself stand close examination. Under the proposal, established blue-chip companies would be quoted in London, while high-growth technology stocks would be quoted in Frankfurt. Long-term, it seemed, London would end up trading shares of dinosaur companies – assuming the British and the Germans could ever agree on what was blue-chip and what was high-growth.

Amidst all this came the final humiliation. Sweden's OM Group, operator of the Stockholm Stock Exchange, not hitherto one of the world's great bourses, launched a bid for its London rival. The offer failed, but that it had ever been made in the first place was a signal of the exchange's greatly weakened position. The German merger proposal collapsed in November 2000.

You may be wondering how quite such a shambolic outfit has kept its position as Europe's premier stock market. And you would be right to do so. But the clowning around by the top brass is only half the story. Down in the engine room, while the officers upstairs have been busy rearranging the deckchairs, the crew has been remarkably consistent when it comes to the key pivot point of exchange policy: liquidity.

In banking – and in life generally, come to that – liquidity is a synonym for large quantities of ready cash. So it may seem there is little about which to congratulate the exchange if all we are talking about is its continued ability to bring people with money to spend through its doors. After all, shares are not issued for free, so a sufficiency of spending power would appear to be the *sine qua non* of doing business.

In the wonderful world of equities, however, liquidity has a different meaning. Here, it is possibly best defined as the ability easily to reverse an investment decision. In other words, seized with enthusiasm for the communications revolution, you rush out on Monday morning and buy 1000 shares in XYZ Telecom at £1 each. Come Tuesday, you read a thoughtful article suggesting telecom shares are not all they have been cracked up to be. You hold fire, but on Wednesday your nerve cracks after you have listened to a radio programme hailing the revival in the art of letter-writing and the sudden unfashionability of mobile phones.

In a liquid market, barring any terrible mishaps between Monday and Wednesday such as the bankruptcy of XYZ Telecom or the sudden arrival of the Fraud Squad at its doors, you ought to be able fairly painlessly to sell your shares back into the market. In other words, to change your mind.

This doesn't mean you will get the full £1,000 back. You may do, of course. You may even make a profit. This is all beside the point. Liquidity does not provide a guarantee against loss, but it does provide the best possible chance of finding a buyer at a price that is within hailing distance of what you paid.

Think of the alternative in terms of the way the housing market functions in Britain. On Monday, you spend £1,000 on shares in XYZ Telecom. By Wednesday, after an earnest discussion over a glass of wine with your spouse, you decide to sell. You select a stockbroker and make an appointment for Friday. Details of your shareholding are photocopied at the stockbroker's office and posted to those clients who have shown some interest in buying shares in this sector of the market. People come round to your house to look at your share certificates, make polite noises, and leave. Your stockbroker suggests dropping the price. Eventually, if you are lucky, someone will decide that the one thing missing from their portfolio is a block of 1000 shares in XYZ Telecom.

Liquidity may be a difficult concept to grasp – illiquidity isn't. On the contrary, it is the deeply felt experience of anybody who has ever bought or sold a property.

So what are the conditions necessary for liquidity?

That is actually a more difficult question than it seems. An obvious answer would be that you need a very large base of potential customers – both buyers and sellers. This is partly true, although it is just about possible to conceive of a highly liquid market made up of relatively few, albeit wealthy, participants. Another suggestion would be that liquidity can be measured in terms of the total pool of funds available for investment. Again this is part of the answer, although it is far from being a complete one.

Let's look at it from the other end, and examine the measures the London Stock Exchange has put in place to guarantee liquidity. After all, it is not easy to define 'the Queen's peace', but a good try can be made from the observation of the activities of police and magistrates.

To begin with the policing theme, why does the exchange spend so much time, effort and money on keeping the market clean? The would-be sophisticate's answer is: 'To put up a show of respectability behind which "the chaps" can carry on as usual rooking the investing public by insider dealing and all the other little tricks of their trade'.

But this cannot be quite right. In the 1990s, the exchange hired some of the world's leading experts in artificial intelligence to create a market monitoring system dubbed 'the billion dollar brain'. It can trace every deal and spot even the most well hidden patterns in the market. This seems a little excessive for a mere 'show of respectability'.

But neither is this huge effort in terms of people and systems primarily a moral crusade. In conversation, the exchange's market surveillance personnel are remarkably hard to work up into a lather about the iniquity of market abuse. This is not because they lack ethical sense, but because market abuse, in particular insider dealing, is not primarily a moral issue. It is an issue of liquidity.

Let's return to your troubled purchase of XYZ shares. Assume a market in which insider dealing is rife and imagine the thoughts going through your head on the Monday morning as you prepare to place your order with a stockbroker. You know full well that the chances are that he is armed with information about XYZ that you simply do not have. Nor is there a way of you getting that information any time soon. How would you react? To begin with, you may well decide not to buy the shares. After all, even if XYZ itself is sound, you simply cannot trust the price your broker is putting on those shares.

Alternatively, were you a more seasoned investor, you may haggle with your stockbroker to reduce the price. He, in turn, may have been expecting you to do this, so even had he not padded the price initially, he may have done so to protect his own profit against your haggling.

Whatever the outcome, liquidity has been seriously damaged. Should you decide not to buy the shares, trading in XYZ's stock has started to seize up. Should you and the broker haggle, then the price of XYZ shares has become subject to very wide 'spreads' between buying and selling prices.

You will hear a great deal about 'spreads', much of it made to sound terribly complex. In fact, it is simply the difference between the market-maker's offer to buy and offer to sell, the former being lower than the latter. Anyone who has bought foreign currency for their holidays at a high street bank or money changer will grasp the principle.

What is this likely to mean on Wednesday, when you wish to sell? Even if he is honest, there is no guarantee that your broker will be interested, for the simple reason that if every other investor is behaving as you behaved on Monday, he will find the stock hard to sell on. Reversing your investment decision is not easy, but difficult. That is an illiquid market.

Indeed, wide 'spreads' between buying and selling prices are a sure symptom of market illiquidity. They represent players' attempts to protect themselves against what they fear to be a secret advantage enjoyed by the other party. If you assume the other party to the deal is armed with hidden information concerning an asset, then you will be seeking either a deep discount (if you are buying) or a steep premium (if you are selling) to counteract the edge enjoyed by the other side.

Of course, this makes multilateral trading well nigh impossible. It is bad enough to be face to face with the economic actor you believe to have the edge over you; dealing through anonymous screens simply gives 'them' even more opportunity to deceive you. In place of multilateral dealing between anonymous parties will be a much more cumbersome series of bilateral one-on-one deals, akin, as we saw, to selling a private house.

Such deals are the symptom of a highly illiquid market.

Liquidity by contrast relies upon a reasonable parity of information among all the potential parties. This is an essential precondition for the anonymity – or at least the confidence to deal with players you do not know – that is itself a key feature of a liquid market. Parallel to this is the need for the commodities traded (in this case, company securities) to be similarly anonymous and standardised. Were your XYZ shares to be as peculiar to you as is your house, carrying slightly different entitlements to income, capital and control both from each other and from everybody else's XYZ shares, then a liquid stock market would be an impossibility; your stockbroker really would be 'showing people around' your portfolio!

These, then, are two essential pillars of a liquid market: standardisation of products, and standardisation – as far as human nature will allow – of the knowledge available to the market participants. With these pillars in place, much should follow. This is not to say that the exchange has not, at different times, placed various obligations upon market participants to deal in certain shares to which they are committed. But such regulations ought to be decreasingly important the more closely a market's structure conforms to the essential features required for liquidity.

This does not mean that all securities are uniformly liquid. Far from it. Shares may no longer be banded, as they were in the 1980s, according to their liquidity, but the FTSE 100 elite represents the first division of liquidity, while the more exotic 'tiddler' shares at the bottom of the market may be traded only among a handful of enthusiasts. Football club shares – the majority of them, anyway – tend to fall within this category. One (very senior) cynic at Barclays Stockbrokers offers a terse piece of advice to fans contemplating a stake in their local team: 'Buy a scarf instead'.

Nor is a liquid stock market necessarily better than an

exchange that has set itself different priorities. The Tokyo Stock Exchange has long prized orderly trading above liquidity. In the wake of the 1987 crash, the ability of Japan's Ministry of Finance to dragoon the country's big brokers back into the market place to support share values was much admired in the West. This admiration is voiced less frequently now after assorted scandals in the 1990s involving ministry personnel enjoying wild nights on the town, courtesy of the banks they were supposedly regulating. Nevertheless, it is entirely legitimate for a stock market to choose an overriding priority other than liquidity. One exchange may value confidentiality above all else; another may place great store in the minimising of price volatility. Indeed, the New York Stock Exchange, with its 'circuit breakers' and its 'sidecars', available at times of market panic, would seem more concerned to keep trading within acceptable bounds than is the London market.

London's special focus on liquidity may come to be seen as its unique selling point, should competition between international centres intensify and a truly global market in securities trading opens up. It is a tribute to the exchange's sense of long-term purpose that it has kept maximum liquidity as its compass through thick and thin – very often thin, as we have seen. And there is no doubt that liquidity works as it is intended to as regards share dealings. Reversibility is a reality. In the vast majority of share deals, there really is no need for your stockbroker to make contact with individual 'prospects'.

But liquidity is claimed to have wider benefits. It is not simply a state of affairs that allows dithering buyers of XYZ shares to change their minds willy-nilly. Nor is it solely a mechanism to ensure smooth trading among market participants. Liquidity is of the greatest benefit, it is claimed, not to market participants at all but to the 'end user' of the exchange, the companies quoted thereon.

We saw earlier how an illiquid market expresses itself through wide variations between buying and selling prices. Precisely the same principle applies to the raising of funds via the exchange. A company coming to an illiquid market is going to have to work hard to persuade would-be investors to take its shares. Put another way, it is going to have to offer a relatively high return on the investment to compensate the investor for the risk that she will find it difficult to sell shares and realise the value of her investment. Multiply this a thousandfold throughout the economy, and the effective cost of funds to business and industry is very much greater than it otherwise would have been.

In a liquid market, by contrast, investors will be more moderate with regard to the return they expect on the investment because they will no longer be seeking an additional premium to cover the risk of illiquidity.

This then is the true beauty of liquidity. Just as it reduces the total demands made by investors against each other, so it also reduces the demands made by investors as a group as against companies seeking finance.

There's just one problem. It doesn't. Once the illiquidity principle leaves the Stock Exchange, it breaks down. Were it to be working properly, one would expect companies listed in Britain to be paying significantly lower dividends than companies listed on less liquid markets. The reverse is true.

Figures from the Bank for International Settlements (BIS) – the central bank for other central banks, based in Basle in Switzerland – measure 'dividend yields' paid by companies in different countries. The dividend yield is calculated simply by dividing the dividend per share by the price per share. As dividends increase, so does the yield. For example, XYZ Telecom, as we saw, has issued shares costing £1 each. Were XYZ to pay a dividend of 2p per share, the dividend yield would be 2p divided by 100p, or two per cent. But were XYZ to increase the dividend to 5p per share, the yield would have increased to five per cent.

So how does liquid London compare with other countries? Surely UK-listed firms will be able to get away with much lower dividend yields than their competitors who have raised funds on other exchanges?

Not at all. BIS figures show an average UK dividend yield of 4.7 per cent a year, against 2.8 per cent a year in Germany, a country that until recently had relatively undeveloped stock markets and a heavy reliance on bank finance for industry. Similarly France –

whose bourse opened for only a couple of hours around lunchtime well into the 1980s, and all bar three of whose stockbroking firms received their licences during the Napoleonic era – would be expected to show much higher dividend yields over the years. Far from it: France's average dividend yield is listed at 4.5 per cent – lower than Britain's.

The same is true of Japan (3 per cent), Belgium (4.3 per cent), Italy (2.3 per cent), Switzerland (2.9 per cent), and Canada (3.4 per cent). Funnily enough, only the Netherlands – like Britain, an economy with a strong tradition of equity ownership and shareholder rights – boasted higher average yields, 4.8 per cent.

These figures are far from perfect, because not all begin in the same year. However, the story is much the same in recent years, using strictly comparable figures; while low inflation combined with higher share prices have helped to reduce yields, Britain still leads the pack. The BIS lists the lowest average annual dividend paid in each of these countries since 1981. At 2.8 per cent, the British average is approximately 50 per cent greater than the next highest figure, 1.8 per cent in the Netherlands. For the record, some of Britain's other competitors line-up as follows: France 1.7 per cent; Belgium 1.6 per cent; US 1.5 per cent; Canada 1.4 per cent; Germany 1.3 per cent; Switzerland 1 per cent; Italy 0.8 per cent and Japan 0.4 per cent.

Of course cultural, legal and taxation factors all play their part in the level of dividends paid in different countries. So-called political risk – such as a threat of nationalisation or social disorder – also affects the returns investors will demand. As, of course, does the nature of the investments on offer. A stock market dominated by risky ventures is likely overall to offer higher returns than one largely made up of solid blue-chip companies.

Nevertheless, it is interesting to note that the liquidity theory works no better in the economy as a whole than does the notion that the Stock Exchange exists primarily to raise capital for business. It is tempting to conclude from this that the stock market exists primarily for itself. This accusation has been the subject of numerous reports and investigations. None has proved conclusive.

The cliche accusation levelled against the stock market in this regard is that it is a casino. Yet this need not be the put down that it appears. British casinos are well regulated, with both personnel and cameras keeping a close eye on the players and the games. The house 'edge' is strictly laid down by law. Staff are graded according to tightly-controlled criteria. Upstairs, away from the hubbub of roulette and blackjack, are the private card rooms, where wilder spirits play each other, not the house, with rules and stakes of their own devising.

Overall, you may think, not a bad model for the equity market. In that spirit, let us take a closer look in this most exclusive of gaming clubs, starting with the most important ingredient of any game: the counters on the table.

The chips aren't down

At the last count, there were 2431 British companies listed on the London Stock Exchange and 491 international businesses. These figures are deceptive, however. The international concerns, while making up only one sixth of the total by headcount, dwarf the purely domestic businesses in terms of size. The market value – that is, the value of all the shares added together – of UK companies comes to about £1,500 billion. By contrast, that of the international companies comes to £2,400 billion. It is the same story when it comes to the value of turnover in the shares of the two groups of companies. In September 2001, this stood at £157 billion for UK companies and £275 billion for the international companies.

Raising money, as we have seen, is not the preoccupation that the exchange would have you believe. Nevertheless, even here the international companies give the home team a run for their money, frequently raising more money than their British counterparts. In September 2001, British firms maintained a narrow lend, raising £6.4 billion, while international companies raised £6 billion.

This should not be read as evidence that British industry is all washed up. By definition, only the larger international firms are likely to seek a London listing. Smaller businesses will trade their shares closer to home. That said, the top ten international companies listed in London are big beasts indeed. They are headed by America's General Electric, with a market capitalisation in March 2001 of £325 billion, followed by Exxon Mobil at £245 billion and Japan's Toyota Motor Corporation at £94 billion. Other giants follow: Royal Dutch Petroleum at £85 billion, Finland's Nokia, at £80 billion and tobacco group Philip Morris at £79 billion.

Our home team contains some big boys too. Top of the list in March 2001 was BP Amoco, valued at £131 billion, closely followed by Vodafone at £125 billion and Glaxo SmithKline at £115 billion. Banker HSBC was next at £78 billion followed by AstraZeneca at £59 billion, Shell at £54 billion, Royal Bank of Scotland at £47 billion, Lloyds TSB at £38 billion, Barclays at £36 billion and British Telecom at £34 billion.

The total market value of the top ten international quoted companies was, on these figures, £1,180 billion. That is well over a third of the total value of all the listed international companies in London. Britain's top dogs take up even more kennel room; their total value is £717 billion, or 44 per cent of the value of all UK listed companies. Put together, the top ten British companies and the top ten international companies and they have a total stock market value of £1,897 billion – equivalent to 40 per cent of the total value of all companies listed on the London Stock Exchange.

It is the same story when it comes to trading in shares of these monster corporations. With one exception, Barclays, the ten largest UK companies were also the ten most actively traded shares in the first quarter of 2001. Cable & Wireless filled the gap left by Barclays. The value of turnover in these top-ten shares was £202 billion, nearly half the total £549 billion worth of action seen by all quoted UK companies.

The picture is slightly different on the international side, because of the disparity between the amount of trading in their shares that takes place in London as opposed to in their home markets. For example, neither Exxon nor General Electric features in the figures for the first quarter of 2001 covering the top ten international companies in terms of number of bargains struck in their shares.

Nevertheless, one thing is clear. To describe these vast financial and industrial concerns as simply customers of the stock market is highly misleading. It would be more accurate to describe them as making up the environment in which everybody else has to operate.

And who is everybody else? Well, whatever accusations can be levelled at the Stock Exchange as regards its alleged failings as a source of support for smaller British companies, there is little doubt that the minnows of the business world are well represented both on the main market and on AIM. As of September 2001, using figures for just UK companies, there were 131 with a market value of £2 million or less and a further 228 valued at between £2 million and £5 million.

Moving a little further up the league, there were 261 companies upon whom the market in its wisdom placed a value on the shares of between £5 million and £10 million. The biggest single category by number – 394 companies – was made up of those firms with a market value ranging from £10 million to £25 million. 'The second largest, with 297 companies, enjoyed a valuation ranging from £25 million to £50 million. In other words, in September 2001, the number of quoted British companies valued at less than £50 million was 1,311, while the number valued at more than £50 million was just 834.

At the top of the range, there are 97 companies worth £2 billion or more, and 56 valued at between £1 billion and £2 billion.

Overall, the total number of both British and international companies whose shares are traded on the main list and on AIM has changed little in the last five years. There were 2,972 in 1997, 2,967 in 1998, 2,881 in 1999, 2,801 in 2000 and 2,922 in 2001. Turnover, by contrast, has changed greatly during the same period, marching ever up in total value of shares traded from £574 bn in 1997 to £715 bn in 1998 through the £1 trillion barrier in 1999 (£1,045 bn) up to £1,526 bn in 2000 to hit £1,616 bn in 2001.

Interestingly, much of this growth has been driven by trade in international shares; by 2001 the total value of UK stocks traded was about double the value in 1997 while the market overall saw an increase nearer treble. Furthermore, each individual bargain has, on average, become more valuable. While total turnover value has moved relentlessly upwards, the number of bargains has fallen. It jumped from 5 million to 12.4 million between 1997 and 2000 but dropped back to 11.9 million in 2001.

Becoming a 'counter' on the board, i.e. floating a company on the stock market, is not the straightforward business of twenty or thirty years ago. Then, an aspirant quoted business had just two or three major hurdles to jump, chiefly finding a suitable merchant bank, providing the exchange with a solid trading record and saying the right things at the inevitable wine and peanuts soirée for potential institutional shareholders.

Today, it is both easier and harder than in days gone by.

Easier, because the exchange and its competitors have acquired a 'business focus' in place of the club ethic of the past. Market personnel are nowadays conditioned to say 'yes' and to treat the aspirant quoted company as a valued customer; twenty years ago, they were conditioned to say 'perhaps', while treating the aspirant quoted company as an upstart would-be member of a very exclusive circle. Hard and fast rules about the number of years of trading records needed before joining the list have given way to a more flexible approach.

Harder, because at least in the old days when you were in, you were in. The Stock Exchange controlled all listing requirements – after all, it was the only exchange – as well as policing its own entry criteria. In that sense, it was a 'one-stop shop' before the phrase was invented. Now, listing requirements for all exchanges in Britain are drawn up and supervised by a public body, the United Kingdom Listing Authority, itself part of the City's regulator, the Financial Services Authority. Clearing the UKLA's many and various hurdles is merely the prelude to another steeplechase, this one to clear the hurdles required to list on whichever exchange the company has chosen for the trading of its shares. It is rather like the practice of West End cinemas that, during the first few weeks of a blockbuster film release, issue one ticket to those queuing round the block that gives them the right to join the main queue for the box office.

Helping the would-be quoted company around these various obstacle courses is the gaggle of well-paid people referred to always as 'The Advisers'. You will not spend long in the City without picking up references, during discussions of one or other quoted company, to 'The Advisers', often spoken in the reverential tones more appropriate to a mention of the College of Cardinals. You will probably gain the impression that the speaker is referring to the most venerable of merchant banks, probably working hand in glove with a huge law firm. And you may well be right.

In fact, only two types of advisers are mandatory for a firm wishing to trade its shares on a UK exchange, and there is no requirement that they be the sort of colossus conjured up by the 'adviser' tag. The first is an auditor, in other words an accountant or accountancy practice with a licence to audit company accounts. This is hardly startling, given that only a public limited company can offer shares to the public and every PLC (along with all sizeable private limited companies) has to appoint an auditor whether it wishes to trade its shares or not.

The second is an adviser (not to be confused with 'The Advisers'). This is usually a broker, investment banker or corporate finance specialist firm and it has one key role – the management of relations between the exchange (and, by extension nowadays, the regulators such as UKLA and the FSA) and the quoted company. It is the adviser who will request a share suspension should it learn that the client company is in difficulty. It will be the adviser who scrutinises every word of every statement the client company makes either to or through the exchange. And it is the adviser who will endure an uncomfortable interview at the Stock Exchange Tower or at FSA headquarters in Canary Wharf should the client be found to have shown a deplorable lack of respect for the rules binding publicly quoted companies.

A third type of adviser is ubiquitous, although not mandatory. This is the 'broker', which, confusingly enough, could well be an investment bank rather than a stockbroker. While the adviser keeps the channels open with the exchange and the other authorities, the broker maintains a two-way communication with investors, to ginger up interest in the shares when times are good and to calm fears when the company hits trouble.

But these three types of professional assistance are pretty well the bare minimum. The reality nowadays is that even fairly modest-sized enterprises wishing to join the exchange will launch their shares with a protective escort of Advisers. At the head of this impressive fleet will probably be an investment bank, fulfilling the broker role, as well as underwriting the shares (i.e. promising to buy them itself if all else fails) in order to guarantee their successful debut. Occasionally, with smaller or more uncertain flotations, the investment bank will decline this role and offer instead simply to do its best to sell the shares. Not surprisingly, cautious investors see this as a vote of no confidence by the chief Adviser, and see no reason to risk their own money on an opportunity snubbed by its main promoter.

Along with underwriting, the lead bank is likely also to shoulder the burden of marketing the shares to investors and setting the price at which they will be sold. The bank may also act as Adviser, although it is common for this function to be performed by a different Adviser.

Jostling in behind will be a City law firm, checking every dot and comma of the 'prospectus' – the key public document in which the about-to-be-quoted company (supposedly) lays bare its inner workings in terms of profits, trading outlook and so forth, and hopes the investing public likes what it sees. Then there will be the clearing bank that (allegedly) stuck with the company through thick and thin and now wants some of the credit. The audit firm will be somewhere in the background too, keen to sell the company some of those 'consultancy' services that pay so much better than mere auditing. And then there are the financial public relations advisers, whose success in insinuating themselves into the charmed circle of Advisers is a public relations coup greater than any they have ever achieved for their clients.

For a large flotation, the list of Advisers starts, rather than stops, at this point. There will be the investment banks and brokers acting as sub-underwriters, taking on some of the risk from the lead underwriters in return for an appropriate fee. There will be a further flotilla of bankers and lawyers to deal with US and international investors. Scottish brokers will handle the issue north of the border. A Brussels law practice will ensure conformity with European Union regulations. A second PR company will focus on putting the message across to the trade and technical press. And so on.

Until now we have been discussing 'flotation'. This is but one of the ways on to the exchange. There are 'placings' of shares with a predetermined group of investors; at the moment of placing, the shares become quoted but they will not become traded until one or more of the original institutions starts selling. There is the 'introduction', in which a PLC that already enjoys a well-stocked share register simply brings itself and its shareholders to the market.

Nor are shares the only instruments to be issued by quoted companies, although they are far and away the most common. So-called 'warrants' are also sometimes issued, for tax and other reasons. Strictly speaking they ought to be in chapter nine on derivative products, but they have been part of the Stock Exchange scene for so long that they fit more happily here. A warrant is simply a piece of paper that can be traded, allowing the holder to buy the company's shares at a predetermined price and at a predetermined time. Should the price in the open market fall below the price specified in the warrant, then the warrant becomes effectively worthless.

But whatever the method of obtaining a quotation, and whatever types of paper are issued, a battalion of Advisers will be required to lift the company from industrious obscurity to the bright lights of a stock market listing.

Arranging a listing takes months, sometimes years. And those Advisers don't come cheaply. But, finally, our company has made it to the big time and its directors can luxuriate in the knowledge that their neighbours can see the company's name in the newspapers, on the share-price page, every day of the week. Or, if you prefer, the directors can luxuriate in the knowledge that they are now able to tap a deep source of capital that will allow them to build their business, to the greater benefit of the economy as a whole.

They are also, of course, now able to print a currency all of their own – their shares. That doesn't mean they can simply run off thousands of extra share certificates without telling anybody, sell them and pocket the proceeds. That would be fraud, because the existing shareholders would have had their stake in the economic value of the company diluted without their permission. For example, someone who bought shares equivalent to one per cent of the company's equity is entitled to one per cent of the monies paid in dividends, one per cent of the increase in the capital value of the company as measured by the value placed by the market on all of its shares, and a one per cent say in the control of the company.

Any additional share issue must be with the general or specific consent of the shareholders and it must offer those shareholders first refusal on enough of the new shares to keep their stakes in the enlarged company identical to their current stakes. In other words, if a company is given permission by its shareholders to increase the number of its shares by ten per cent, then a holder of one per cent of the shares must be given first refusal on one per cent of the extra ten per cent. Hence the name for such an issue is 'rights issue' – the existing shareholders' rights are preserved.

All that, however, lies in the future. For now, our company has achieved its great ambition. It is a counter on the board.

The tables are set

To use the word 'bargain' – as the Stock Exchange does in referring to equity trading – conjures up images of face-to-face haggling at car-boot sales or market stalls. And, indeed, before 1986 this was pretty much the way company shares were traded. From the Stock Exchange gallery, the visitor looked down upon a scene recognisably similar to that on display at any country town on market day, with the exceptions, of course, of the absence of livestock and the cut of the clothes. The customers, the brokers, wandered from one hexagonal 'pitch' to another comparing the prices on offer from the traders, the jobbers.

This has long gone. So have many of the country markets, but that is a different story. Today, shares are traded electronically and not all shares are equal.

Most unequal of all are the two hundred shares traded on the flagship market, Stock Exchange Electronic Trading Service, or SETS. Launched in October 1997, SETS takes in the hundred shares in the main FTSE index plus one hundred further blue-chip stocks. This system is based on the order book principle in which member firms display buying and selling prices on the shares in which they deal, along with the blocks of shares they wish to buy or sell. When an order and an offer match, they are automatically cleared through the system.

Various different types of orders can be placed on SETS. These range from 'limit', which specify the exact size and price at which the firm wishes to deal, through to bloodthirsty sounding 'fill or kill' and 'execute and eliminate' orders – respectively orders that must be matched immediately and orders that can be filled in part, the remainder being deleted.

According to the Stock Exchange, SETS is saving market players a small fortune. For investors using the market, costs have more than halved between 1997 and 2000. One huge area of savings comes from the ability immediately to push a client's order through SETS rather than through the member firm's own trading book, which ties up the capital of that firm, incurring a cost that has to be paid for.

It is worth looking at the principle behind SETS a little more closely, not least because it would appear to represent a U-turn by the exchange on the principle of maximum liquidity.

Indeed, it would be so were it not for technical developments that allow deals in high volume stocks to be cleared quickly through the exchange itself, as opposed to being parked on traders' own books for a time. Because of technological advance, bids and offers that match can swiftly find each other without the need for a trading book. It is as if all the houses for sale and all the house-hunters were to 'meet' each other through a large computer market place, with the particulars offered by the first group clearing instantly when they matched the requirements of the second group. There have been suggestions that the internet will make just such a housing market possible, although the unique nature of most houses, and the unique requirements of most house-hunters, make this unlikely.

In fact the housing market has yet to reach the market-making stage, which would require a number of wealthy property companies to act as intermediaries, buying homes from sellers and then separately awaiting orders from buyers.

Back on the exchange, the advantages of the order-book system could, thanks to technology, be introduced without draining liquidity from the market. Indeed, it was essential that it was; European exchanges had embraced the order-book system with the result that costs on the Continent were sharply competitive, since the inevitable overheads involved in maintaining a number of trading books had been all but eliminated.

Market-makers remain, not only for the majority of stocks, but also in handling aspects of trading in the SETS stocks. When a very large client, usually an investment institution, wishes to execute a very large order immediately, a trading book remains essential, as does the willingness of the market maker to shoulder the risk should the price move adversely while the shares in question are still on his book.

Cynics may guess that the SETS-style order-driven system has something else to commend it, in that it strengthens the role of the exchange versus what had been its mightiest – some would say over-mighty – subjects, the market-makers. Because trades are cleared through the machinery of the exchange itself, the exchange and its governing personnel have paradoxically tightened their grip on the market, contrary to predictions that it would loosen.

The vast majority of shares, however, continue to be traded through the market-making system, the Stock Exchange Automated Quotations system, SEAQ. Here the principle is very different. Member firms wishing to make a market in a particular share offer competing quotations of the prices at which they are prepared to deal, usually with other member firms who are acting on behalf of clients. In contrast to SETS, SEAQ screen prices are merely a reference point for telephone dealing, although the SEAQ Auctions facility allows market-makers to match orders electronically twice a day. A third member of the SEAQ family is SEAQ International, upon which overseas securities are quoted.

AIM stocks and some smaller shares on the main list are quoted on the baby of the exchange's gaming tables, the Stock Exchange Alternative Trading Service, or SEATS Plus. This system carries quotes from market-makers along with orders from member firms for particular shares.

So much for the gaming tables, what about the players?

The London Stock Exchange list 256 member firms based in London. This figure should be treated with some caution because the peculiarities of the exchange directory require some quite small outfits to list each branch separately, while allowing mighty Goldman Sachs, for example, just one entry.

Some of the old names survive, albeit as almost an after-thought: Crédit Suisse First Boston de Zoete & Bevan is an obvious case. Elsewhere, it is almost frightening to note how many of what were once thought of as giant entities in their own right have had to marry and marry again in order to maintain critical mass: Dresdner Kleinwort Wasserstein is one example. Global colossi are well represented: Chase Manhattan, Deutsche Bank, Merrill Lynch, UBS and Citibank.

George Soros is here, on Pall Mall. France's Indosuez group is in Leadenhall Street.

As we saw earlier, Britain's contingent tends these days to be of the cottage industry variety. There is the famously discreet stock-broker Cazenove, the equally illustrious Rothschild, the only slightly less grand Lazard Bank. Lower down there are what may prove to be tomorrow's top players: Canacord Capital (Europe), formerly T. Hoare; private-client broker Brewin Dolphin, and others.

There are oddities, including stockbroker JP Jenkins, the only Stock Exchange member firm to operate its own stock exchange, the

OPEX market for smaller companies. There is a branch office of the mighty Yorkshire broker Redmayne-Bentley, which has both its heart and its head in its native Leeds. There is the share-dealing service set up for members of what was the Norwich and Peterborough Building Society.

But this dense and sometimes exotic undergrowth ought not to blind the observer to one key fact: as with the companies traded on the exchange, it is the big boys that dominate all trading activities. As the players' chief customers – the institutional investors – themselves get larger, so do the size of trades that they want handled. Very large immediate deals require huge amounts of capital on the part of any investment bank keen to take on the business. This is not simply because large sums of money are needed to fund a trading book, but equally large additional sums are needed in order to cover the risk that the shares will misbehave in terms of value during the time that they are on the bank's own book.

Not only do the big investors dominate the business; they also get the best treatment. In 1999, British private clients accounted for 9.2 per cent in value terms of all turnover in British equities. On the back of that, they accounted for a whopping 29.1 per cent of commission revenue. British institutional investors, by contrast, accounted for 61.1 per cent of the turnover but paid just 40.6 per cent of the commission revenue. Foreign clients and other business accounted for the balance.

The lobby group International Financial Services London calculates: 'Commission rates vary widely from more than four per cent on the smallest trades to 0.07 per cent on deals of more than £1 million'.

In the light of this, it may not be surprising to learn from IFSL that: 'Individual shareholding [as a proportion of all shareholding] has been on a downward trend since the 1960s, from more than 50 per cent in 1963 to about 15 per cent in 1999'. This does not include shares held through the now defunct personal equity plan (PEP) or its replacement, the individual savings account (ISA). Furthermore, these figures disguise the fact that a great many wealthy individuals remained actively involved in direct share ownership. IFSL notes that, in 1998, it was estimated that the 16,000 richest private clients of London stockbrokers, each with a portfolio worth at least £1 million, held shares worth a total of £41 billion.

And while the proportion of shares held by private shareholders has fallen, the ranks of those private shareholders has been swelled from 4 million in the 1960s to about 12 million now, largely a result of privatisation of state industries and de-mutualisation of buildings societies and insurance companies.

It has become commonplace to say that the market is dominated by institutional investors, chiefly pension funds and insurance companies. And it is true that these institutions hold more than half of all UK equities. But their share has dropped from about 60 per cent in the 1980s and 1990s as they have been elbowed aside by overseas investors, whose slice has risen from less than 10 per cent in 1963 to nearly 30 per cent today. To a large extent, this penetration reflects a large number of trans-frontier corporate mergers, in which the combined company is listed in London but brings with it a large number of overseas shareholders.

On a face of it, strenuous official attempts in the 1980s to build a 'shareholding democracy' on the back of the big privatisation issues have been a failure. It is indeed true that the wilder hopes of weaning the British off their fixation on property ownership and turning them into a nation of Stock Exchange speculators never materialised and were never likely to. But IFSL looks on the bright side: 'European comparisons show that the proportion of shares held directly by UK individuals is lower than in France, Spain and Italy, where it is around 30 per cent, and higher than in Germany, where it is around 10 per cent. However, the greater size of the UK equity market relative to these countries indicates a much more significant penetration of the UK market by individual investors'.

It is worth noting also that private clients account for 54.6 per cent of all bargains struck on the exchange, while UK institutions account for only 24.2 per cent. As we have seen, however, by far the greater slice of turnover by value is accounted for by the institutions, for the simple reason that their bargains, although fewer in number, are very much the larger in both size and value.

Tomorrow belongs to them?: The upstart exchanges

It is a little-known fact that the European Union came very close indeed to strangling Britain's newcomer stock markets at birth. During interminable negotiations during the late-1980s and early-1990s on the creation of a single European investment market, one of the proposals on the table covered what was known as a 'concentration requirement'. For those unversed in fluent bureaucratese, that translated as: one country, one stock exchange.

The UK representative spotted this and had it thrown out. Britain was not in the business of creating national monopolies, and certainly not one controlled by the London Stock Exchange, then still embroiled in the Taurus debacle. Shortly afterwards, it became fashionable to claim that the whole idea of a large central stock market was pretty well dead and buried and that small, ultra-cheap and decentralised electronic systems would take over. Since then, while a hundred flowers have not exactly bloomed, and while the Stock Exchange still presides over more than 90 per cent of equity trading, newcomers have managed to make their mark.

As *The Economist* noted on 28 July 2001: 'As businesses go, stock exchanges are rather curious. They are under pressure to consolidate, yet trading platforms proliferate. Considerable economies of scale exist in their activities, yet tiny upstarts and small national exchanges can do well'.

Britain has three such upstarts. The largest and best-known is Virt-x, which came into being in 2001 as a partnership between Tradepoint (Britain's most successful home-grown upstart) and the Swiss Stock Exchange, SWX. Tradepoint was launched in September 1995, offering electronic trading in the top 2,000 British shares and a raft of top European equities. Its target market was the professional, both the fund manager and the broker. By July 2001 Virt-x claimed to have taken 10 per cent of all trading in the top fifty pan-European companies' shares. On the other hand, its proportion of trades in European stocks overall was much smaller. It took just 0.2 per cent of total trade in the top 100 FTSE shares. Virt-x denies being a direct competitor for national exchanges, claiming instead it wishes to carve out a new constituency of professionals trading across borders inside Europe.

The next upstart has a European flavour too. Jiway, launched in November 2000, offers a pan-European electronic share trading system for stockbrokers specialising in private, or 'retail', clients. Jiway is 60 per cent owned by OM, the Swedish company that owns the Stockholm Stock Exchange, and 40 per cent by US investment bank Morgan Stanley.

Finally, OPEX is an offshoot of the stockbroker JP Jenkins. OPEX is, strictly speaking, not a full-scale stock market but rather a 'secondary market facility' – jargon for a place where shares already in issue can be traded. OPEX came into existence in October 1995 after the Stock Exchange closed down its Rule 4.2 market place, which offered a similar service.

Great bond themes

It is 1992 and a major British corporate empire is undergoing radical surgery under the watchful eyes of its bankers. That is hardly a unique experience in these recessionary times. Championing the cause of one particular group of creditors is a well-known investor – let us call him Mark Smith. Given Smith is very much man of the moment in this big corporate restructuring, a financial journalist takes him out to lunch. Smith is a cautious American financier, and seems at first one of the less lively lunch dates in the journalist's long history of eating out in the line of duty. Smith declines the journalist's original suggestion that they meet at The Gay Hussar, apparently fearing Soho's famous Hungarian restaurant to be something other than simply Soho's famous Hungarian restaurant. Finally ensconced in L'Escargot, Smith refuses wine with the meal and eats sparingly. Despairing of getting anything of much interest out of the ultra-discreet financier, the journalist passes the time with small talk, eventually making a vague remark about the troubled company and its founder, to the effect that one cannot help but feel sorry for the man as his creditors closed in.

Smith comes alive, alarming fellow eaters by bellowing a well-known expletive derived from the excreta of an uncastrated male of the ox family. Feel sorry for the founder? Is the journalist out of his mind? Smith concludes: 'What about the flaming bondholders?' Or words that effect.

Quite right too. What about the bondholders? Or, more importantly, what about the bonds? The bond market enjoys a fraction of the attention devoted to its sister, the equity market, although in size terms, as we saw above, the corporate bond market easily gives the equity market a run for its money. But before going further, it is important to get our terminology straight. The word 'bonds' is really an Americanism for what we traditionally call 'stocks'. Just to keep everyone merrily confused, Americans use 'stocks' to describe what we call 'shares'.

Bonds (or stocks) are the mirror image of shares (or stocks). They generate a fixed, guaranteed series of payments from the issuer to the investor, but confer no ownership rights. Shares, by contrast, generate an erratic, far-from-guaranteed series of dividends but (usually) carry ownership rights.

A share is a little piece of the company; a bond is a little piece of a loan to the company. Once the bond matures, the original sum is repaid to the holder and the bond is cancelled. Shares, by contrast, enjoy an unlimited life, until removed from the market by takeover, bankruptcy or management buy-out.

The current fashion is to lump corporate bonds together with government securities, under the umbrella title of 'fixed interest'. We shall look at British government stocks – 'gilts' – in a later chapter, as it is my view that government and corporate bonds are fundamentally different entities. Nevertheless, some key data for the bond market combines public and private sector bonds in a way that is impossible to break down. Therefore as far as possible I will restrict this chapter to an examination of the corporate bond market, and apologise in advance for any overlap. The role of the government bond market as an instrument of policy and source of public funding will be reserved entirely for chapter five on gilts.

As with equities, 'raising money' for industry plays a very minor part in the life of the global corporate bond market; the vast bulk of activity involves secondary trading of existing bonds. Figures are harder to come by than for the equity market because of the dispersed nature of the world of bonds, but in 1999, $1,200 billion of new bonds were issued, while secondary trading topped $18,000 billion.

Who issues bonds? The simple answer is – large companies. Fixed costs make it uneconomic to issue a bond for less than about £15 million, immediately ruling out most small and small / medium enterprises. Even without such overheads, bond investors would demand an interest rate from an unknown, small company far higher than they would ask for on bonds issued by an international household name. Corporate bonds can run for three, five or ten years, sometimes longer – Coca-Cola has issued 100-year bonds – but such instruments are extremely rare. More usual is a three or five-year bond issue that can then be refinanced as the old bonds are redeemed and new ones issued. A company's first bond refinancing increasingly tends to separate the sheep from the goats, with investor-resistance building against companies suspected of being likely to face potential problems in honouring their commitments and defaulting on their bonds should the economy turn down.

At the time of writing, midsummer 2001, a number of bonds issued in 1997–98 are coming up for refinancing. During an economic boom, bond investors tend to be less discriminating and to give issues a fair wind. But as one persistent critic of the bond markets, economist and lecturer Peter Warburton pointed out: 'A first bond issue is really just an auction of promises. It is on the second bond issue that many companies come unstuck'. The notion of 'default' is, to a bondholder, what a mongoose is to a snake – something to be avoided at absolutely all costs.

Why do companies issue bonds? The stock answer from any finance director or his investment-banking adviser is that bonds form 'the key component of a company's long-term debt structure'. Equity, short-term debt (bank loans, essentially), money-market instruments (of which more later) and bonds make up a solid three-legged financial stool. Big corporations employ the brightest and the best to review constantly the balance between debt and equity and are able to tweak it to the company's maximum advantage.

Should your interlocutor be of the romantic type, he may wax lyrical about the 'creativity' needed to 'profile' the funding picture from one day to the next. Should you be of the cynical type, you may ask how it is then that these creative geniuses so frequently produce a turkey rather than a masterpiece, forcing their masters to beg banks and capital markets for one more 'restructuring' before the receivers are put in. It is true, however, that – whatever the outcome of all this 'creativity' – major corporations are constantly balancing the relative attractions of debt and equity, of bonds versus shares, as the rates demanded by the two markets shift by minute fractions that would mean nothing to the private citizen but can make (or cost) millions of pounds for a large-scale corporate borrower with colossal funding.

Through the looking glass, investors are doing exactly the same thing, from the reverse perspective. They want to pay as little as possible for the greatest possible return, while the corporate fund-raisers want to drum up the maximum amount of capital at the lowest cost. Just as most issuers of equity are also issuers of bonds, so most equity investors are also bond investors. There is a small but significant group of individual bondholders who, for reasons of their own, prefer the anonymity of the bond market (especially the 'bearer' securities, unregistered anywhere and portable as cash).

For both buyers and sellers, the pivot on which the scales balance when the attractions of bonds are weighed against the attraction of equities is the yield. For bonds, the yield is calculated by dividing its market price – either at issue or afterwards – by the annual interest payment that it carries. As with shares, a fall in the price means an increase in the yield, as the purchaser is being asked to pay less for the same income. But, as with shares, there may be good reasons for the fall in the price – the spectre of default may be looming. So-called junk bonds – paper issued by borrowers with a low credit rating – offer generous yields for those with strong enough nerves to invest in them. Household-name bond issuing corporations, by contrast, offer the smallest yields they can get away with. Governments historically offer the lowest yields of all, on the basis that they rarely default on their obligations. This is a curious notion, given the historical experience. During the past 500 years, France and Spin have defaulted on public debt numerous times; Britain itself defaulted twice, in 1671 and 1685. More recently, a respectable western sovereign state has actually gone bust (Newfoundland, in 1933) and in August 1998 Russia defaulted on its external debts, plunging the financial world into crisis.

Third World states have defaulted too many times to mention, and municipal governments from New York to Liverpool have effectively filed for bankruptcy. The safety of sovereign debt is one of those comforting notions cherished by the market but unsupported by the evidence.

Nevertheless, government bonds are the 'benchmark' for yields and so of risk. On this platform, a rickety structure of corporate bond yields has been constructed. The price of a corporate bond is often expressed in terms of the 'spread', or difference, between that bond and a government bond of similar 'maturity', or lifespan. Whereas the abovementioned calculation – a bond's annual interest payment divided by its market price – gives what is known as the 'current yield', market professionals calculate also the 'yield to maturity', which takes into account the capital value of the bond as well as its interest-bearing worth.

With the bond's yield worked out, investors can then compare it to that available on equities. Central to this process is the notion of the 'yield gap', and its twin brother, the 'reverse yield gap'. Much excitement – and a great many lucrative careers – have been generated by 'gap spotting', but the idea is simplicity itself. Essentially, the yield gap is the average yield on shares in a particular market minus the average yield on bonds. Why minus? Because, the received wisdom has it, equities are inherently riskier than bonds, thus will always, over time, have to pay a higher yield than bonds in order to attract investors.

High inflation in the 1970s and 1980s turned this equation on its head, and the 'reverse yield gap' was born, helped into the world by the crumbing reputation for probity and competence enjoyed by the 'benchmark' bond issuers, national governments. Roaring inflation led bondholders to factor in heavy erosion of future interest payments, thus they demanded a bigger current yield, and the yield gap frequently went negative, with bonds yielding more than equities.

The reverse yield gap's great moment of glory occurred in October 1987, when true believers noted that the canyon-sized gap that had opened up that summer had made a sharp 'rubber-band effect' inevitable – equity prices were so high, and their yields so low, that an exodus into the bond market was bound to occur.

One hears less about yield gaps of either type nowadays. Partly, this is because the dividend has become a less helpful guide to the value of shares given the growth of tax-efficient alternatives, such as 'buy-backs' from companies purchasing equities themselves, thus returning money to shareholders in a way that does not show up in the dividend figures. Partly it is because low inflation over a long period has made the reverse yield gap a less plausible stick with which to beat 'profligate' national governments. Today, the more prosaic explanation when the yield gap goes negative is that, on average, bondholders expect most of their profit to come from the bond's interest payments, while shareholders, on average, expect most of their profit to come from a rise in the price of a share. Thus bondholders demand, and receive, higher yields over time.

Two types of risk determine the short, but sometimes glorious, life of a bond. The first is the inherent riskiness of the issuer. The second is the external risk of changes in interest rates and inflation.

As we have seen, a junk bond issued by a low-grade borrower will need to offer a generous yield at the moment of issue in order for the bonds to launch successfully. That means a high interest payment (or 'coupon') relative to the issue price. Both the coupon and the price are critical. No investor is going to buy lavish interest payments expensively, and certainly not from a low-grade, high risk borrower. Similarly, a bargain bond price will not compensate for a

Scrooge-style coupon. As we have seen, (allegedly) zero-risk government bonds provide the benchmark – the basic current price of a set amount of money in terms of coupon and price. Building on that floor is entirely about calculating risk.

Now, the official line on risk assessment is that venerable credit-ratings agencies – chiefly Moody's Investors Service and Standard & Poor's, both New York-based – investigate each major bond issue in depth, probing the economic, financial and political background to the issue and, after much cogitation, award it a rating, from the coveted treble-A to the plague-warning D (or C, in the case of S&P). In between is a finely-calibrated scale of grades, reminiscent of the essay marks beloved of Oxbridge tutors: Aa3, BBB+, Caa1, AA-.

As the abovementioned *Economist* guide notes: 'All of the ratings agencies emphasise that they rate only the probability of default, not the probability that the issuer will experience financial distress or that the price of its bonds will fall. Nonetheless, ratings are extremely important in setting bond prices. Bonds with lower ratings almost always have a greater yield than bonds with higher ratings. If an agency lowers its rating on a bond that has already been issued, the bond's price will fall'.

So far, so good. But the ratings agencies, while providing a service chiefly of benefit to investors, are usually paid by the bond issuer. It was not always so, but during the past twenty-five years it has become commonplace for agencies to charge a fee to the bond issuer in return for a credit rating. These fees can run into tens of thousands of dollars and intense negotiations take place between the issuer's bank and the agency, with the former determined to obtain the best possible rating and the latter keen to preserve its reputation. The result is often some sort of compromise, rather than the gimlet-eyed assessment of a bond's creditworthiness that investors may expect.

Banking's big bond issuers are headed by Schroder Salomon Smith Barney, with 11.2 per cent of the world market share in 2000. Next is Deutsche Bank (9 per cent), JP Morgan (14.5 per cent), UBS Warburg (13.5 per cent), Barclays Capital (13.2 per cent), Morgan

Stanley Dean Witter (12.9 per cent), Lehman Brothers (12.9 per cent), Merrill Lynch (12.8 per cent), Goldman Sachs (11.1 per cent) and Crédit Suisse First Boston (10.9 per cent).

These banks dominate the international bond scene, defined as bonds raised for large sums of money, using whatever currency or currencies suit the borrower, and which are marketed worldwide. Both public and private sectors issue international bonds, and the total raised this way has exploded from $10 billion a year in the early-1970s to $1,200 billion in 1999. The US is the location for 37.5 per cent of international bond isues, followed by Germany (22.1 per cent), Britain (10.2 per cent) and France (6.1 per cent). The dollar and the euro are far and away the most popular currencies for the denomination of international bonds, with sterling coming a very poor third.

By far the greatest proportion of these issues are accounted for by traditional fixed-rate bonds, which take nearly 70 per cent of the total. Most of the remainder is accounted for by floating rate notes, which are a type of bond structured to pay a coupon that floats in relation to one or more variables, such as the rate of interest in the market at large.

Twenty years ago, much space in any discussion of the bond market would be given over to 'Eurobonds', which – confusingly enough – have nothing to do with Europe's single currency and are usually issued in dollars. Back then, the notion of a corporation in one country raising money in a market in a second country in a currency issued in a third country seemed either exciting or disreputable, depending on your point of view. Today it seems routine.

Eurobonds were simply loans raised in Eurodollars, a Eurodollar being defined as any currency (usually the US dollar, hence the name) held outside its country of origin. In the post-war period, when governments tried to control capital movements and to lay down limits on interest rates, Eurobonds were genuinely radical and different from the conservative national bond market. They represented lending and borrowing outside the grasp of national authorities. Today, when capital flows freely around the world and provincial solicitors have access to multi-currency mortgages, all international bonds are Eurobonds, and the phrase really ought to be given a decent burial.

Increasing numbers of bonds are asset-backed, meaning they represent an entitlement to a stream of future payments owed to the issuer. This market originated in the pooling of thousands of mortgage loans into packaged securities that were then sold on to other investors. The mortgage payments formed the income stream for which the investors were paying. Meanwhile, the mortgage lenders could focus on homeloan activities, leaving someone else to worry about the management of the asset represented by those homeloans.

Today, asset-backed bonds include packaged credit-card loans, hire-purchase deals, car loans and other types of mass-market borrowing. By 1999, Moody's estimated a total value for the global asset-backed market at $550 billion, a 4 per cent rise on 1998. Of this total, the US market accounted for $415 billion. The European market exploded in 1999 to $83 billion, an 84 per cent rise on 1998. London was the largest single European centre for asset-backed issues, generating $26.2 billion-worth of such bonds. In 1990, the figure had been just $3.8 billion. Much of the UK asset-backed business is related to commercial and residential mortgages.

A last word on asset-backed bonds. Their name is suitably solid-sounding, but you may have noticed that the income stream they represent is actually rather more unreliable than are the fixed, guaranteed payments offered by a standard corporate bond. After all, mortgage-holders default, credit-card customers have their cards snipped in two and a distressingly high number of cars disappear, along with their drivers, before the last hire-purchase payment falls due. On the legitimate side of the street, mortgages are repaid early and credit-card shopaholics cure their addiction. All these events reduce the income available to the bondholders. Investors know this full well, thus the returns they are offered are more generous than would have been the case on a straightforward company bond.

But the outsider could be forgiven for assuming an 'asset-backed security' to be far safer than the alternative, presumably non-asset-backed, bond offering. This is as good a time as any to note that investment banks and other institutions go to great lengths to dream up reassuring and attractive names to disguise the level of risk investors are being asked to take. The most obvious example is 'security', as in 'securities dealing', 'securities portfolio' and so on. Actually, a security – a share or a bond – is rather less secure than a bank deposit, but you wouldn't think so from the name.

Then there is 'secured lending'. It is only recently that the regulators have required banks and others to point out to customers that the lending is secured on the borrower's home. It makes the lender feel secure, but the borrower rather less so. One may have assumed that a 'hedge fund' was designed to hedge its investors against risk; in fact, its purpose is to take on vast and sometimes unbridled risks on its own account. Once, banks lent money to 'the Third World'. By the end of the 1970s, it looked as if the Third World may decide not to pay up, thus 'sovereign debt' became the preferred term, with its overtones of Good Queen Bess and guinea pieces. Sad to say, 'sovereign debt' was no more likely to be honoured than 'Third World debt', so – after a flirtation with 'LDC lending' (that's 'less developed countries') – the 'emerging markets' were born. True, rather too many of these proved to be submerging markets, but, as Winston Churchill said in defence of calling his dingy wartime canteens 'British Restaurants', if the public can't have anything else, they can at least have the name.

Ultimately, perhaps 'investment' is the most misleading expression in the entire financial dictionary, suggesting, as it does, an act of long-term prudence – indeed, an act of trust. That so many 'investments' turn out to be divestments does not deter the financial advisers.

And there's another one. 'Financial adviser' conjures up images of wood-pannelled offices and glasses of sherry, whereas the reality is a commission-hungry salesmen whose bread and butter is getting private investors to sign on the dotted line. At the level of high-finance, it is the same. A major corporation, you will read in the financial pages, is 'holding talks with its professional advisers' regarding a takeover or a share issue. From this you may assume these 'advisers' to be solicitors or accountants but, while m'learned and numerate friends will be much in evidence, the main 'advice' comes from corporate financiers whose reputations depend on generating huge fees for their employers. The point is this. The language of finance is grotesquely self-serving and misleading. Whole chunks of it seem designed to camouflage vested interests. Often it is the direct opposite of the language of the ordinary person. Were your neighbour to describe the labour market as 'tight', you would assume he meant that jobs were hard to come by. When a City economist talks of tight labour markets, he means that workers are hard to come by.

Be sceptical of the language and grammar of the City. Fat cats not only screech the loudest, but they have the knack of persuading the rest of us to screech the same tune. On that cacophonous note – back to bonds!

Aside from straightforward corporate bonds, floating rate notes and asset-backed securities, there is an exotic array of different types of bonds, many designed specifically for one particular issue and never to be repeated. At the far frontier of the bond world, it begins to shade into the world of derivatives. At the other end, bonds overlap with equities insofar as preference, or 'A', shares have more in common with a bond than with an ordinary share – payments are fixed and holders of 'prefs' take precedence over ordinary shareholders in the queue for dividends. Another feature shared with bonds is that ownership of 'prefs' usually confers no say in the control of the company.

One type of bond, however, does carry the right to exchange the bond for ordinary shares. This is the convertible bond, which can be swapped for a predetermined number of shares at given times during the bond's life (convertible preference shares operate in a similar way). Convertible bonds are much in demand, given the holder can draw guaranteed interest payments right up to the moment of conversion. For that reason, they are usually more expensive than straightforward bonds.

Zero-coupon bonds, by contrast, pay no interest at all. Or rather, the return they generate is not actually called 'interest'. A 'zero' is sold at a sharp discount to its redemption value, so the bondholder takes his return in the form of the balance on the redemption date.

STRIPS – or Separately Registered Interest and Principal of Securities – are a sort of smashed-up bond, with each of the resulting fragments sold as a separate security, or STRIP. So a five-year bond could become six separate securities, five representing the annual interest payment and the sixth representing the principal. Each is sold at a discount as a zero-coupon bond in its own right.

Perpetual bonds generate interest payments indefinitely, although there is usually the ability for either issuer or bondholder to trigger a redemption process.

Out on the borderline with derivatives are the 'structured notes' or 'structured bonds'. These are often lumped together with what are known as 'callable' and 'putable' bonds, which, respectively, give the issuer the right to buy back the bonds before the redemption date and the investor the right to sell the bonds back to the issuer before the redemption date. But structured bonds are fundamentally different. Callable and putable bonds are still, essentially, bonds. Structured bonds actually contain at their heart a complex derivative product, and are dealt with in chapter nine on derivatives.

Who buys bonds?

Well into the 1990s, the smart answer was: 'Belgian dentists', by which the speaker meant conservative, wealthy individuals of any nationality with a passing interest in the anonymity (and hence untaxability) conferred by 'bearer' bond certificates. Given the opaque nature of the market, it is impossible to obtain reliable current figures for the split between private and institutional bondholders. But it is certain that private investors, although still vital to the health of the market, have seen their share decline as institutions have both bought and, more importantly, traded corporate bonds. Traditionally, corporate bonds were traded once – at issue – and then tucked away by the abovementioned Flemish or Walloon tooth-doctors until they matured, at which point they were cashed in. All that has changed. Secondary dealing, as we saw earlier, has ballooned. In 1990, secondary trading globally was worth about £3,000 billion; in 1999, it was a shade under £20,000 billion.

The process of issuing a bond has changed too. Twenty years ago, a merchant bank would be appointed to handle the issue and would then set about assembling a syndicate of other banks to 'underwrite' it, effectively to buy or promise to buy the bonds from the issuing bank and to help sell them to investors. Many relatively-undercapitalised banks would compete on price and service to be appointed as an underwriter. Today, the spate of bank mega-mergers in the second half of the 1990s has greatly reduced the number of such institutions and the choice available to the issuing company is correspondingly smaller. Critics mutter about an 'underwriting cartel', to which the retort is that a global capital market needs global-sized institutions, and that the dismantling of financial frontiers around the world has maintained the level of competition overall – as the number of banks has shrunk overall, those that remain are truly international.

Once the bond issue is safely 'away', the secondary trading we looked at earlier can now begin. Relatively little trading takes place on stock exchanges; the real action is in face-to-face or telephone dealing between bond dealers and investors. Attempts at trading bonds electronically have been frustrated, in part, by the same factor that frustrated attempts to trade precious stones over dealing screens: no two are the same. Ironically, screen trading would have had more chance of dominating the market in the days before the technology existed, when bonds were more standardised and bright young things in the investment banks had yet to STRIP them, or pack them full of one-off derivative products.

That said, screen systems do operate, successfully and profit-ably, but with a limited scope. They are likely over time to focus mainly on public-sector bonds which are less exotic and more amenable to mass, anonymous trading.

The bond market has changed out of all recognition in just two decades. A staid, conservative investment forum has been transformed into the epitome of aggressive trading. Books such as *Liar's Poker* and *The Bonfire of the Vanities* have propelled the quasi-psychotic bond trader – forever snarling obscenities down the telephone and boasting of 'blood in the water' and 'ripping the face off' a counterparty to a deal – to the forefront of the public consciousness. It is no exaggeraton to say the bond trader is to our current capitalist mythology what the top-hatted merchant banker was to the folklore of the 1930s.

And behind the bond trader are the 'fixed income analysts', the 'bond gurus'. Now compared to equity analysis, bond analysis is fairly straightforward. There is the yield, and there is the risk of default. A half-decent computer can tell you whether Eurotunnel paper is attractive compared to the latest issue from DaimlerChrysler and can keep you updated in real time. By comparison, equity analysts have to juggle a huge number of imponderables when judging a company's shares. Fixed income analysis seems something of a doddle. Needless to say, the bond gurus don't see it in quite that way. As interest rates are key to bond performance, and as interest rates are set by governmental bodies, the bond guru sees himself as moving in the realms of High Policy.

But the real changes behind all this flim-flam are very real indeed. Bond markets have opened up an ocean of liquidity to borrowers who previously lacked access to funds. Whether it be the 'emerging market' government, the junk-bond takeover tycoon or the unemployed person able to command hire-purchase and credit-card borrowings, it is the power of the bond markets that has turned these one-time pariahs into feted customers.

Given that even bond traders cannot create new money, their ability to conjure up these funds is something of a poser. Peter Warburton, a British economist, and persistent critic of the bond markets, explains that bond markets have made more money available by increasing the velocity of the existing global capital stock. In other words, cash that twenty years ago would have been dozing in a building society account is now tearing around the international system, available to be borrowed and borrowed again. Warburton believes this explosion in debt has been accompanied by a sharp decline in the quality of the loans being made, and is forecasting very serious trouble by the end of 2003.

We shall know quite soon whether he is right – but one fact is beyond dispute. Because of their sheer size, and because of their intimate connection with public-sector finance, bond markets have become enormously powerful. On 10 August 2001, the eFinancial News on-line service reported the following:

> The Organisation for Economic Cooperation and Development is considering going to the bond markets to raise debt capital. The OECD, which has just received a rating from international rating agency Standard & Poor's, needs cash to redevelop its offices in Paris ... The OECD ... picked up a AA long-term credit rating from S&P and an A1+ short-term rating ... three notches short of the coveted AAA status. S&P noted in its rating that almost 90 per cent of sovereign states in the OECD are rated AA+ or AAA, but said its 'consensual decision-making process' and 'need for unanimity' could hamper its ability to move swiftly in difficult market conditions.

So there you have it. The OECD, a prestigious forum for economic policy discussion among the richest countries in the world – all of whom guarantee the organisation's credit – cannot achieve an AAA rating. But then, shortly after his election in 1992, President Bill Clinton learned that his mildly reflationary economic strategy would not be practical because of the adverse affect its implementation would have on US government securities. Clinton expressed bemusement that his policy should effectively have been vetoed by 'a bunch of flaming bond traders'.

Or words to that effect.

4

The magic money machine

Q: Do you have ten fingers?
A: Yes.
Q: Count them.
A: One, two, three, four, five . . .
Q: And the other hand makes ten,
   so, ten, nine, eight, seven, six.
A: Yes.
Q: What are five plus six?
A: Er . . .

**Children's playground riddle,
Sussex, c. 1970**

Trading while insolvent: how the City turns dross into gold

Does the City of London actually make any money?

The question may seem bizarre. Not only are we constantly told of the enormous contribution to our balance of payments that is made by financial services, but it would defy economic gravity, surely, were the whole of the Square Mile and its associated districts, with all its skyscrapers, rock-solid bank buildings and fashionable restaurants to be effectively insolvent?

Yet we all know the story of the emperor's new clothes, and a glance at some key official data raises the question: 'if not whether then at the very least how does the City make any money?'

A century and a half ago, such a query could be answered in a trice. Britain was the world's leading industrial nation and her booming domestic companies – then among the mightiest commercial concerns on the planet – naturally supported an equally dominant financial services sector. Those conditions have long since ceased to apply. But since the war, it has become commonplace to hear that the City's chief source of wealth lies in its extensive portfolio of overseas assets. To critics, this portfolio is the product of the City having evaded down the years its responsibility to support British industry; to fans of the Square Mile, it is a national nest-egg that has permitted Britain to run an enormous deficit on trade in manufactured goods.

Both camps, however, have a problem. This crock of foreign gold does not exist. Figures available in early 2001 for the net external asset position of the United Kingdom for 1999 paint an apparently alarming picture. Britain has a negative external asset position, with liabilities exceeding assets by something like £100 billion.

In share investment, Britain had liabilities of £576 billion against assets of £400 billion. On bonds and similar paper, the picture was a little brighter, with assets of £330 billion against liabilities of £217 billion. And on direct investment in foreign companies, assets of £416 billion easily outstripped liabilities of £243 billion.

However, with money market instruments, liabilities of £90 billion are set off against assets of £42 billion; on sterling bank deposits and loans, assets of £76 billion sit alongside liabilities of £168 billion. The position on foreign currency deposits and loans is even worse, with liabilities of £860 billion towering over assets of £544 billion.

Nor are things getting any better in this regard. On the

contrary, Britain's net external asset position was broadly flat in 1995 and has deteriorated seriously since then. Its current negative state gives the lie to the notion that Britain is living off a solid portfolio of foreign investments built up during the heyday of industrial and imperial supremacy. As Professor Roger Bootle, the respected economist now working for his own consultancy Capital Economics, pointed out in April 2000, Britain today is neither the workshop of the world nor 'a pure rentier country, drawing in goods and services from the rest of the world [paid] for with the income from its investments'.

The mystery deepens. How exactly are we paying for a colossal deficit on trade in goods heading towards £30 billion? We looked in Chapter One of this book at the City's contribution to invisible earnings. But how does it do it, given we owe the world more than the world owes us? Could it be that the City isn't really earning at all in the overall picture?

It would be entirely possible to answer yes. There is one enormous industry, every bit as visible as the City, that makes no money – net – at all for the United Kingdom. It is tourism. True, the country is planted thick with hotels, inns, holiday cottages and holiday camps. There is a minister for tourism; there are tourism boards; there are subsidies to tourism and there are committees awarding stars and crowns to hostelries and restaurants, the better to guide tourists to the best that Britain has to offer. Yet the contribution of all those planeloads of tourists and all those enormous coaches full of foreign visitors to the balance of payments is entirely negative, for the simple reason that we spend more abroad than they spend here.

Is the City in the same position? Happily not – or, at least, not exactly. The asset position is only part of the story. Think of it as the base of a large wedding cake. The net external asset position is the figure left over after the world's claims on the UK have been deducted from the UK's claims on the rest of the world. As we have seen, this figure is negative. But the next layer of the cake is rather more enticing. It represents the net investment income earned on those investments. Common sense would suggest this figure also should be negative, but common sense would be wrong. In 1999, the City earned about £7 billion net on the back of this unpromising position. How? By living on its wits; by managing to pay less for the money it has effectively borrowed and by receiving more for money it has effectively lent.

That's the optimists' version. A gloomier view suggests the City as a whole is taking very large risks with its foreign investments, putting money into more hazardous ventures and being paid – for the time being at least – higher rewards. Such a strategy is bound to come to grief eventually, according to this school of thought.

The third tier of the cake represents fees earned by Britain for the investment of other people's money and for tendering them technical and financial advice, legal counsel and other financial services. Here, the City notched up net earnings from the rest of the world of nearly £18 billion in 1999, a very large figure in its own right and a huge increase on the £10 billion earned just two years earlier.

Professor Bootle sums up the City's ability to earn a large return on a negative asset base thus: 'It would be more accurate to think of Britain as a sort of giant investment bank.' Andrew Smithers, of economic consultancy Smithers & Co, prefers to talk of 'hedge fund Britain'. This will sound alarming to anyone who knows anything of the hedge funds which, despite their title, do not 'hedge' against risk but deliberately take on some of the riskiest investments available on behalf of their wealthy clients. We shall examine them more closely in chapter nine. Smithers warns: 'The UK has a marked mismatch between its external assets and liabilities. It acts like a huge hedge fund. This has been very profitable, but is extremely risky. In addition, the UK derives a large surplus from banking and other financial services. This is equally vulnerable to a change in the world financial climate'.

International Financial Services London, whom we met earlier, takes a jollier view, as one would expect, and has the figures to back it up. It reckons the financial sector contribution of 5.8 per cent of Britain's gross domestic product in value-added terms, which we noted in the last chapter, should really be bumped up by another three percentage points once related services such as accountancy, law and management consultancy are included. IFSL calculate total earnings from the City at £31 billion net for 1999, from £29.8 billion in 1998 and £25 billion in 1997. These figures should not be compared directly to those we looked at earlier, derived from Britain's net external asset position, because they relate specifically to City financial institutions, whereas the external asset numbers include firms and households across the country and exclude much banking business. Nor should they be compared directly to the invisible earnings figures we looked at in Chapter One.

Nevertheless, it is interesting to note that this £31 billion breaks down into £18 billion worth of income from services and just £13 billion worth of income from investments. Two years earlier, service income totalled just £10 billion, against £15 billion income from investments. Again, Britain emerges less as a 'rentier' nation and more as a beehive full of ultra-bright 'knowledge workers' whose services are in heavy demand. These services are becoming increasingly important in terms of employment. Legal firms working in financial services now employ close on a quarter of a million people, with accountancy not far behind. Management consulting, with a payroll of 180,000 people, dwarfs securities dealing, which employs just 54,000 people. Whether this development is a net gain or loss for society is a matter of personal taste. As, indeed, is the judgment on whether Britain has ultimately benefited from having such a very large financial centre perched on top of a rather small economy.

What is not in doubt is that our Magic Money Machine is a wondrous thing. Whether in banking – where Britain represents about 20 per cent of the world total of cross-border lending – or insurance (the British market is the fifth largest in the world), a ream of statistics routinely puts the City at or near the top of the international league: more than a third of foreign-exchange dealing; the top slot for institutional portfolio management; the leading centre for shipbroking, shipping insurance and other maritime services; more foreign banks than anywhere else on earth.

Given the unpromising nature of Britain's economic position in the post-war period, this is quite an achievement. As Professor Ira Scott noted as far back as 1969: 'the Empire may have disintegrated and the UK may now be a third-rate power, but the City of London has staged a comeback which would be the envy of any child movie star reaching maturity'.

How did it happen?

Bouncing back: dollars in exile and a brand new board game

Anybody with the slightest interest in the City, or indeed anybody over the age of thirty, will have some awareness of the earthquake of change that transformed the Stock Exchange in the mid-1980s. The thumbnail sketch of these reforms runs roughly as follows: the Square Mile, being run by a gaggle of old duffers and ex-public schoolboys, was facing extinction at the hands of international competitors. Enter Margaret Thatcher, who gave them a jolly good roughing up, threw the City open to international competition and sat back to watch business and profits rise like a well cooked soufflé.

Actually, the City revolution started not in the stock market but in the foreign exchanges and short-term money markets. It was here that the new City took shape in the 1960s both in terms of personnel – beholden to neither the old way of doing things nor the City establishment – and in terms of providing the background of huge capital movements that was to make change inevitable in securities trading.

Control of currency movements had been a key of the post-war economic order around the world. With one or two recherché exceptions, such as Macao and Tangier, every non-Communist territory tied its own currency to the US dollar. In turn, the dollar was tied to gold at the immutable rate of $35 a Troy ounce. This system conferred one great advantage on the Americans. As supplier of the world's currency, they could borrow, in terms of both private and government debt, vastly greater quantities of money than would normally have been the case. But it conferred also great restraints, without which the 'dollar standard' could not have functioned. One of these was a prohibition barring individual American citizens from owning or trading in gold bullion. Another was the duty upon the US government to make available enough dollars around the world to stimulate international trade and prevent another depression. A third was the duty of the United States to pay out in gold any foreign citizen or government that presented dollar bills for exchange.

These various constraints were reflected in a complex web of financial controls within the United States that belied its self-image as a bastion of economic freedom. American banks were generally prohibited from conducting business in more than one state of the Union; this greatly hobbled their ability to reach the size needed to compete internationally. They were prohibited also from offering rates of interest on deposit accounts matching those on offer from the savings and loans institutions – effectively small banks fulfilling many of the roles of Britain's building societies. The savings and loans institutions, in turn, were prohibited from supplying current accounts and chequebooks.

The capstone of this edifice of control was Regulation Q, the legal ceiling on interest rates in the United States. Combined with capital controls that effectively prevented foreign borrowers bidding for dollars on Wall Street, Regulation Q could almost have been designed to create an alternative dollar market outside the United States. Which is precisely what happened.

As the US government supplied dollars abroad to oil the wheels of world trade, increasing numbers of these dollars stayed 'out there' and never came home. Sitting in European and other banks, these dollars became available for loans both to subsidiaries of American companies operating abroad and to non-US borrowers keen to get their hands on the 'good as gold' dollar. By the early-1960s, London's merchant banks had started bundling up these stateless dollars – inaccurately but indelibly named 'Eurodollars' – into huge loans, Eurobonds, whose terms and rates of interest were entirely beyond the reach of the US federal monetary authorities. City banks had always been good at this sort of thing; they had their roots in the days of the gold standard, and the Eurodollar boom was, for them, just like old times.

As Hamish McRae and Frances Cairncross noted in 1985: 'At last London again had a currency in which to operate worldwide'. Free of regulation by either Washington or the even more intrusive British authorities, the merchant banks and other specialists in the Eurodollar and eurobond market could get on with doing what they did best.

Two far-reaching consequences flowed from this explosion in unregulated foreign currency-based securities trading. The first was a parallel development of a much larger foreign exchange trading capability in the City. The second was the enormous growth outside the traditional Stock Exchange of dealing in foreign securities; Eurobonds at first, but increasingly foreign equities.

Meanwhile, as the costs of America's involvement in the war in Indochina escalated in the late-1960s, the number of dollars in circulation worldwide increased. The Washington authorities had chosen not to risk unpopularity by raising taxes to fund military spending, so instead they effectively printed the money.

The flood-tide of surplus dollars did more than simply lift greatly the Eurodollar markets. It undermined the post-war economic order by shaking confidence in the cornerstone of the system, the US currency. By the end of the 1960s, the pretence that Fort Knox held enough gold to back these new dollars was effectively abandoned. By 1971, the dollar was cut free to float against other currencies; inevitably, those other currencies followed suit. Inevitably also, foreign exchange trading not only ballooned but became respectable; no longer did people talk of 'speculators', in much the same tone as one may describe 'pornographers', but of the more sober-sounding 'dealers'. Their views were sought on arcane matters of state policy such as the appropriate size of Britain's public sector borrowing requirement.

In parallel, the justification for exchange control – the restriction of currency movements beyond national frontiers – was fatally weakened. For the tourist irritated by the currency declaration form at the back of his passport, the old rationale – that it was a worthwhile sacrifice to maintain international stability and full employment – no longer applied. Furthermore, a growing body of economic opinion – tagged 'monetarist' or 'neo-liberal' in media shorthand – believed such controls to be undesirable in themselves, regardless of any supposed benefits they could deliver.

By the late-1970s, the new City was taking shape around the Stock Exchange, creating a parallel Square Mile largely beyond the control of the exchange and out of sympathy with the exchange's way of doing things. Furthermore, the prospect of the removal of exchange controls threatened to leave the exchange dangerously exposed to competition from foreign markets.

Alongside all these developments, an ominous fuse was burning. In 1976, the scope of the Restrictive Practices Act was extended to cover services as well as manufactured goods. Within a short space of time the Labour government had referred the entire Stock Exchange rulebook to the Office of Fair Trading, the competition watchdog. Two issues in particular had placed the rulebook at odds with the OFT's doctrine of total competition at all times: minimum commissions on share deals (which prevented wholehearted competition for business), and single capacity, which separated brokers, who dealt for and on behalf of the client, from jobbers, who made markets in stocks and shares and with whom brokers would transact deals. Brokers could not trade shares themselves and jobbers could not deal directly with the public.

The OFT in turn referred the rulebook to the Restrictive Practices Court which began a long process of mulling over whether or not the exchange's rules conflicted with the public interest. In the event, the court was never to reach a verdict. In 1979, Britain elected a Conservative government which lifted the issue out of the legal system in order to settle the future of the exchange by negotiation between ministers and the market itself.

The eventual result was Big Bang, but before discussing that particular earthquake here is a little alternative history, with apologies to all concerned. This is very much what did *not* happen in the mid and late 1980s, but is, with luck, a way of illuminating what *did* happen.

Parkinson's Pleasure: Why Big Bang never happened

Q What exactly was Big Bang?

A It was a slang phrase for a radical plan to throw the London stock market open to foreign competition and to break up the old way of doing things.

Q What did that mean in practice?

A Pretty much the throwing open of the exchange and indeed all securities-dealing to all-comers. It was extraordinarily radical. The old City would have been completely destroyed. No more stockbrokers, no more merchant bankers, no more jobbers. High street banks would have been allowed to buy merchant banks (although some, such as Barclays, already had one), and the merchant banks would have been allowed to buy brokers and jobbers. What had been three separate little crafts would have been brought under one roof at 'securities houses', or 'investment banks'. The exchange itself would ultimately have lost its monopoly position and had to fight it out with rival markets. Big would have been beautiful, foreigners would have been welcomed with open arms and anybody would have been allowed to buy any British institution.

Q Hang on. Who are these brokers and jobbers and merchant bankers, and what was the big deal about letting them get together?

A A broker dealt for clients (rather as an estate agent does). You wanted to buy or sell shares and the broker would then try to find the best deal by shopping around the jobbers. Now, the jobbers *traded* shares on their own account; in other words, they made a market in them. The broker was paid by the client; the jobber made money from the 'turn' between buying and selling prices. Merchant bankers provided what we would now call corporate finance (helping big companies through the maze of issuing shares, bonds, and so forth). They were not allowed into the circle of brokers and jobbers, although they had been trying to get in for some years. The Big Bang idea would have allowed all three types of instititions to merge.

Q Why is that so bad?

A Well as you know, there are one or two maverick voices now saying it would not have been bad at all. They claim the shelving of Big Bang was a missed opportunity.

Q But that isn't the majority view?

A Not at all. It certainly isn't the establishment view.

Q Was this plan ever taken seriously?

A Not according to the people around at the time – politicians, stock market bigwigs and so on. A recent investigative documentary on Channel 4, however, suggests that it was taken very seriously indeed. There was a strong school of thought at that time suggesting the City simply could not survive unless it tore up its old rulebook, admitted bankers and brokers from all over the world and embraced new technology. This school contained lots of different people with different motives. There were those in the Thatcher government who saw the Stock Exchange as just another trade union. There were partners in exchange member firms who reckoned they could sell out to British and foreign banks for very large sums. There were ideologues in the Conservative think-tanks who detested any restriction on financial market activity. There were even some Labour people who were still under the impression that everyone in the City dreaded losing the old rules and that Big Bang would somehow be a punishment for them. But they were all to be disappointed. Instead of Big Bang, they were to get Genesis.

Q Everyone has heard of the Genesis reforms, but I always thought the name was a bit of a puzzle. Now I suppose we know where it came from.

A That's right. Genesis was framed in deliberate opposition to the Big Bang plans. Certain Treasury officials and some people in the Bank of England tried to bounce Cecil Parkinson into Big Bang; he responded with Genesis.

Q How was Parkinson involved?

A He had been appointed Secretary of State at the reunited Department of Trade and Industry after the 1983 general election. One of his first tasks was to conclude negotiations with Sir Nicholas Goodison, chairman of the Stock Exchange, on the terms under which the court case would be dropped. On 22 July, 1983, both men announced an agreement had been reached. Fixed commission would go by the end of 1986 and within the same period outside capital would be permitted in Stock Exchange member firms.

Q How did that differ from the Big Bang proposals?

A It didn't, to start with. The devil was in the detail. Parkinson realised this by the end of 1983. It was obvious to him that a powerful lobby was building up in Whitehall and the City determined to go much further than simply the introduction of price competition and the admission of outside capital. The endgame, Parkinson realised, was the destruction of single capacity, the set-up we noted earlier whereby brokers and jobbers were kept apart. Neither Parkinson or Goodison had envisaged this the previous summer.

Q Why was that important?

A Because it had been seen by everybody since its introduction – or rather, its codification – in 1908 as essential both to consumer protection and to keeping the City clean. Clients could approach a broker knowing the broker would get the best deal available and would not simply try to stuff the client with shares from his own book. Furthermore, by keeping merchant banks out of the Stock Exchange, the authorities could be confident that clients were not being loaded up with shares in the bank's corporate customers. By the end of 1983, Parkinson had decided to take a stand on single capacity. He had always been something of a consumer champion.

Q How did he win?

A With difficulty. Ranged against him were not only some of the bigger exchange member firms, who could see a lucrative future as part of a securities house, but also older partners who were interested simply in being bought out by incoming banks at the highest possible price. They realised that the price would be greatly reduced were single capacity to be retained. On top of that, Parkinson had to contend with ideological deregulation freaks in the Treasury and elsewhere, who were wholeheartedly committed to Big Bang. Fortunately, Parkinson had the authority to beat them all off. He had been in the Falklands War Cabinet and had gone on to lead the Tory party to victory as chairman during the 1983 election. His status as heir apparent to Margaret Thatcher gave him tremendous clout. Perhaps most importantly, he had the prime minister's support. And Lloyd's of London was the clincher.

Q How come? Lloyd's was an insurance market. It would never have been included in the Big Bang package.

A Exactly. At about that time, after a number of scandals involving conflicts of interests, Lloyd's was moving from double capacity to single capacity, by separating insurance brokers from underwriters. How could it be explained to the investing public that something that had become mandatory at Lloyd's was entirely dispensable a few hundred yards down the road at the Stock Exchange?

Q You said the prime minister supported Parkinson. What did Mrs Thatcher have against the Big Bang plan?

A It was more a case of what she had against the City. The Chancellor, Nigel Lawson, noted in his memoirs that 'Margaret had no love for the banks'. In 1988, City bigwigs complained she had snubbed them in the New Year's Honours list. The City had crossed her earlier her premiership in a complicated row over something called monetary base control.

Q Monetary what?

A Essentially a method of controlling the money supply that did not rely on high interest rates. Not surprisingly, the City preferred the high interest rates and, in cahoots with the Bank of England and the Treasury, defeated Mrs Thatcher. This was a perfect opportunity for her to take her revenge.

Q OK, so Parkinson beat off the Big Bang idea. How did he go about drawing up an alternative blueprint?

A Well, once he made single capacity his compass, it wasn't as difficult as the Big Bang lobby had made out. That said, there were tricky obstacles to be negotiated. With exchange control gone, how do you keep business in London without allowing the free-for-all involving highly capitalised securities houses? And without minimum commission, how do you keep single capacity?

Q How do you?

A Parkinson and his advisers squared the circle by blending regulation and reform together in one mixture. This was in sharp contrast to the Big Bang lobby, which, insofar as it had thought about regulation at all, assumed it could all be sorted out at a later date. Under the Parkinson plan, all practitioners would be required to register as brokers, or market-makers or merchant banks or whatever. Each had a defined business area which was regulated by its own special committee. This was part of the beauty of the plan. With Big Bang, inevitably you would have ended up with some enormous super-regulator costing millions.

Q Fine, so he kept banks away from the brokers and the brokers away from the market-makers. But wasn't Parkinson already committed to allowing in outside capital? And wasn't new capital essential if London were to compete?

A Absolutely right. But Parkinson could see no reason why new capital should necessarily go hand in hand with control of the businesses. Nor could Mrs Thatcher. It's no secret that the prospect of foreign control helped keep her on Parkinson's side during heated discussions in 1984 and 1985. She became particularly agitated when someone suggested that Morgan Grenfell could end up being owned by Deutsche Bank!

Q Ha ha ha!

A So Parkinson dreamed up the idea of limited-liability joint ventures allowing outside investors, British or foreign, to put up capital for modernisation and trading and in return to share in profits, but to have no say in management. This kept the partnership system intact on the Stock Exchange but allowed those partnerships to go into partnership themselves with wealthy corporate backers. Some wag called it 'Parkinship'.

Q I bet not everybody was happy.

A Not everybody, no. Those who had hoped to sell out total control of their partnerships to large foreign banks saw the pound signs fading before their eyes. But the moderate opinion of the Stock Exchange was reasonably content. Coupled with a new Companies Act, requiring public companies issuing shares or other securities to do business only through recognised brokers, bankers and market-makers, the Parkinson reforms achieved the objective of stimulating much greater internal competition while also making London, to a more limited extent, competitive internationally.

Q But firms could still snub the exchange and use cheaper markets overseas to raise capital couldn't they?

A They could, but under the new Act, it was made clear to them that they needn't come crying to the British courts or British compensation schemes if it all went wrong. The same principle applied to investors. That was why the Government was so tough in 1988 on the people who lost money in Barlow Clowes in Gibraltar. They didn't get a penny piece.

Q What did the Americans make of it?

A Some of their banks weren't too happy. They had hoped to buy their way into London on a rather more ambitious scale than was allowed for by the 'parkinships'. But the authorities were delighted. The Securities and Exchange Commission and others had feared the Big Bang proposals would have allowed American banks to do in London what they were forbidden to do at that time in the United States – American laws separating ordinary clearing banks from investment banks were even stricter than our own.

Q And the Europeans?

A They were even happier. At that time none of their stock exchanges amounted to very much and they feared a fully liberalised London would be a great big cuckoo in the European nest. Furthermore, the Parkinson package was very much a model upon which they could base modernisation of their own bourses. Which is pretty much what happened.

Q So everybody was happy?

A Up to a point. A treaty was signed establishing London as the hub of the Pan-European Stock Exchange. But there are critics who say the whole Genesis package was a cop-out, and that London should have moved much more radically towards deregulation. That would have given the Americans the push they needed to dismantle their own Glass-Steagall Act, the chief law keeping commercial banks out of investment business. And that, in turn, could have pushed the Europeans towards much greater liberalisation of their own markets. On this reading, the Parkinson scheme was nothing more than an extension of the inward-looking City of old, complete with its small-scale firms and special protection against foreign competition. But Parkinson's fans claim that it was the Genesis scheme that put us at the heart of European securities dealing. Which is ironic really, because we'd have been at the heart of it anyway under the Big Bang proposals, albeit not in quite the same sense.

Q What you mean?

A Well, it has since emerged that had Big Bang gone through, it is quite likely that the French bank Paribas would have bought the stockbroker Quilter Goodison.

Q So what?

A Paribas was nationalised at that time.

Q And?

A Where do you think Sir Nicholas Goodison was a partner?

Q You mean . . .?

A That's right. The chairman of the London Stock Exchange would have been a French civil servant!

Q That's unthinkable!

A Of course it is. But it does illustrate just how impractical and ill-considered the Big Bang plan had always been.

Watch it come down: The short life and inglorious times of British investment banking

It never happened, of course. None of it, beyond the Parkinson-Goodison outline announcement in summer 1983. Nor is there any evidence that Parkinson really would have made a stand on single capacity or on anything else. We shall never know. In the autumn of 1983 he was forced from office by a sex scandal and the countdown to Big Bang continued unimpeded.

The point of our potted alternative history is simply to show that, contrary to current belief, there was nothing inevitable about Big Bang. Indeed, at its inception, many of its architects – Goodison included – expected the outcome to be very different from what emerged three or four years later. Our question-and-answer session reminds us also that Britain was very much a policy leader in the mid-1980s, whether on privatising state industries or on stock market reform. Far from there having been any pressure from the

American authorities for the City to be liberalised, their concern was that liberalisation could go too far and give the US banks and brokerages an offshore platform from which they could behave in ways still prohibited at home, in particular hopping over the US legal barrier separating clearing banks from investment banks.

Much the same was true of Europe. Those who are rightly sceptical about repeated claims from successive British governments that 'the European argument is going our way' ought to suspend their disbelief when it comes to financial market regulation. Here, very largely, the argument has indeed 'gone our way', whether on the removal of exchange controls or the regulation of securities markets. Had our lead been in a different direction, Europe's bourses could look very different today.

Not half as different, it must be added, as the City itself. Face-to-face trading on the Stock Exchange floor was probably doomed whatever route to reform was taken. The same is not true of many of the great names in banking and broking that have long since disappeared into foreign control. Who knows? Our fictional Lord Parkinson could today be sitting out his retirement as non-executive chairman of Rowe & Pitman, Pinchin Denny or Wedd Durlacher Mordaunt. He could even have ended up as chairman of Barings Bank.

As it is, the development of the City in the quarter-century since that fateful revision to the Restrictive Practices Act has been a series of hasty retreats from pre-prepared positions. Position one was that the 1979 Tory victory would see the termination of the outgoing Labour government's case against the exchange in the Restrictive Practices Court. When that failed to happen, position two was that Parkinson and Goodison would cook up some face-saving formula that would allow things to carry on pretty much as before. When this, in turn, did not happen, the new conventional wisdom was that only minimum commission would have to go by the board, and that single capacity would be retained.

This in turn proved to be the opposite of the truth, but in 1985–86, the notion gained ground that the new securities houses would be little more than holding companies beneath whose capacious umbrellas the old cottage industries would survive. This comforting thought was given some support by the appearance of interim stationery and business cards printed by the aforementioned houses. In the case of SG Warburg, its official title managed to include both its own name and those of the gilts broker Mullens, the jobber Ackroyd & Smithers and the Queen's broker Rowe & Pitman. As with stages of the Apollo rockets, however, these names dropped away as the securities houses soared skywards.

Funnily enough, the most comforting illusion of all was probably Big Bang itself. The idea that 27 October 1986 represented some sort of sound barrier, the breaking of which was the only achievement necessary to qualify as a major world financial centre, was widespread at the time. Lip-service was paid to the need to 'update systems', to 'maintain our cutting-edge' and, of course, to 'avoid the burden of over-regulation'. But this was little more than background music. The City had changed, as required. The much feared American and Japanese banks had been allowed in. The bitter pill had been swallowed once and for all.

Little did the City know that the pill in question was but the first dose of an extensive and painful course of medication. By the end of the treatment, there would be not a single British-owned investment bank of any size left in the Square Mile. Yet if this were a retreat, it was a retreat with a difference – a retreat into prosperity. By the turn of the century, the rewards available for top players in the City were eye-popping, not only by the standards of the pre-Big Bang era but even by those of the late 1980s; the 'years of greed' of 1985–88 were beginning to look rather more like an era of lost innocence. In light of this, it is perhaps not surprising that as the colonisation of the Square Mile by foreign banks proceeded apace, it proved to be an occupation like no other – those who had expressed doubts at the time tended to accustom themselves to the new dispensation as the money rolled in.

Nobody, it turned out, had been in the Resistance.

There are exceptions, of course. Rod Kent of Close Brothers, the merchant bank, believes that foreign ownership is an issue. Philip Augar, whose campaign medals include NatWest, Schroders and, in the dim and distant past, stockbroker Fielding Newson Smith, became so concerned that he left the City to write a book about its occupation by foreign bankers. In his view, the City establishment has quite simply sold out.

But mavericks such as this are very much in the minority. Big institutions like to have them in for lunch now and again; they can always be relied upon to 'say something interesting'. The official line is unchanged: ownership simply does not matter. If the financial market is a casino, then the important thing is to ensure that London has the widest range of games, the most agreeable surroundings, unobtrusive yet effective regulation, the best trained (and most honest) staff and the finest food and wine in the restaurants. Should the high rolling gamblers proved to be foreign, that is of no concern.

It is a remarkable turnaround from the conventional thinking of the mid-1980s, when no City dinner was complete without abundant reassurances from speakers that British firms would continue to dominate securities trading in London. Augar himself recalls the then Bank of England governor Robin Leigh-Pemberton (now Lord Kingsdown) on the subject: '[We] would not contemplate with equanimity a Stock Exchange in which British member firms played a clearly subordinate role'.

Today, the thumbnail sketch of what went wrong suggests the worldwide stock market crash that began on the 19 October 1987 was the 'reality check' for Britain's fledgling investment banks. This is true only in a very limited sense; if anything, it was the foreign invaders that took the bigger beating in the late 1980s. True, Britain's Morgan Grenfell – before 1986, the premier British merchant bank – pulled out of securities trading shortly after the crash, the first casualty of a savage new price war in the Square Mile. But so did Citicorp of the United States, whose huge South Bank securities operation was bleeding money. Citicorp – better known as First National City, one of the largest banks on earth – had bought two London firms, Vickers da Costa and Scrimgeour Kemp Gee, for a total of £38 million. By the time it bowed out, Citicorp had poured a total £355 million into Citicorp Scrimgeour Vickers and had received back a paltry £25 million. Another casualty was a Big Bang pioneer, Security Pacific. Way back in 1983, the bank had paid more than £8 million for just under a third of stockbroker Hoare Govett. This increased to 80 per cent ownership once London rules allowed. By 1991, Security Pacific was looking to return the broker to its original owners – the management. At that time, Hoare had cost Security Pacific a total £230 million and repaid just £28 million.

Chase Manhattan, possibly the grandest name on Wall Street, was also heading for the door. Chase's London subsidiary, Chase Investment Bank, owned two City brokers, Laurie Milbank and Simon & Coates. In 1989 it shut the entire operation, foreshadowing by exactly one year Citicorp's own withdrawal.

To the outsider, the sequence of events was obvious. The crash had wiped out everyone's profits and the weakest players were going to the wall. To an extent, this was true enough. Pre-tax profits for Stock Exchange member firms went negative to the tune of nearly £400 million in the last quarter of 1987, but profits had been under pressure anyway as costs had exploded – up from £493 million in the first quarter of 1987, topping £500 million in the second quarter and reaching a record £650 million in the third quarter. The crash, to the extent that it played any part at all in the Square Mile's agonies of the late 1980s, probably did all concerned a favour, in that it exposed the grotesque overcapacity in securities trading that had followed Big Bang. There was quite simply never going to be enough business to go round. Worse, this excess capacity was costing more per head than the old system ever had. Prior to 1986, the ability to trade securities was an individual privilege, granted by those already enjoying that same privilege. Not surprisingly, this meant very tight restrictions on the numbers of people permitted to join the charmed circle. After 1986, all quantitative restrictions on market participants had been lifted; anyone judged fit and proper and working for an authorised firm was allowed in to try their hand. One would have thought that this change would have devalued each individual market participant, in much the same way that the worth of a London taxi driver's badge would be devalued were the Mayor of London to double the number of badges in issue overnight.

Displaying its usual shaky grasp of economics, the City allowed average salaries to take off like a firework at a time when staff numbers were ballooning. In 1980, a trainee stockbroker could expect to start work on about the same earnings as a skilled blue-collar worker at Ford's Dagenham plant. In 1986–87, starting packages of seven or eight times that amount – and perhaps ten times average male earnings – were commonplace. Brian Winterflood, the outspoken ex-jobber who quit NatWest's securities arm to set up Winterflood Securities, estimated at the time that jobbers doubled their salaries overnight once they were re-named 'market-makers'.

In the summer of 1987, various fantasy 'explanations' were circulating in the Square Mile as to why there was no need to worry about the City's bloated new shape and cost base. Britain's privatisation programme, then in full swing, was creating a 'shareholder democracy' whose citizens would provide all the demand needed to keep the new City in business. The Single European Act, passed the previous year, was unifying European financial markets; in a ghostly echo of post-war British *folie de grandeur,* it was assumed quite naturally that London would be the centre of this 'single investment space'. Most amusing of all was a 'Japanese wall of money' declared to be heading for London from the Pacific during the high summer of 1987. This notion was based upon the misconception that the June 1987 election result had ever been seriously in doubt (it hadn't been). The wall of money, apparently, represented huge quantities of Japanese investment held back until Tokyo's financial wizards could be satisfied that Mrs Thatcher's Tories had been returned to office. The Tories were duly returned. Reference Point won the Derby. Princess Anne became the Princess Royal. But, as the rather wet and heavy summer progressed, of this mythical mobile wall there was no sign.

One final factor made the traumatic shake-out of 1988–91 inevitable: not only were there too many investment banks employing too many expensive people, but too many of these investment banks were exactly the same as each other. In the old City, most firms had their own specialities – in economic jargon, they were producing 'non-competing specialised outputs'. In the new City, giant amorphous entities offered much the same services as their rival giant amorphous entities.

Speaking in February 1991, Tom Jones, chief financial officer of Citibank, explained the thinking behind the closure of Citicorp Scrimgeour Vickers: 'In this case we just honestly didn't think that even if we stayed around for years of pain there were going to be the rewards, and we also ... had no particular strength versus the customer. The offering was becoming less significant to the customer. The market was overburdened with capacity. We just didn't think that it made sense. Had we thought it made sense long-term, we would have been prepared to stay and put money in'. Mr Jones added that, in 1988, 'virtually no player made money', and even in 1990, profits were wafer-thin.

He was speaking as the London Business School published a report estimating the total net cost of Big Bang to the forty biggest City securities firms (or, more likely, to their new owners). From the first Security Pacific stake in Hoare Govett up to February 1991, the school put the figure at an astronomical £4 billion.

Morgan Grenfell apart, the chief casualties as we have seen were American. Relief combined with smugness summed up the reaction of the surviving British. Only two or three short years before, it had been the US banks that had been expected to clean up after Big Bang. Commentator William Kay noted in 1986: 'The Americans in the City quietly reckon that the Big Bang is tailor-made for them ... It [the City] is, quite simply, becoming more ruthless ... This is an ideal breeding ground for newcomers, who must fight for new business by luring potential customers away from the long established British banks and brokers'.

Merrill Lynch had been a particular bogey for the British investment banks. America's biggest stockbroker made no secret of its desire to be a serious player in the reformed City. As if to symbolise the new order, its London head, Stanislav Yassukovitch, was chairman of the Securities Association, the regulatory body that had replaced the Stock Exchange as the supervisor for market-based business. And on the Friday before Big Bang, 24 October 1986, the

Exchange Telegraph news service reported ominously that, while the final hours of the old Stock Exchange trading floor dissolved into an impromptu party involving champagne, tears and a huge pantomime horse, 'the new American and Japanese masters looked on in silence'.

By 1990 it was all, on the surface, very different. One of the senior executives at SG Warburg felt able to joke of Merrill Lynch: 'They thundered in, looked around, then thundered off again'. This was a reference both to Merrill's long-standing nickname – the thundering herd' – and to its lower-than-expected profile in the City at that time. Doubtless our Warburg man had a ready quip five years later when Merrill Lynch snapped up British broker Smith New Court.

All that lay in the future, however. At the dawn of the new decade, the better placed British investment banks displayed a self-confidence at odds with the idle cranes and derelict building sites left behind by the general economic recession. Profits had started to recover from the turmoil of the late-1980s, and with key American players retiring hurt, upward pressure on salaries and bonuses had temporarily abated.

And there was little doubt which was the biggest British beast in the jungle. From its palatial headquarters in Finsbury Square, SG Warburg was the likeliest candidate to be the country's flag-carrying securities house. If anybody could look the giants of Wall Street in the eye, then Warburg could. Its chairman Sir David Scholey was frequently spoken of as a future governor of the Bank of England.

The shock was that much the greater, then, when in December 1994 Warburg announced it was in talks to merge with the American investment bank Morgan Stanley. Warburg's fan club in the City and the financial press continued to insist that the proposed marriage merely underlined Warburg's global status. The truth emerged early in the New Year – the British house had lost a great deal of money the previous year in an ill-fated attempt to break into the big time on bond trading. They were very much the junior partner in the merger. Worse, Morgan Stanley scarcely bothered to conceal its indifference to Warburg's banking side, as opposed to the fund management arm Mercury Asset Management. Once it became obvious that MAM, which enjoyed quasi-independent status, would not be bought on Morgan Stanley's terms, the deal collapsed.

In March 1995, once-proud Warburg sank gratefully into the arms of Swiss Bank Corporation. In other words, the nation's champion in investment banking – a business at which the British were thought to excel – was taken over by an institution from Switzerland, a country whose banks had long been looked down on as excelling at nothing very much beyond supplying secret bank accounts to dubious characters. But by the time of that final humiliation, British investment banking had suffered an equally serious body blow. On Sunday 26 February 1995 it emerged that Britain's oldest merchant bank, Barings, was effectively insolvent. A series of ultimately fatal bets on Far Eastern derivatives markets had run up a bill totalling nearly £1 billion. The Bank of England had held secret talks all weekend to try to put together a consortium of banks prepared to stand behind Barings' and guarantee its independence.

By the Sunday night, the Bank accepted defeat.

In his book on the Barings affair, journalist Stephen Fay comments:

> In fact, the collapse of Barings was a moment when the City of London redefined itself. Ever since Big Bang, its image as a quintessentially English place, nourished by its history and yet flexible enough to welcome new ideas and new men, had been changing. Now the emphasis had switched entirely to the new men and their money. The collapse of Barings, and the prospect of the sale of other merchant banks, wrenched the City from its roots.

With Barings down, other dominoes were quick to fall. In June 1995, Kleinwort Benson was sold to Dresdner Bank. In the same month, Merrill Lynch snapped up Smith New Court. The pace accelerated as the decade drew to a close. In October 1997, Barclays announced its withdrawal from investment banking and the effective closure of its securities offshoot BZW, perhaps the only serious challenger just a few years earlier to Warburg's claim to be the only British institution capable of feasting in Wall Street's fabled 'bulge bracket' of investment-banking giants. Two months later, NatWest followed suit. In January 2000, Schroders sold itself to Citicorp, now returning to the City after its unfortunate withdrawal 10 years earlier. Shortly afterwards, Robert Fleming was sold to another US bank returning to London, Chase Manhattan.

It was the 'Yanks' revenge'. Only Security Pacific, now subsumed into Bank of America, was missing from what could have been a golden opportunity to crow at the stricken British.

Meanwhile, as UK investment banking was given as decent a burial as possible, explanations for its demise varied widely. True believers in the forward march of globalisation pointed to size as the great handicap of the British securities houses. Their balance sheets, it was argued, had never been able to support truly international ambitions. The future, inescapably, was American.

Philip Augar, former senior investment banker with NatWest and Schroders and author of *The Death of Gentlemanly Capitalism*, blames a complex mix of factors: the public school backgrounds of the senior partners responsible for guiding firms after 1986, with the emphasis on 'effortless superiority' – too often translated into effortless inferiority – rather than hard management graft; the easy money paid to those partners for their shares, freeing them from personal financial worries and robbing them of performance incentives; lack of grip in the management of the new entities and a chronically short-term approach by those commercial banks trying to assemble investment arms. Furthermore, he believes the Bank of England and the authorities in general were far too hands-off: 'The occasional intervention in a manner that central banks have done over the years would have ensured the survival of at least one British investment bank without damaging in any way the City's reputation for openness.'

In retrospect, the Big Bang era looks rather less an expression of thrusting Thatcherite entrepreneurial values and rather more a last gasp of Britain's post-war great power fantasies. Whereas in the 1950s, 'the big three' placed Britain at the top table in terms of military power, in the 1980s the same phrase now put the City alongside New York and Tokyo as a great financial centre. Indeed, the one aspect of the new City that seemed truly to reflect the tough unsentimental business approach much touted in the 1980s and 1990s was the collapse of institutional loyalty. This went far beyond the old merchant banks and brokerages and expressed itself in 'demutualisation' – an ugly word for the once and for all sale of organisations previously owned by their members – of such pillars of the City as the International Petroleum Exchange, the London International Financial Futures and Options Exchange and the Stock Exchange itself. In such a climate, a new 'non-institutional' mentality rules. This is particularly true of the banks, and may well explain their reluctance to spend decades building investment banking offshoots. Peter Ellwood, currently chief-executive of Lloyds TSB, has described banking as essentially a very simple business: 'There is a cost stream and an income stream'. Banking, he explains, is all about minimising the first and maximising the second. Martin Taylor, Barclays chief executive at the time it dismantled BZW, said much the same thing, albeit in a rather more complicated fashion involving H-shaped matrices. Taylor was reported at the time he pulled Barclays out of BZW to be both puzzled and irritated the by the idea that 'investment banking is special'.

This is a far cry from the traditional notion, which held that banks of all types were 'special' – indeed, that they were nothing less than the system itself. The great insurance houses had a scarcely less inflated opinion of their own importance. And Lloyd's of London was an institution so grand it had its own Act of Parliament to prove it. At the time of writing, Lloyd's is preparing to 'let go' those underwriters who have 'underperformed'. Insurance, it seems, is seeking to reduce its own 'cost stream'.

The Ellwood–Taylor view is entirely defensible – and could well be unavoidable, given the current lack of sympathy in high government circles for anything that smacks of a 'cosy cartel'.

(Cartels, for some reason, are never austere, or even moderately comfortable.) Nevertheless, the point with which we began this chapter – how does the City make its money? – is intimately bound up with the question of institutions and attitudes. Let us look again at Andrew Smithers' critique of 'hedge fund Britain'. He suggests just two explanations for the City's ability to make a positive return on a negative asset position: one is that the Square Mile routinely makes better selections abroad in terms of shares and other investments than foreigners make here. The other, as we saw earlier, is that the City is making not better but much riskier investments abroad, and that these risks, because of the greater hazard attached to them, pay better returns – for as long as they are paying any returns at all.

Such a strategy would hardly commend itself in a financial centre dominated by tightly-knit institutions whose members had a personal stake in the long-term future of the organisation for which they worked. But just as life in City firms has become more short-term and 'transactional', so perhaps has the attitude of those firms to the City itself, treating it in much the same way as their own employees treat them: somewhere to make hay while the sun shines and to enjoy it while it lasts, because it never does. As Stephen Fay puts it: 'The City may be surrounded by London, but it no longer really belongs there. The new City of London has more in common with Wall Street and Marunouchi in Tokyo than with Glasgow or Birmingham. Everything in the City has its price, and patriotism is not worth very much'.

As the twentieth century drew to a close, the tycoon Sir James Goldsmith died. As tributes were uttered and obituaries penned, the consensus was that the great political causes to which Sir James had devoted his later years were in pretty good shape: environmentalism, the questioning of global free trade and the insistence that the British people be consulted in a referendum before Britain join the single European currency. But regarding his commercial legacy, the general view seemed to be a chuckle and the assertion that 'you couldn't get away with that these days'. Which is strange, given that

Sir James pioneered the freewheeling, non-institutional business style that now permeates the City.

Sir James's two great commercial characteristics were, first, a hatred of companies as institutions – he described them variously as 'ministries', 'mausoleums', 'memorials' and 'private bureaucracies' – and, second, a love of gambling. In his heyday, Sir James was routinely described as 'an outsider' in the City. Today, one can't help but imagine that he would feel very much at home.

But if Goldsmith is the spiritual father of the Magic Money Machine, we ought not to forget its two Parliamentary begetters. Both now sit in the House of Lords. The first extended the scope of the Restrictive Practices Act in such a way as to encompass the City, while it was the second, her successor as Secretary of State for Prices and Consumer Protection, who made the fateful decision to pack the Stock Exchange rulebook off to the OFT. They are respectively Lady (Shirley) Williams and Lord (Roy) Hattersley. Perhaps their statues could share a plinth with Sir James's, somewhere prominent in the Square Mile.

5

Soldiers of the Queen.
Part one – The Bank of England, the gilt market and the money markets.

We're going to nationalise the Bank [of England]. We don't know how, but we're going to do it. Get the appropriate fellow to draw up the plans.

Hugh Dalton, Chancellor of the Exchequer, July 1945

Ever faithful? The Bank's secret history

The City is often portrayed as a bastion of free enterprise – a 'jungle' to its critics, a sure fortress against the false doctrines of socialism to its supporters. In fact, the City has been intimately bound up with Government and governments for hundreds of years.

As we saw in the introduction, the earliest common interest between the City and Westminster was money. The City had it, and governments wanted it. Later, as markets became more sophisticated and more prone to catastrophic breakdown, some of the traffic was in the opposite direction, with the City approaching the politicians for bail-outs (or 'liquidity', which is a superior sort of bail-out available only to the City). But cash is not the only mutual attraction between the two. Questions of law and regulation have brought political considerations into the heart of the City, as the legislators have sought to bring order to a world they barely understand. And national-interest issues have proved an equally powerful link, whether primarily external – the balance of payments, the exchange rate, the country's stock of bullion and foreign currency – or primarily internal, such as questions of support for industry, general financial stability and the protection of consumers.

For centuries, the chief border crossing, the clearing house for the politics of finance, has been the Bank of England. Massive, stone-faced and impassive, the Bank's premises at the heart of the City exude constancy and stolidity. Here, surely, is the original 'immovable object' against which the forces of inflation, financial instability and imprudence dash themselves in vain? Indeed, as you ascend the escalator from one of the Bank's four Tube or light-rail stations – that the rest of us should enjoy public transport facilities such as this! – it will not be long before you pick up the threads of a narrative not unlike a financial version of Thomas Hardy's epic of faithful love rewarded, *Far from the Madding Crowd*.

Here are the bare bones of the plot. For centuries, the Bank is the custodian of the eternal verities of sound money, honouring one's debts and living within one's means. But in the middle of the twentieth Century, the world goes mad. Crazed with the fashionable ideas of John Maynard Keynes and other economists, the politicians throw over the Bank and all it stands for in favour of the flashy, trashy notions of economic demand management – a euphemism for inflation and borrowing beyond all reason. Indeed, they turn the Bank into a nationalised industry, they seize control of interest rates, (which they always set too low in order to buy popularity from the voters), and they create a vast state sector made up of bankrupt state industries and an ever-expanding army of bureaucrats. This humiliation continues for decades, during which time the Bank – to continue the Hardy analogy – suffers largely in silence, a stoic Gabriel Oak tormented by the sight of his beloved Bathsheba Everdene running around with the meretricious Sergeant Troy.

But all is well that ends well. Finally, on a glorious May day in 1997, the scales fall from the politicians' eyes and the worthlessness of the Troy way of doing things becomes apparent. They turn to the steadfast Bank, beg forgiveness and return control of interest rates – the key instrument of economic policy – back where it had always truly belonged, with a Bank free of political interference. Wedding bells ring; there is not a dry eye in the house. The Bank reaps the reward for unswerving fidelity to the true canons of sound money.

In fact, nothing could be further from the truth. Far from standing firm against the tides of economic fashion, the Bank has spent fifty years as a fashion victim without equal. Worse, it has managed to be wrong about almost everything.

In the early-1930s, the Bank promulgated the message of orthodox finance and adherence to the gold standard, in the teeth of the worst depression of the century. But within little more than a decade, as the Allied powers prepared for the post-war world, its advocacy of planning, controls and state economic management was so fierce as to draw protests from Keynes himself.

Come the era of Bretton Woods – the fixed international currency system established after the war – and no other institution defended currency fixing with the fervour of the Bank. When that position became untenable after the devaluation of sterling in 1967 and the dollar in 1971, the Bank bounced the Treasury into a package of financial liberalisation measures – the Competition & Credit Control paper of 1971 – that unleashed a flood of new credit into the British economy, stoking inflation and pumping up an unsustainable speculative bubble. Beyond a mild suggestion that banks ought to curb their lending to property speculators, the Bank did nothing as inflation soared out of control and the economy slammed into the crash of 1973–74.

Within a few short years, however, the Bank was in full agreement with the canons of monetarism – or, at least, it said it was. By the time of the Lawson boom in the late-1980s, the Bank was assuring one and all that Lawson's huge tax cuts were not inflationary. They were.

Help was at hand with a brand new craze sweeping the British establishment – membership of the European Exchange Rate Mechanism. None cheered more loudly than the Bank in October 1990, when sterling's disastrous membership of the ERM began, exulting in the 'discipline' this would exert over wage bargaining and other proletarian activities detrimental to the national well-being; none was more shattered two years later when sterling was unceremoniously ejected.

In the late-1980s, when Britain's top people favoured British membership of European monetary union, the Bank was in there with the best of them. Indeed, Bank Governor Lord Kingsdown signed the Delors Report that paved the way for the creation of the euro. In the late-1990s, when the establishment was cooling on the whole idea, Lord Kingsdown's successor Sir Edward George was appropriately downbeat.

Before May 1997, the Bank's role as a supervisor of the banking system – banks had 'supervisors', whereas downmarket and untrustworthy people such as share traders and commodity dealers had 'regulators' – was entirely non-negotiable, a resigning issue. Take banking supervision away from the Bank, and chaos would follow. After May 1997, when banking supervision was indeed taken away from the Bank, it seemed that the Old Lady of Threadneedle Street could, after all, live with this outrage.

Critics may detect in this sorry history of twisting and turning a performance worthy of the Vicar of Bray, the seventeenth century churchman who was, in a colourful career, by turns an Anglican, a Catholic, a Protestant, a Whig and a Tory, but whose career had a common theme, namely, in the words of the song, that: 'Whatsoever king shall reign / I will be Vicar of Bray, sir!'

Supporters may prefer to suggest that the Bank has acted merely as the faithful servant of the politicians, and that its apparent ducking and weaving simply reflects the fact that it has at all times been properly under the control of our democratically-elected masters. Indeed, this is a point well worth making, given the Bank's central place in left-wing demonology as a rogue institution forever 'ramping' well-meaning but muddled politicians into following a City agenda of public spending cuts, a strong pound and high interest rates – all at the cost of jobs, living standards and social tranquillity. The Bank can either be hopelessly suggestible, a dedicated follower of fashion, or it can be a sinister cell inside the governmental structure, secretly promoting a hidden capitalistic agenda.

But it cannot be both.

Perhaps it is more useful to see the Bank as engaged in a perpetual struggle for institutional survival. There is nothing dishonourable about this notion, and it does help explain how it is that the Bank has been so many different things, played so many different roles, during the comparatively short period since the war. The Bank has been a custodian of the exchange rate, from 1945–71 and in 1990–92. It has been a bank supervisor, informally until 1979 and formally from 1979–97. It has been a policeman, enforcing exchange controls from 1945–79. It has been a friend to business and commerce, from helping to set up the venture fund Investors in Industry (later 3i) after the war, to strong-arming foreign and domestic banks to support the Eurotunnel project in the 1980s.

It has been custodian of the gilt market, unofficial City enforcer and troubleshooter, the government's bankers, the regulator of money markets and boss of the bullion market. But through all these costume changes, an entity called the Bank of England has survived and (mostly) thrived in Threadneedle Street, EC2. Now would seem to be its hour of triumph, as it has once more assumed the role it considers to be the veritable Hamlet of the central-banking repertoire – the conduct of monetary policy. But in doing so, the Bank has placed a very risky bet on its own survival, as we shall see.

Gambling on red: the birth of the Monetary Policy Committee

Since May 1997, the phrase 'Bank of England independence' has been bandied about in a lazy fashion to describe the changes in the respective roles of the Treasury and the Bank in setting interest rates. Point one: the Bank of England is not independent. It is a national-ised institution with a bare majority of the votes on a body that meets monthly to set short-term interest rates. Point two: this body, the Monetary Policy Committee (MPC), is working to a target inflation rate set by politicians, currently 2.5 per cent a year. By contrast, the European Central Bank, and, before European economic and monetary union in 1999, Germany's Bundesbank, set their own inflation targets.

In the jargon, the MPC has 'operational independence' – it can move rates without political approval in order to try to hit this target – but it does not have 'target independence', the right to decide what inflation ought to be. By the criteria laid down in the European Union's Maastricht Treaty, the Bank does not qualify at all as an 'independent central bank', both because it lacks target independence and because it is itself merely a delegate, albeit the one with the most votes, to an external interest-rate committee. Were Britain to vote to join the euro, the MPC's statutes would have to be torn up. Effectively, the committee is a sub-contractor to the Treasury. It is in the same position as an outside catering firm. The caterer delivers coffee, sandwiches and hot pies to the Treasury canteen at an agreed standard and price; the MPC delivers an agreed inflation rate.

This unglamorous sub-contractor role is sniffed at in both continental Europe and the United States, whose Federal Reserve Board similarly takes no instructions from mere politicians as to the appropriate level of inflation. But the Bank seized it with both hands. Why?

In part, because it was the best deal on offer. No British politician was likely to go 'all the way' and create a British 'Fed' or Bundesbank. The doctrine of Parliament sovereignty militates in favour of the sub-contractor concept and against the notion of the central bank as an estate of the realm. It is no coincidence that New Zealand pioneered the sub-contractor model, given that New Zealand shares Britain's belief in the supremacy of Parliament.

But above all, the Bank practically took Chancellor Gordon Brown's arm off in May 1997 because, as I mentioned above, monetary policy is the job that every central bank wishes to do. Banking supervision is all very well, but has connotations of gumshoe activities and 'police business'. Management of the market in gilts, British government securities, was rather classier, and 'open market operations' – Bank intervention in the wholesale money markets and the foreign exchanges to influence interest rates and / or the level of sterling – were very close to being the Real Thing. Very close, but not quite, since these operations wee at the behest of a monetary policy decided a mile and a half to west, at the Treasury.

By 1997, the consensus around the world was that 'real' central banks operated an independent monetary policy, while a sort of junior division took orders from politicians. Offered five-ninths of the Monetary Policy Committee, the Bank took less than a second to say 'yes'. But in doing so, it placed nearly all its eggs in one basket. Banking supervision was shifted to the new Financial Services Authority, as was regulation of the wholesale money markets. Management of the national debt was next to go, heading off to the new Debt Management Office, a Treasury offshoot. True, the Bank remained a banker to the government and to the banking system as a whole, but this later role is itself more an arm of monetary policy than anything else. And, true, the Bank retains some private bank accounts and is responsible for looking after both the national currency reserves on behalf of the Treasury and its own reserves, which it is allowed to use independently in pursuit of monetary policy.

Then there is Lolar, which sounds like a shady lady but stands more prosaically for Lender of Last Resort, the ability and duty to pump liquidity (the up-market hand-outs we discussed earlier) into any financial institution whose troubles could threaten 'systemic risk', i.e. widespread damage to the financial system as a whole. Lolar is at the heart of the Bank's 'financial stability' remit, which aside from the MPC is probably the most substantial role left for the Bank today. Needless to say, the Bank is playing up 'financial stability' for all it is worth, with one of its deputy governors, currently David Clementi, in charge of this duty. Given the other deputy governor, at the time of writing Mervyn King, is in charge of monetary stability, one may gain the impression that the Bank has two, equally important, responsibilities, and that the Bank is about much more than merely supplying most of the MPC's membership. This impression is spoilt, however, somewhat when one learns that Mr Clementi sits on the MPC, as, of course, do Mr King and the Governor, Sir Edward George.

There is a 'financial stability committee', which also meets once a month and is made up of Mr Clementi, a Treasury representative and a senior officer of the FSA. But you wouldn't know it. In fact, the committee worked effectively behind the scenes to shield the City from the fall-out when Russia defaulted on its debts in 1998. Nevertheless, financial stability is very much a junior partner to monetary policy, which is now the central role of the Bank.

As for the Bank's alleged third 'key function', promoting the City's effectiveness as a financial centre, its openness to innovation and its flexibility and so forth; this is sheer flim-flam that can be and is done elsewhere – the FSA has a pretty much identical remit.

So if monetary policy is the chief role of the Bank, it is hardly surprising that the institution seems less than keen on Britain joining the euro. In that event, Sir Edward would be just one voice at bi-monthly meetings of the European Central Bank, and the institution he heads would suffer the humiliation of becoming a 'legacy bank'

– a sub-branch of the ECB. Furthermore, deprived of the ability to create liquidity, it is hard to see how the financial stability role could be satisfactorily discharged. By contrast, the regulatory role will survive and thrive whether Britain uses sterling, the euro, the dollar or the Spanish doubloon as its national currency, as will the job of managing the gilt market.

It is, indeed, a gamble. At the time of writing, the MPC is seen to be on a 'hot streak', with its record contrasting favourably to the lamentable performance of the ECB. But four years is a drop in the great ocean of time that is economic history, and hot streaks have a habit of going cold.

Unit 5 plus 4: Inside the Monetary Policy Committee

If the Anglican Communion is three churches in one – Catholics, Evangelicals and Liberals – then the MPC is similarly three sub-committees that meet together once a month. There are the central bankers: Sir Edward, Messrs King and Clementi, Bank executive director Ian Plenderleith and Bank economist Charles Bean. There are the academics: Steve Nickell and Christopher Allsopp. And there is the real-economy, pro-business faction : Sushil Wadhwani and Kate Barker. Very broadly speaking, this last group is biased towards lower interest rates, the first group in favour of higher interest rates and the academics swing between the two.

Not that you will learn any of this from the MPC's spokespeople. Indeed, they will hotly deny any such divisions, and stress that all nine members are working together to the great goal of price stability. So be it. I suggest you check the voting records. They are available in the MPC minutes, on the Bank of England website.

In four short years, two conventions have already established themselves at the MPC's monthly meetings. The first is that Sir Edward is never on the losing side. This does not mean the Governor lays down the law and the rest follow. Far from it. On occasions, it seems the Governor has swallowed his own misgivings and voted with the consensus. The second is that all the different options are boiled down to just one set of alternatives, which is then voted on. In other words, the MPC does not vote first on one members' suggestion of a rate increase, then another's on no change then yet another's on an interest-rate cut. The MPC takes one vote on a single proposition, which will be one of three: a cut, a rise, no change. There is one alternative also on offer, which will be one of the following: a larger cut than suggested, a cut, no change, a rise, or a larger rise than suggested. The Treasury is allowed to send one non-voting representative.

In general, the MPC moves rates in quarter-point stages (0.25 per cent) and, Bank watchers have noticed, it is something like three times more likely to vote for a change in one of the four months of the year that see the publication of the Bank's quarterly Inflation Report than in the other eight months. The committee met twice during the 2001 election campaign; critics, friendly and otherwise, suggested its statutes be amended to avoid any hint of political interference.

Elsewhere on the political front, the Chancellor appoints the independent members, although the MPs on the Treasury Select Committee, the backbench committee that scrutinises the Treasury, the Bank, the FSA and the MPC, have suggested they ought to have US Senate-style powers to veto appointments. Don't hold your breath.

The monthly meeting is spread across two days; on the second day, the MPC's decision is announced immediately, and, two weeks later, the minutes are published. These are, sad to say, not a verbatim transcript but they do, as I said, give the voting records. So the MPC has met and voted. Interest rates have, let us say, been changed. The newspaper headlines and radio bulletins spread the word.

What happens now?

Remote control: monetary policy in action

When the Bank 'sets interest rates', what does that mean? In the immediate post-war period, it meant just that: banks and other lending institutions were pretty well obliged to fall immediately into line. That was when the official interest rate was called Bank Rate and central economic management was the name of the game. It doesn't mean that any more. The Bank does not bark out orders to the banking community. But then, it doesn't have to. So how does monetary policy 'bite'?

The Bank's power over monetary policy derives from its position as the monopoly supplier of the monetary base, which is made up of notes, coins and money held on deposit by the banks at the Bank of England. In days gone by, it used this basic power to try to control the amount of money and credit in the system – for example, by ordering banks to increase their deposits at the Bank, thus curbing their ability to make loans. Today, it keeps that power firmly in reserve, preferring instead to keep the banking system short of money every day, and therefore in a position of having to borrow from the Bank, at a rate set by the Bank. This is the base rate, the 'price of money' as established by the most recent meeting of the MPC.

How does it keep the system short? The answer is: with great ingenuity.

Here is what happens. Every day, the twenty-two 'settlement banks' – the main banking institutions of the UK – are required at close of business to show a positive balance on their accounts, which are held at the Bank of England. Now obviously, one bank may have paid money to another bank, but that shouldn't mean the system overall is short of money, because there is a brisk 'inter-bank' lending market, in which the banks trade their surplus balances with each other every single day.

But let us suppose clearing bank customers are paying taxes to the government, whether as companies or individuals. Then you have a net drain of cash out of the system as a whole and into the government's accounts, which are held, by happy chance, at the

Bank of England. Thus on some days, for sure, the system as a whole will be sort of cash and will need to go cap in hand to the Bank. But how can there be a shortage on most days?

In two ways. First, the Bank manipulates the flow of money from the banking system to the government with the deliberate aim of creating a shortage. Second, there are 'obligations' – IOUs of one sort or another – held on the Bank's books from previous rounds of assistance to the banking system. These give the Bank another tool to manipulate the flow of money in such a way as to create at least the prospect of a shortage. Having created the drought, the Bank then helpfully offers water – at a price. That price is the base rate, or 'repo' rate. It wades into the wholesale money market with up to four rounds of assistance, supplying the funds needed to relieve the shortage. The Bank offers to buy 'eligible' bills from the banking system – chiefly short-term Treasury paper and local authority debt – thus injecting cash back into the system. It also enters sale and repurchase (thus 'repo') agreements, lending money to the banks and taking gilts as security.

A third tool in the battle to ensure a shortage was the weekly auction for Treasury bills, which both raised cash for the government on a short-term basis and helped the Bank influence the amount of liquidity in the system. In years gone by, the large-scale use not only of Treasury bills but of the longer-term gilts to manage the money supply was commonplace. Now it is out of fashion, and oversight of the gilt market, as we saw earlier, has been passed to an independent Treasury agency. Since 2000, the Treasury bill function has also been passed to this agency.

Also out of fashion are the 'discount houses' that, until the 1990s, sat between the Bank and the banks, effectively making a market out of the shortage, being under contract to buy every issue of short-term Government paper (Treasury bills) in return for the Bank acting as their lender of last resort. Off duty, the discount houses built an enviable reputation for agreeable lunches. They are now extinct in their old form, and the Bank deals directly with its counterparties in the money markets, mainly the banks themselves but also building societies and approved securities dealers.

The Bank's fourth tool is the $8.8 billion pot of foreign currency reserves available to the MPC for intervention in the foreign exchange markets should sterling's level threaten the inflation rate. This could happen were sterling too low (because import prices would rise, boosting inflation) or if it were too high (because exports would be too expensive and the economy would start to 'deflate', i.e. to sink into a recession). To date, this pot has been left untouched, as has the Treasury's much larger pot, totalling $46 billion, available for the same purpose and for any other national emergency. In theory, the Treasury could take one view and start selling sterling, while the Bank was taking the opposite view and buying it, but this is marginally more likely to happen than the discovery of fairies at the bottom of the Governor's back garden.

On the subject of foreign-exchange reserves, they break down as follows. The Treasury's reserves are made up of about $13.7 billion net funds – i.e. Britain's own money. Of this, gold takes, at the time of writing, about 29 per cent, down from 44 per cent at the time of Labour's 1997 election victory, after which the Treasury decided to reduce Britain's gold holdings in favour of paper currencies. It is set to fall ultimately to 20 per cent. Another 10 per cent is made of up 'special drawing rights', which may sound like a charter for graffiti artists but actually refers to a nominal currency issued by the International Monetary Fund, representing a basket of international currencies. Of the remaining $8.2 billion in the net reserves, 40 per cent is held in dollars, 40 per cent in euros and 20 per cent in yen.

These net reserves, along with the balance of $32.3 billion borrowed by Britain on international capital markets, is managed by the Bank on the instructions of the Treasury. The Bank takes no instructions on the use of its own reserves; in addition to the $8.8 billion it has $2.8 billion lodged as a deposit with Target, the euro zone's payments system.

As impressive as the Bank's reserves seem to be, however, it is the 'shortage' that makes the banking system sensitive to changes in the repo rate and gives the Bank, and thus the MPC, its leverage over interest rates throughout the economy.

So far, so good. But what does it get for its leverage? As always, let's look first at the official version, as set out by the Bank itself:

> Monetary policy operates by influencing the cost of money, i.e. the short-term rate of interest. The Bank sets an interest rate for its own dealings with market and that rate then affects the whole pattern of rates set by the commercial banks for their savers and borrowers.
>
> This in turn will affect asset prices (e.g. shares and property), consumer and business demand and, ultimately, output and employment . . . If rates are set too low this may encourage the emergence of inflationary pressures so that inflation is persistently above target. If they are set too high there is likely to be an unnecessary loss of output and employment, and inflation is likely to be persistently below target.

There you have it, the alpha and omega of monetary policy. It sounds extraordinarily simple, and that is part of the problem. Because behind the creation of the MPC was the notion that interest rate decisions were easy to judge, but difficult to take. Difficult, because they were being taken by politicians with a short-term seat-of-the-pants terror of bad poll numbers and general unpopularity. If only the decision could be placed in the hands of dispassionate experts, then all would be well. Making the judgment was easy, and so – if those charged with putting the judgment into effect were insulated from the voters – implementing the judgment would be easy as well.

It has not worked out quite like that. In August 2001, the MPC cut interest rates because manufacturing industry was in recession. But the rest of the economy was not in recession: house prices were spiralling and consumer credit flowed like water. Mr King – who voted with two other members against the cut – admitted afterwards it was a finely-balanced judgment, and nobody knew whether it was the right one or not.

Nor did the outbreak of hostilities in the wake of September 11 do much to clarify the picture. At an emergency meeting on September 18, seven members voted for a further cut of 0.25 percentage points, but two held out for 0.50 percentage points. Come October, eight voted for a cut of 0.25 percentage points, while one held out for 0.50 percentage points. But given little sign of an end to the consumer credit boom, the question facing the MPC in August had scarcely changed.

There are ways of cutting interest rates to help industry without stoking up consumer demand. It is possible to accompany the cut with a steep rise in sales taxes, or with a rise in Stamp Duty to penalise share speculation and property price inflation. It is even possible to raise income tax. But these weapons have been stood down as an orthodoxy has taken root that monetary policy is the sole instrument to be used in economic management. The MPC is to be the remote-control handset, pressing whose buttons will result in the desired economic picture popping up on the screen. Just as the Bank as an institution has put all its eggs in one basket, so too have the Bank's masters at the Treasury, entrusting the basket in question to the MPC. If the Bank has gambled its future on the MPC, then the Treasury has gambled all our futures. Let us hope the right numbers come up.

Good as gold: the gilt market

Compared to the birth of the Monetary Policy Committee, the parallel launch of the Debt Management Office passed largely unnoticed by the public at large. Everyone has heard of Sir Edward George. How many know of Mike Williams, chief executive of the DMO? Television reporters routinely deliver their reports standing in front of the Bank of England. Few ever take their camera crew for the short walk to Eastcheap Court, head office of the DMO.

Yet the notion of an independent agency for the issue of gilt-edged stock – British government securities, the certificates for which were once edged in gilt, hence the name – is in its way every bit as radical as the idea of an independent committee to set interest rates. For decades, gilts had been an intensely political and highly contentious area of policy. There have been 'gilt strikes' by investors. There have been 'revenge hits' by the government, cunningly timing a large issue at the most propitious moment. A fairly recent example came on the night of the April 1992 General Election, when the surprise victory for John Major's Conservative party – generally welcomed in the City and the international investment community – gave the Bank an opportunity to strike while the iron was hot. Fortunately, the Bank had kept a gilts team on site all night for just this eventuality – the moment Mr Major's victory was announced, they 'hit the phones' and 'got away' a vast £1 billion-odd issue at an excellent price.

In the broader sense, too, gilts have long been seen as instruments of policy. In the post-war period, gilts were a key weapon in economic management. Not only did they raise money for the government; they could be used to massage the stock of money in the system, thus influencing credit growth and, ultimately, economic performance. When the chancellor judged there to be too much money in circulation, an issue of gilts would drain liquidity from the system as funds were transferred from the private sector to the state. And when the chancellor judged there to be to little money in the system, the Bank could be ordered into the gilt market with tempting offers to buy gilts.

No more. The buzz words at the DMO are 'precommitment and transparency'. Roughly translated, this means the Treasury says upfront at the start of each year (or even earlier) how much it plans to borrow, and when most of the borrowing will take place. The DMO fine-tunes the details, and the sixteen accredited 'gilt-edged market-makers' (GEMM) bid for the stock at auctions spaced across the year. Currently, there are about ten gilts auctions annually.

Who are the GEMMs? Pretty much the usual suspects, the giant banks and investment banks. HSBC is there, as are Goldman Sachs and Deutsche Bank. It remains a telephone market, with the GEMMs bidding for issues of five, ten and thirty-year government paper. As we saw in the section on corporate bonds, the GEMMs' focus is on the yield – the interest rate paid in relation to the price of the issue. Currently Britain's credit is good, the government is borrowing very little and inflation is under control, thus yields have been down in the four per cent region since 1998. By contrast, the crisis years of the mid-1970s saw yields explode to something like 19 per cent, as investors demanded greater reward for greater risk. In effect, 1974–75 saw an investors' 'strike' that was only ended when Britain re-introduced wage controls in the summer of 1975.

Supplementing the auction of gilts is the weekly auction of short-term Treasury bills, which are currently issued for one month and three months, although there is the facility to issue six-month and twelve-month paper. The importance of this market has declined under current government policy to place most of the funding burden on longer-term gilts.

Once they have successfully bid for the issue in question, the GEMMs can get down to trading the stock – to each other and, more importantly, to outside investors. The daily turnover in the gilt market is £6 billion, or £1,518 billion a year, which dwarfs the current government annual borrowing of £13.5 billion.

Gilts, as with just about every other security, support a vast superstructure of 'derivative' contracts – the futures and options that we shall meet in the chapter nine. Along with corporate bonds, they form part of the fixed-interest market that is in a constant battle for attention with the equity market. Investment has become an unsentimental business, and it would probably take another war before we see people again buying gilts for patriotic reasons.

It was all very different in days gone by. From 1786 to 1982, the position of government bill broker – effectively, the Bank of England's broker – was practically an hereditary one, being vested in the broking firm of Mullens & Co. From Benjamin Cole, the first Mullens bill broker, to Lord Cromwell, the last, this relatively small brokerage (long since vanished into the maw of SG Warburg) provided what was quaintly known as 'Broker to the Commissioners for the Reduction of the National Debt'. Change was not immediate, however. True, Lord Cromwell was succeeded by someone from outside Mullens, Nigel Althaus, senior partner at stockbroker Pember & Boyle. But he promptly became senior partner of Mullens, so the change was hardly radical.

Real change, however, could not be long delayed, and in 1986 the position of Government bill broker was abolished. The Bank itself dealt directly with the market, and did so until the 1997 reforms set up the DMO. As with the MPC, however, the big question has to be whether the DMO could stand a real economic storm or whether government would itch to resume a more hands-on management of its borrowings. Just as saving is easy when pay rises are frequent and prices low, so the virtues of transparency and long-term thinking are more comfortably sustained when the economy is booming and inflation subdued. For both these institutions, all we can say with certainty is that they seem to work very well – just as long as everything else is also working very well.

Vast and invisible: the London money market

Logic may dictate that this section ought properly to have preceded the whole discussion of monetary policy, because only when the banks are unable to satisfy their immediate shortages in the money market do they need to borrow at the Bank of England. That is not to say that the London money market exists primarily for the convenience of the banks, although they are the biggest players and the biggest users. It is a market in short-term debt maturing usually within twelve months.

In the days when most lending between banks and other financial institutions was channelled through the abovementioned discount houses, the money market was known as the 'parallel market', which gives a vaguely disreputable impression. It was noted that there was no lender of last resort in this market, as there was for the discount houses. More to the point, the money markets had access to the vast pool of dollars and other foreign currency lodged in London that went by the name of 'Eurodollars'. This was not a welcome development in the eyes of the Treasury and the Bank, and added to the air of disrepute surrounding the 'parallel' market.

Today, all that has changed and there is no longer anything much for the money market to be 'parallel' to, unless you count the daily rounds of Bank of England assistance to the banks. Nor, as I explained in the section on bonds in chapter three, does it any longer make much sense to talk about 'Eurodollars'. Around the world, both exchange controls and (most) attempts to impose limits on interest rates and borrowings have disappeared. Today's Bank official or Treasury mandarin positively exults in London's role as a centre for dealings in currencies of all types. The 'eurobond' market is now, in effect, subsumed into the bond market, and the 'Eurodollar' market is, depending on whether one is trading or borrowing, a branch of either the foreign exchange market or a branch of the money market.

Nor is the 'money broker' of yesteryear the figure of suspicion that he once was. In a market dominated by the most respectable banks, there can be no discredit in doing business there. Today, one hears rather more of 'managers of money market funds' – a breed enjoying new-found respectability as the most conservative pension funds, and wealthy private investors, invest a portion of their assets on the money market.

So where is this market? It is anywhere that very large 'wholesale' amounts of money are lent and borrowed for short periods of time. There is no physical exchange; this is a bilateral market, telephone-based for the most part, and invisible to the naked eye. At its heart is the inter-bank market, where colossal sums are lent, usually overnight, from one bank to another. Longer-term loans stretching several years ahead can be made, but are rare. This is a market whose lowest unit of currency is £250,000, but more usually £5 million. Money traders live short, glorious and well-remunerated professional lives before collapsing in a nervous heap at around the age of thirty and heading off to farm chickens in Norfolk. This is a market where the cost of money can and does move dozens of times in a single minute. Contrary to the stereotype of the bawling City trader expostulating down a telephone, the money trader needs a neutral tone of voice, so as not to alert the counterparty to any emotion – desperation for funds being the most obvious emotion to keep hidden. Banks rely on each other to play by the rules and pay up, so collateral is not asked for in these deals. A money trader's word is his bond; besides, most telephone calls nowadays are taped.

The inter-bank market may be largely submerged, but its conning tower is clear above the waterline – the London Inter-Bank Offered Rate (LIBOR). This is used as a benchmark interest rate around the world, and has inevitably become the narrow plinth upon which has been built a towering structure of 'derivative' products.

But if money itself is, as one would expect, the primary commodity on offer in the money markets, and if the inter-bank market manages very nicely without contracts and tons of additional paper, that is not to say there are not a range of instruments peculiar to the money markets. There are.

The oldest and best-known is the bill of exchange, or 'bankers' acceptance', an IOU issued by a large company, usually for three months. These bills were originally issued to finance a particular piece of trade, usually connected with a sea voyage. I say 'originally', but in the 1970s the finance department of one blue-chip was startled to receive a call from the authorities asking for the name of the ship to whose cargo a particular bill related. A mad flurry resulted, but the company – a specialist in wire products – was able to locate a vessel at sea carrying company material to which the bill could plausibly be attached. Even today, bills are usually connected with goods in storage or in transit.

Bills traditionally had to be 'avalised' – guaranteed – by a merchant bank, which made good sense if the paper of a shaky enterprise were to be traded in the money markets alongside the paper of solid companies. However, it was a cause of some irritation to the solid companies, often many, many times larger than the merchant bank that was 'guaranteeing' their credit.

No such irritations attach to the commercial paper market, which has grown up since the mid-1980s and dispenses with the paternalistic trappings of the traditional bill market. Commercial paper originated in the US, where it has long been a vast market. Companies issue IOUs, usually for thirty days and usually for amounts of £500,000 upwards. It is up to investors to assess the creditworthiness of the borrower; the money market will soon gag on the commercial paper of a company even vaguely likely to default.

Another common money-market instrument is the certificate of deposit, or CD. These are documents issued by banks, confirming that a deposit has been made for a fixed period of time at a fixed rate of interest. The depositor can then sell on the CD into the money markets for a discount, receiving cash now. Alternatively, the depositor can hold the CD until the bank is due to redeem it, thus collecting is full value. It is this flexibility that has made CDs popular with both companies and wealthy individuals. Upwards of £50,000 is needed to buy a CD, which last from ninety days to five years.

Banks and brokerages dominate the money markets, but there are other players too. Local authorities have long had a presence here, borrowing for short periods of no more than six months in order to smooth out their cash requirements. Their activities take place under the beady eye of the Department of Transport, Local Government and the Regions. Large non-financial companies are involved, sometimes lending directly to one another, as are suppliers of hire-purchase, equipment-leasing services and other forms of non-bank credit.

No-one knows the size of the London money market – after all, banks are at the centre of the action and confidentiality is at the centre of banking. But figures from the Bank for International Settlements put the size of the market in money-market instruments internationally at £5,000 billion in 2000, with most of this accounted for by New York, Tokyo, Frankfurt and London.

The market is unregulated in the sense that it is not, in the jargon, a 'recognised investment exchange'. This is not simply because it has no tangible existence, but because every deal is 'bilateral', jargon for 'between two consenting adults', rather than multilateral and anonymous, as on the equity market. Some bilateral trading is regulated, most obviously on the face-to-face commodity markets. However, the powers-that-be tend to be more relaxed than usual when handling wholesale, bilateral markets between professionals in which the small investor is most definitely not welcome. Its main players, the banks and brokers, are regulated in their own right, and the FSA has issued a code of conduct for money-market participants.

I began this section by commenting that perhaps the money markets ought to have preceded rather than followed the Bank of England. Looked at another way, it could be said that the money markets ought not to be found in this chapter at all, and would sit more comfortably with the foreign currency market, far away from respectable folk in the Bank and the gilts market. The money markets are in no sense 'official' and have only recently shaken off their 'parallel' tag.

They are, perhaps, not 'soldiers of the Queen' but soldiers of fortune?

Nevertheless, the money-market as a whole is a key component of the liquidity mechanism, the management of which is central to the Bank of England's remit. Without it, paradoxically, there may well be no 'shortage', because the banking system would simply adjust itself to ensuring, whatever the weather, a positive balance every day on its accounts at the Bank.

On the other hand it probably wouldn't advance very many loans either. Whether this would be a boon or a curse is a matter of person taste.

6

Soldiers of the Queen Part Two – the Financial Services Authority and the Serious Fraud Office

'Well, sir,' said the constable, 'he's the man we were in search of, that's true; and yet he's not the man we were in search of. For the man we were in search of was not the man we wanted sir'.

Thomas Hardy, *The Three Strangers*

You have the right to remain silent: the rise and fall of 'talk-or-else'

The 17 December 1996 was a dull, grey day in the city of Strasbourg, home to, among other institutions, the European Court of Human Rights. There was, however, nothing dull about one item of the court's business that day, which was to deliver a verdict in a case prosaically entitled Saunders versus United Kingdom.

In a half-empty courtroom, watched mainly by a handful of journalists, the judges proceeded to mothball the British fraudbusters' ultimate weapon, known colloquially as 'talk-or-else'. The court ruled Saunders's rights had been violated in that evidence he had been compelled to produce was then used against him in his 1990 trial. The court did not rule that Saunders was innocent of the case against him; he had engaged in illegal support operations to keep up the price of Guinness shares in its bitter bid battle for the drinks group Distillers. Nevertheless, the verdict was to reverberate through the regulatory and investigative structure right up to the present day.

Increasingly during the 1980s, suspects in fraud cases had found that the right to silence did not apply to them. In some cases, the power to compel answers that could be used in court as evidence against the person giving the answer was long-standing. Official Receivers had enjoyed a limited ability to compel answers and documents for many years, as part of their inquiries into company failures. Inspectors appointed by the Department of Trade and Industry had, similarly, been able to require answers and documents in the course of their inquiries into the affairs of a company.

What changed in the 1980s was a very great extension of talk-or-else powers, both in the leeway granted by the courts to existing holders of that power and, critically, in the numbers and types of officials entitled to use the power. The key statutes were the Financial Services Act 1986 and the Criminal Justice Act 1987. The first of these established a number of regulatory bodies, each responsible for policing one part of the City: stockbroking, retail financial services, fund management and so forth.

These bodies were 'membership-based'; anyone wishing to engage in, for example, fund management would be required to join the Investment Management Regulatory Organisation (IMRO). Once a member, the person concerned would be bound by the rules of IMRO, which included an obligation to answer questions posed by IMRO's investigation and enforcement personnel. But this power applied only to members; should someone genuinely object to answering IMRO's questions, he or she could simply leave the industry. IMRO was, in that sense, no different from any professional association policing its membership in a closed-shop environment – the General Medical Council and the Law Society come to mind, not to mention the London Stock Exchange in its old role as regulator as well as market place.

The 1986 Act, however, contained a key additional feature. While the regulatory bodies such as IMRO derived their powers from membership, they sat beneath a master-regulator that derived its powers from statute, the Securities and Investments Board (SIB). Now, SIB, funnily enough, did have a few direct members of its own, some large banks and insurance companies plus some smaller operators. Ironically, given the Strasbourg ruling of December 1996, SIB had to be open to members wishing to join because – under the European Convention on Human Rights – any person or company has the right to be directly regulated by a 'public law forum'. Legal advice in 1986 was that the membership-based regulators would not fit this definition.

SIB, in relation to its own membership, could, of course, compel answers. But the Act gave it a second power – that of compelling answers from any other person in the United Kingdom. It was rarely if ever used. But it was a huge change.

An even larger change was ushered in the following year with the Criminal Justice Act. This created an entirely new organisation under the auspices of the Attorney General – the Serious Fraud Office. Nothing like the SFO had ever been seen in Britain. It was both investigator and prosecutor. It contained police officers, but was not a branch of the police. It could refuse to take on cases, but could not instigate its own inquiries, having instead to wait for a case to be referred from a police force, the DTI or another official body. The detectives working for the SFO were not members of its staff, and were supplied at the grace and favour of the Commissioners of the Metropolitan Police and the City Police, along with the chief constables of the provincial forces. And – above all – it was armed from day one with talk-or-else powers, enshrined in Section Two of the Act.

The SFO was structured around Section Two. Its top personnel – the director, the half dozen or so assistant directors and the case controllers and investigators beneath them – all tended to be lawyers and accountants. But they were not, and could not be, police officers. The police are covered by the Police and Criminal Evidence Act 1984 (PACE), under which the right to silence explicitly binds their conduct. So the detectives working for the SFO could not use talk-or-else, and could hold no management role in an organisation that did.

Given this structure, there were and are formidable legal obstacles to placing a non-police officer in charge of police officers. Thus the SFO could not employ detectives, it could simply borrow them from police chiefs who would remain, theoretically, in command of those detectives throughout their stint at the SFO. Some officers have become almost permanent fixtures at SFO headquarters in Elm Street, central London, so this is a little bizarre, to say the least.

Although talk-or-else seemed to be pulling the whole structure into some very strange shapes, the SFO never doubted its correctness for a moment. Every director from John Wood in 1987 through Barbara Mills to George Staple, who was holding the baby when the Saunders judgment came in, has insisted that Section Two was essential in dealing with 'these very complex frauds'. Anyone who hung around Elm Street in these years came quickly to recognise the mantra-like status of 'these very complex frauds'. It was to the SFO what 'London's position as an international financial centre' is down the road in the City.

Funnily enough, Section Two was actually less draconian than the powers available to DTI inspectors. Whereas a number of court rulings had confirmed that the inspectors were entitled to compel answers and then hand the results straight over to the police and the Crown Prosecution Service, the SFO could use Section Two material only if a defendant deviated from his answers when in the witness box. For that very reason, Elm Street clung, even after the Saunders verdict, to the hope that Section Two may not be affected. After all, the SFO hadn't even been in existence when the Guinness inquiry began in December 1986. Saunders had been questioned by the DTI, who had effectively been working in cahoots with the police, grilling Saunders under talk-or-else and getting the police to hold off charging him, at which point Saunders' PACE rights would have kicked in. Surely it was this to which the case referred, not Section Two?

Alas, the British Government chose to bite the bullet all at once. Labour, who were in power by the time the verdict needed to be digested by the UK legal system, prohibited the use of all talk-or-else material in criminal proceedings under any circumstances. Talk-or-else could still be used to extract information from suspects and witnesses, but none of that information could be produced in court.

The first shoe had dropped. The second followed in short order.

Labour's new master-regulator, the Financial Services Authority, needed a new Act to give it the powers to supersede SIB and its sub-stratum of membership-based organisations. That instrument, the Financial Services and Markets Bill, was not long in arriving. But by late 1998, it was obvious that the bill – FiSMA, as the final version became known once it passed into law – was on a collision course with the Saunders judgment.

The FSA was to have powers of criminal prosecution in exceptional cases. And, as under the old system, it would have disciplinary powers over its members. But much more significant was the swathe of new powers under the heading 'market abuse'. This covered not only insider-dealing but any form of abusive conduct in any regulated market, i.e. just about anywhere in the financial services industry. And it gave the FSA powers over everyone in the country.

Now, 'market abuse' was a civil, not a criminal, procedure, and so the original Treasury view was that it was unaffected by the Saunders judgment. But the European Court had warned member-nations in the past that it would not tolerate quasi-criminal penalties being dished out under cover of a 'civil' hearing, and the ability of the FSA to demand unlimited fines from those convicted of this 'offence' could well fall into that category. Furthermore, the fact that market abuse cases would initially be heard before an internal FSA 'court' did little to reassure those who feared the whole concept was wide open to abuse of a different kind.

Labour ministers tried to tough it out, especially in view of their long-held attitude in opposition that 'City swindlers' had it far too easy in general, and that only the prospect of 'rough justice' would bring order to the Square Mile. Besides, Labour had for years con-trasted the SIB-based system unfavourably with the US regulator, the Securities and Exchange Commission. While SIB pussyfooted around, said Labour MPs, the SEC clapped fraudsters in irons and carted them off to the federal penitentiary. Of course, few Labour MPs had much real idea of how the SEC worked. The fact that crim-inal fraud was dealt with by the US Attorney's Office, rather than the SEC, was a distinction lost on most of the SEC's new fan club, as was the fact that it did not regulate banking or insurance at all.

Ultimately, however, the Treasury gave in. Market abuse defen-dants were granted the right to silence, and the FSA's private court was transformed into a fully-fledged 'court of first instance'. It was the end-result of a long process that had started with the 1979 Banking Act; that of replacing the club-style regulation of the City – in which the Bank governor's famous 'raised eyebrows' were enough to warn off the 'bad hats' – with a legal structure, complete with rights for defendants and the accompanying battalion of lawyers on each side. The 1986 Act had proved an unworkable hybrid of the two; it was not possible simultaneously to threaten the sharp practitioners with proper, criminal penalties and to hope they would 'do the decent thing' and accept behind-closed-doors punishments just as in the old days.

Ironically, Labour in power tried to keep precisely this sort of hybrid in being, having criticised it so ferociously in opposition. In 1997–98, it was felt in Treasury circles to be almost unsporting of alleged fraudsters to stand on their rights. This delusion did not last long. After all, today's FSA defendant is as likely to be a German or an American as an ex-public schoolboy, and is unlikely to share any assumption that mounting a proper legal defence in a market abuse case is somehow 'cheating'.

So the 1990s – which were to have been, particularly after 1997, the decade in which the 'pinstriped twisters' who flourished during the 'years of greed' in the 1980s would be brought to heel – ended, ironically, with a flourish of new 'Twister's Rights' – rights unimaginable during the 'greed' years, when suspected twisters had very few rights of any kind. But then, the view of the old system as a 'club' was always a caricature, as we shall now find out.

Aphabetti Spaghetti: from PF(I)A to FiSMA in 40 easy years

There is a scene in the television series *Yes, Prime Minister*, in which the fictional premier interviews a candidate for governorship of the Bank of England. These were the days when the 'Governor's eyebrows' were still thought to rule in the City.

The candidate, a bufferish chairman of a clearing bank, is asked what he would do were he to suspect a City type of committing fraud. The candidate boasts that he would not hesitate – he would take the chap straight out to lunch and ask him, man to man, if he were a fraudster.

And if he said no?

Well, said the candidate, so be it. You have to take the chap's word.

As I say, this was a caricature of the old set-up, for two reasons. First, the law did have teeth in dealing with financial fraud. The Prevention of Fraud (Investments) Act of 1959 may have been flawed but it did provide a legal means of dealing with white-collar criminals. Beyond this, the law governing 'agency' – the holding of a position of trust on behalf of another – provided further redress, and county fraud squads tended to be rather better staffed in 1959 than in 2000, when at least one squad has been disbanded altogether and others have downgraded the position of head of the squad to the rank of sergeant. Furthermore, dealers in securities were required to be registered with one of two organisations; the Stock Exchange or the Board of Trade, later the Department of Trade and Industry. A third organisation, the International Securities Regulatory Organisation, was accredited later on.

Second, the management of the economy as a whole was a huge curb on the activities of the City generally. Exchange control, which was policed by the Bank, hobbled the ability of all City players to operate in international markets. The existence of a very large public sector, encompassing at one point steel, coal, railways, road transport, telecommunications, civil aviation, aircraft manufacture and car-making, greatly reduced the size of the pool in which 'sharks' could swim.

At the same time, the boom years of the welfare state encouraged the notion of an all-providing public purse; only the wealthiest were thought to be interested in share-ownership or any kind of financial speculation. Well into the 1970s it was assumed by many that the public sector would continue to grow at the expense of private sector financial and commercial activity of all kinds. The creation in 1975 of the State Earnings Related Pensions Scheme added to the general sense that the state was assuming all the major rights and responsibilities of both the direction of industry and the care of those who worked in it.

This was stony ground for the would-be fraudster. It was hard for the sharp-practitioner to fleece people whose only notion of financial risk was the football pool or the ERNIE premium bond system.

Indeed, the growth of the 'regulation industry' has moved in step with the growing belief since the early-1980s of the alleged desirability of expanding the private sector – privatisation – and the linked (although distinct) idea of a 'share owning democracy'. It was felt politically unacceptable to expose millions of people to the sort of market sharp practice that 'professionals' may feel comfortable with.

For the professionals themselves, there was a quite different but vital incentive to clean up the market, one that we touch on again and again throughout this book – market liquidity. The narrow spreads between buying and selling prices that are a precondition of liquidity cannot co-exist with sharp practice, because narrow spreads reflect trust. At the wholesale level too, then, there was a compelling reason to stamp out the 'colourful' practices of old. We ought not to not be surprised to note, therefore, that the 'decade of greed' was also the decade of regulation. On 1 January 1980, the Banking Act – the first legal instrument granting the Bank explicit powers to regulate other banks – was less than a year old and insider dealing remained legal. There was no explicit regulator for the sale of investment products to the public and the DTI's regime for monitoring licensed dealers would be exposed as leaving a lot to be desired.

By 1 January 1990 the landscape was very different. The master-regulator, the Securities and Investments Board, presided over four sub-regulators covering independent financial advice, tied financial advice, fund management and exchange based business. Furthermore, the resources of the City and the Metropolitan Police fraud squads, along with the smaller teams working in most county and regional forces, had been (as we have seen) significantly augmented by the creation in 1988 of the Serious Fraud Office. Maximum penalties for insider-dealing now matched those for grievous bodily harm. and in the meantime, the Bank of England had collected a new Act of Parliament tightening its grip on all banks operating in London and the country as a whole.

The Government weighed in with what seemed increasingly aggressive use of its own powers under the Companies Act; Guinness was just one case in which Government inspectors were uninhibited when it came to extracting evidence from suspects under compulsion that would later be used against them in court.

*

All seemed set fair for the 1990s to be marked by orderly financial markets going about their business under the watchful eye of a beefed up regulatory machine. It was not to be. The early-1990s were marked by the greatest scandals seen in the City in the twentieth century. True, the scandals had their roots in the 1980s. But the failure of the new corps of regulators properly to get to grips with the alleged wrongdoers – despite hugely increased budgets, payrolls and legal powers – left the regulatory community reeling by the end of the decade, its self-confidence a shadow of what it had been ten years earlier.

The scandals fell neatly into two types and fitted pretty well into two halves of the 1990s. In the first half, such scandals were essentially forms of large-scale theft. In July 1991, worldwide regulatory action led by the Bank of England closed down the Bank of Credit and Commerce International. Within a short space of time it emerged that BCCI was riddled with black holes totalling £13 billion. Much of the fraud had been masterminded from the bank's City headquarters in Leadenhall Street. This whole affair reflected poorly upon the Bank, although the SFO did obtain major convictions some years later.

Five months later, the publisher Robert Maxwell died at sea. Within a few weeks it became clear he had plundered £425 million from company pension funds in an attempt to keep his debt-laden empire in business. This time it was the regulatory organisation IMRO and the Government's barely visible pensions watchdog that bore the brunt of public opprobrium.

But while BCCI and Maxwell hogged the headlines, a thicket of smaller frauds hit investors at local and regional level. Most followed, on a smaller scale, the pattern of the Barlow Clowes scandal of 1988, in that investors had been fraudulently promised high returns on 'solid' investments that proved not to have existed. In many cases the initial returns had been paid from new investors' money. In one case, financier Robert Miller disappeared having lost millions of pounds belonging to a close circle of friends. He was reported to have attempted suicide in a Paris hotel room. In the case of Wessex Trust, two lay preachers were said to have systematically defrauded members of their congregation. Another notorious case was that of Garston Amhurst Associates. Here, millions of pounds of investors' money were telegraphed abroad.

Nor were the 'draconian' penalties always all they had been cracked up to be. In the case of Roger Levitt, a person convicted of serious financial offences received only a community service sentence.

By the second half of the decade, the emphasis had shifted from outright theft to 'rogue trading' – reckless gambling on a spectacular scale without proper authorisation. In February 1995, the venerable Barings discovered to its horror that a relatively junior trader, Nick Leeson, had exposed the institution to £800 million of losses by betting on Far Eastern derivatives. Shortly afterwards, the activities of Sumitomo copper trader Yasuo Hamanaka came to light. His attempts to corner the copper market cost his employer $2 billion. Other smaller cases helped imprint the 'rogue trader' firmly on the public consciousness.

None of the regulatory or investigative organisations set up with such fanfare in the 1980s emerged unscathed from the decade of scandal. In particular, the regulatory bodies established in 1986 explicitly to protect the new breed of small shareholder were, by the mid-1990s, clearly living on borrowed time. Initially five agencies had policed five distinct market areas. It made sense, then, for the top tier Securities and Investments Board to act as mother hen. But the merger process – itself an admission of some degree of failure – had reduced the number to three, casting doubt on the need for the SIB.

Each had endured its own scandal or scandals: the independent finance brokers' body FIMBRA had been plagued by a dozen more serious cowboy operators up and down the country, in many instances involving a million pounds or more of investors' money at risk. Its sister agency regulating brokers tied to one life assurance or other investment company, LAUTRO, had suffered the antics of Garston Amhurst. IMRO, the fund-management regulator, lost chief executive John Morgan and chairman George Nissen in the wake of the Maxwell pension-fund affair; both felt honour-bound to resign, despite the fact IMRO had no explicit responsibility for pension funds. Nor, as it turned out, did anybody else. And the Securities and Futures Authority, the regulator of exchange-based business created in 1991 by the first merger, that of the futures brokers' agency and the Securities Association, found its relative immunity to these downmarket goings-on shattered once the rogue traders crawled out of the woodwork in the late-1990s.

It did not help that these regulatory bodies all hated each other and took enormous pleasure in each other's discomfiture. For a financial journalist in the 1990s, the easiest way to get a story about one regulator was to have lunch with another. Only one thing united the self-regulatory organisations: their loathing of the senior regulator, SIB. 'Remind me,' was a favourite lunch-table line, 'what *does* SIB do?' SIB's revenge came with its report into the lessons learned from the Maxwell affair, published in 1992. The title, *Making the Two-Tier System Work*, left the sub-regulators in no doubt as to their lowly position in the post-Maxwell order. But this was far from the end of the in-fighting. In some ways it was only the beginning.

In the mid-1990s, FIMBRA and LAUTRO were merged into the Personal Investment Authority, a name chosen after the choice of Investment Regulatory Authority was felt to carry an unfortunate set of initials. SIB backed the PIA, at least until it became clear that the creation of the PIA had robbed SIB of one of its previous key roles, the overall supervision of retail financial services, those sold to the ordinary private investor.

PIA chief executive Colette Bowe, an outspoken Merseysider with an interesting Whitehall past (she had resigned as a DTI press officer in 1986 for her role in the scandal surrounding helicopter firm Westland) was not everybody's cup of tea. Furthermore, her chairman Joe Palmer's day job was bossing Legal & General, one of the first assurance companies to be castigated over the pensions mis-selling scandal. Hardly the best figurehead for an organisation devoted to protecting the small person from the sharks. Key figures inside FIMBRA and LAUTRO fought a dogged rearguard action against the PIA, and continued to snipe even after it became an inevitability. Meanwhile, senior SFA figures openly floated the idea of removing the SFA and its superior stockbroker types out of the SIB's ambit altogether and recreating something much closer to the old Stock Exchange regulatory system, complete with a more generous compensation scheme covering stockbroker defaults than that operated by SIB.

The regulatory civil war worsened once it became increasingly likely that a Labour government would shortly be taking office. Everyone knew a shake-up of some sort was on the cards, and each organisation wanted to come out on top – or at least to survive. Thus the SFA mooted the idea of a Trading and Markets Authority – a beefed up version of itself. The PIA, as a recently-created, relatively large regulator concerned with the ordinary investor, envisaged itself as the kernel of a new system. The SIB dismissed Labour's oft-repeated call for a fully statutory overall regulator on the ground that such an agency already existed – SIB. And IMRO argued for survival on the basis that nobody else had the expertise or the desire to regulate fund management, an activity quite different from those supervised by the other organisations.

As it was, the whole squabbling lot was to be given the long goodbye.

The Labour Party had long been committed to radical reform of the regulatory system, so it came as no surprise when, on assuming office in 1997, it moved swiftly in this direction. One of its first acts was to announce that the SIB and its sub-regulators would be merged into a new single regulator. That much may have been expected, but chancellor Gordon Brown went further, stripping the Bank of England of its regulatory role. Even though this move was sweetened with the granting to the Bank of interest rate independence, it still led governor Sir Edward George to contemplate resignation.

The Department of Trade and Industry lost its role as prudential supervisor of insurance companies. Even the Law Society was stripped of its ability to regulate solicitors who provided financial advice as a sideline. Smaller bodies regulating insurance brokers, friendly societies and building societies were also folded into the new regulator, the FSA. Finally, after a tortuous progress through Parliament, the Financial Services and Markets Bill became the Financial Services and Markets Act – FiSMA. Many of the original, eye-watering powers dreamed up by Labour in opposition had been dropped, a victim of Labour's other great enthusiasm, the incorporation into British law of the European Convention on Human Rights. But by November 2001, the FSA was finally kitted out with all its legal backing. PF(I)A was dead; the 1986 Act was dead; FiSMA was in business.

Shades of grey: the fraud / regulation spectrum

So does Britain now have a single financial regulator? Not quite.

What we do have is a unified version of the SIB and its sub-regulators, plus the banking-supervision arm of the Bank, the insurance industry oversight function of the DTI, and various smaller oddities such as the regulator for friendly societies. But the whole huge area of consumer credit, from the granting of licences through to supervision of hire purchase and all other credit activities, including pawnbroking, loan sharking, debt counselling and the 'trace' agencies that go looking for bad debtors, has nothing whatever to do with the FSA and is instead regulated by the Office of Fair Trading.

Offences – or suspected offences – under the laws relating to insolvency are dealt with, in England and Wales, by the network of Official Receivers. And investigations under the Companies Acts remain the province of the DTI. Furthermore, there are two autonomous provinces of FSA chairman Sir Howard Davies' sprawling empire: banking business and general insurance. While both banks and insurers have to belong to the FSA, the conduct of their mainstream businesses, neither of which counts as investment business, is regulated by two codes of conduct policed by industry-based boards.

The FSA has meanwhile carved out a new role in an area never originally envisaged as within its orbit. The decision of the London Stock Exchange to become a limited company made it 'inappropriate', in Whitehall jargon, for the exchange to continue its role as the listing authority – changed with ensuring companies wishing to have their shares quoted met the required standards. Thus the UK Listing Authority moved downriver to become an arm of the FSA. At the time of the changeover, in 2000, this was thought to be merely a technical shift brought about by the exchange's pending demutualisation. By summer 2001, it was clear that control of the listing requirements meant, in the words of one FSA insider, 'extending our reach into the heart of corporate Britain'.

The FSA had always been envisaged as a regulator of financial companies. UKLA made it, in part, a regulator of all quoted companies. It would decide whether they would be allowed to list their shares on an exchange; it would decide when and how these companies would file their accounts, and it would have a say in what went in the annual report.

How this will work in practice is difficult to predict. Should UKLA become too heavy-handed, it is easy to imagine an aggrieved company going to the courts to protest about an unauthorised extension of the FSA's powers. Given Parliament explicitly established the FSA primarily as a regulator of financial services companies, it is not too difficult to foresee a number of court rulings limiting UKLA's reach.

So, finally, who does what in the FiSMA era?

Think of a regulatory-fraud spectrum, from left to right. First there are the purely technical breaches of regulations that would spark little moral outrage from the averagely intelligent person, effectively paperwork 'offences'. These would be dealt with by FSA / UKLA.

A little further over are the offences that involve the mistreatment of consumers. This can range from mis-selling of products through to conducting business for which one was not authorised and even to outright confidence-trick activities. At the left hand side of this part of the spectrum, offences occur because of sloppiness or complacency rather than any ill-intent. At the right hand side, we touch the border separating civil from criminal offences. For the most part, such offences would be dealt with by either the FSA or OFT, unless they related to the Companies Act, in which case they would fall to the DTI.

The next part of the spectrum relates to outright abuse of the financial system, in particular the gamut of 'market abuse' offences over which, as we have seen, the FSA has civil jurisdiction throughout the country. But this is where the FSA starts to fade out, because the most serious market abuse case, insider dealing, is also a criminal offence, at which point we shade into the final section – theft, in its various forms. This is the end of the trail covered by the Serious Fraud Office, the Scotland Yard and City Police fraud squads and the various regional and county forces.

From our spectrum, it is clear that, for all its faults, the FSA system is reasonably logical in the patch of territory it is expected to cover. Just to confuse matters a little further, however, the FSA does have a limited power of criminal prosecution in relation to 'perimeter' offences – the conduct of what ought to be FSA-regulated business by people who are not FSA members.

This power was the cause of some friction between the FSA and SFO in the early part of 2000, with SFO director Rosalind Wright known to be opposed to any criminal-prosecution role for the FSA. But while the FSA and SFO are sometimes referred to as if they were parallel organisations, with one handling the civil side of the street and the other the criminal side, this suggests a clear-cut division that doesn't exist. Quite apart from anything else, the much smaller SFO spends much of its time prosecuting people who are not only not regulated by the FSA but would never be required to be so, being commercial companies rather than providers of financial services.

What do you think so far?: The FSA at rising five

For years, the SIB headquarters in Bunhill Row, sandwiched between Old Street and the Barbican Centre, presented a modest red-brick exterior to the outside world. It was within hitting distance of the City. It was within hitting distance of some fine pubs and a good sandwich bar. But it was never going to strike dread into the heart of any would-be fraudster.

The FSA HQ in Canary Wharf is a different sort of building altogether. Not that it presents a menacing face to the world. Quite the contrary; it has the airy spaciousness of a modern corporate head office. Indeed, it could pass as the premises of an investment bank or major stockbroker.

But the changes are far more than architectural. Regulation, FSA-style, is quite different from the regulation practised by the SIB and its quarrelsome satellite bodies during 1988–97. As the old system was being absorbed into the new, during 1997–98, it seemed as if the old agencies (IMRO, banking supervision and so forth) were simply being reborn as sub-divisions of an umbrella organisation. By 2001, that was clearly not the case.

In effect, Sir Howard and his senior team pushed to its logical conclusion the premise of the SIB system, that people should be regulated for doing things, not for being things. The FSA went one step further; organisations should be regulated not for what they do but for how risky they and their activities were likely to be. One of the FSA's three main directorates is devoted to 'regulatory processes and risk'. This combines in one unit three critical tasks: authorisation (deciding whether to admit people and firms in the first place), enforcement (ensuring they obey the rules once in) and risk assessment (assessing how much surveillance each entity requires). The old system went some way in this direction; the FSA has gone all the way. What an institution calls itself, even what it does, is no longer as important as the level of risk inherent in that company. That risk assessment covers both the inherent risk inside the firm and the hazard it would pose to other institutions and the system as a whole were everything to go wrong.

FSA's other two main directorates cover, first, banking and market places and, second, consumer affairs, investment companies and other providers of packaged financial products, along with general insurance. Again, this is fairly logical, in that banking and exchange-based businesses are quite different from the selling of retail financial products.

The 'risk' model has it limits, however. At the time of writing, Equitable Life is on the brink of insolvency; a miscalculation regarding guaranteed payouts on packaged products triggered a legal battle after which investors started pulling their money out, regardless of ever-steeper penalty clauses. Equitable, one of the world's oldest assurance companies, may well have rated as a low risk on the FSA's radar. A fair criticism of the FSA system is that there is perhaps a touch too much management consultancy about the structure and rather too little of the firm, admonitory tread of the inspector as he mounts the stairs on a routine visit. Regulation is not a service industry but a quasi-policing function.

It was a mistake for Parliament to lay a duty on the FSA to have regard to London's competitive position as a financial centre. That is none of the FSA's proper business.

The City can look after its own competitive position. The FSA is there to look after us.

And the beat goes on: the Serious Fraud Office

From 1988 to 1991, the SFO enjoyed a media honeymoon unrivalled in recent years. Journalists salivated in print about its awesome powers to cut through the red tape and hit the fraudster where he lived. When Polly Peck chief Asil Nadir was arrested by armed officers assisting the SFO, the press could hardly control its excitement. Had a shot actually been fired, it is likely that certain media cheerleaders would have fainted clean away.

The delayed peak of this love-in was reached in June 1992, when Kevin and Ian Maxwell were arrested in connection with the collapse of their late father Robert's publishing and media empire. Mysteriously, television cameras were on the scene at Kevin's house for the 'dawn raid'; dozens of journalists later that day jostled outside Snow Hill police station in the City to see the now-charged brothers being led to a black maria.

By that time, the affair was cooling rapidly. Too many cases were going wrong in court. Guinness defendant Ernest Saunders had, in May 1991, his sentence halved by the Court of Appeal. The new SFO director Barbara [now Dame Barbara] Mills was less sure-footed in dealing with the press than had been the gregarious John Wood. The case against two further Guinness defendants, merchant bankers Roger Seelig and the late Lord Patrick Spens, had fallen apart. The Blue Arrow trial of fourteen individual and corporate defendants for allegedly rigging the market in shares of the employment agency from which the case took its name was well on the way to disintegration.

Worst of all, the SFO was failing to live up to the media's fantasies. Journalists were beginning to grasp that this was an organisation run essentially by cautious government lawyers, not some sort of search-and-destroy outfit.

The media winter was to last a good five years before the public image began to glow once more. But the SFO's 1991–96 record was nowhere near as bad as it has been painted. Nor was its 1988–91 record anywhere near as good.

The four Guinness convictions in summer 1990 – Saunders, plus Gerald Ronson, Anthony Parnes and Jack Lyons – represented the fruits of a case inherited from the DTI and Scotland Yard. The 1991 conviction of fraudster Peter Clowes was a triumph, but one largely based on evidence supplied by the liquidators of his investment group. Nadir had originally been investigated by the Inland Revenue. By contrast, 1991–96 saw at least the beginning if not the conclusion of some major courtroom victories, notably the convictions of history's biggest commercial fraudster, Abbas Gokal, the former chairman of the Gulf shipping group. Gokal was a major player in the BCCI scandal and was jailed in April 1997 for fourteen years. Other BCCI-related figures were also convicted. At the time, an SFO insider was modest about the organisation's BCCI successes, noting: 'Jurors don't relate to Asian defendants'. Nor, it seemed, did the media, who seemed to believe obtaining 'guilty' verdicts in these cases required little effort from the prosecution.

Nadir's flight to Cyprus in spring 1993 was portrayed an 'another SFO failure', even though the office had opposed bail in his case. The 1996 acquittal of Kevin and Ian Maxwell brought fresh opprobrium, almost as if SFO personnel had made up the jury as well as the investigation and prosecution teams. Fraudster Roger Levitt's brief 'community service' sentence, following a plea bargain, provoked outrage, although given Levitt's chief victims – a number of wealthy showbusiness and sporting figures – were unwilling to testify against their investment guru, the SFO was lucky to obtain any sort of conviction at all.

The loss of all the 'second-round' Guinness cases – against Lord Spens, Roger Seelig, David Mayhew and Thomas Ward – was more worrying, and more blameworthy. At SFO headquarters in Elm Street, Guinness seemed to have become a great 'cause', when what was needed was clear thinking on the likelihood of convictions against the drinks group's former advisers. Blue Arrow, similarly, was the worst sort of large-scale fraud trial; an overblown, overlong circus that gave the impression of being conducted largely for the benefit of our learned friends. In both the Guinness and Blue Arrow cases, the 'major fraud case' – both investigation and trial – appeared to have transmogrified into some sort of hugely expensive growth industry, with the SFO acting as a snooty and unaccountable board of directors.

The position started to turn round during the 1992–97 tenure of director George Staple, a courteous City solicitor whose old-fashioned habits, such as speaking in proper sentences and answering criticisms as fully as he could, began to give the organisation a rather more normal and less lurid public image. In parallel with the prosecution of major fraudsters, such as hotelier Robert Feld and retailer Stephen Hinchliffe, the SFO began taking on smaller but still noteworthy cases; by the late-1990s, an SFO-hired QC was as likely to be prosecuting a crooked solicitor from Hastings as a former BCCI executive. Elm Street was now the people's friend.

Today, the SFO is in calmer waters. In 2000 and 2001, it gained convictions in cases ranging from fraudulent champagne 'investment' and the corruption of bank executives, to stock market rigging and fraud against the Legal Aid system. Ironically, it seems to be getting better results without the ability to use Section Two evidence in court than it did when talk-or-else was in full operation. But cuts in police budgets are shrinking the pool of fraud-squad officers upon whom the organisation can draw; only Scotland Yard and the City Police maintain sizeable commercial crime departments. Current director Rosalind Wright has suggested a change in the law to give Elm Street its own corps of police officers – a National Fraud Squad. She has suggested also the SFO should absorb that part of the Crown Prosecution Service that deals with lesser fraud cases, thus unifying under one roof the capacity to prosecute white-collar crime.

Wright's predecessor George Staple, meanwhile, has put forward the idea of treating DTI inspectors and the SFO as a 'common resource'. Judging from recent share-outs of cases between the DTI and SFO, this seems to be happening informally already. Doubtless an expert lawyer would be able to explain why the DTI cases were really 'all about' company law while the SFO cases weren't, but to the untrained eye they have seemed much of a muchness.

Down by the lazy river: NCIS, MI5, MI6

At the start of the 1990s, the Bank of England hosted a press conference launching the first set of money-laundering guidelines for financial institutions. The tone was almost apologetic. No, the Bank had no idea of the scale of the problem, but the world was full of drug dealers, terrorists and other black-hat figures, and the City was a major financial centre, so there had to be a problem of some sort. Besides, the guidelines were voluntary.

At about the same time, Robert Maxwell died at sea. Press reports suggesting either the domestic security service MI5 or its overseas-intelligence counterpart MI6 had been tracking Maxwell's luxury yacht at the time of his death, were met with dignified contempt by the secret services. No, they had not been keeping tabs on Maxwell, the message seemed to run – they had rather more important things on their plates.

By the end of the 1990s, 'economic crime' – effectively, money-laundering plus anything else financial that could be presented as a strategic threat – had become a matter of much greater interest in the secret world. Without the Soviet menace, the services were in need of a new role. Fortunately, there was a group of lawyers and fraudbusters able to supply one. Henceforth, they suggested, the services should not merely supply high-grade intelligence, but high-grade evidence, capable of being used in court against major-league organised crime and their bankers, the money-launderers. The services jumped at the opportunity to combat this new 'threat', as did the new National Criminal Intelligence Service (NCIS), a nationwide intelligence-gathering body one of whose key tasks was the gathering of information about money-launderers.

To critics, money-laundering, far from being a great menace to civilisation, is merely a 'coppers' ramp', an excuse for large budgets, expensive surveillance equipment and intrusive new powers against the citizen. Furthermore, it is a cover for the real object of the exercise, which is to combat tax evasion in an era where exchange controls have been dismantled. By forcing banks and others to disclose details of all their transactions, they are better placed to spot offshore tax dodges and the like. Supporters of the money-laundering measures retort that money is the lifeblood of serious crime, terrorism and the drug trade, and that the strictest measures are needed to choke off the supply. The outrages of 11 September 2001 strengthened their hand, although sceptics point out that the terrorists operating out of the Middle East and South Central Asia have their own money-transmission systems that are unlikely to be affected by western legislation.

Mainstream fraud investigators take a tolerant view of the secret services' incursion into their territory. They refer to MI6 as 'the river people', a reference to the service's Thameside headquarters at Vauxhall Cross, and they poke fun at 'river-speak', the circumlocutory phrases beloved of the spymasters. To the average fraud investigator, money-laundering is a bit like global warming – tremendously important, no doubt, but not very tangible.

7

Cuckoos in the nest: Clearing banks and general insurers

The original depositor still had his deposit, his money. The man who borrowed also had money. You see that the bank, by making the loan, had created money. So it was then, and so it has been ever since.

JK Galbraith and Nicole Salinger,
Almost Everyone's Guide to Economics
(Andre Deutsch, 1979)

Safe as houses? Banking and insurance in the City

In a sense, neither the high street banks nor the insurance companies really belong in the City, and it is no surprise that both have increasingly deported thousands of workers to vast sheds in Peterborough or Leeds while maintaining smaller flagship premises in the Square Mile for the exclusive use of senior executives and their support staffs.

The reason these two big faces don't fit is simple. Neither banking nor insurance is a risk business in the sense that, say, investment banking or commodities trading are risk businesses. That is not to say there isn't any risk in running a bank – or an insurer. Far from it. Banks go 'phut' with astonishing regularity, by which I mean that it is astonishing they have maintained their stolid image despite the routine bank failures – not that the failures themselves are astonishing. They are only too predictable, given the dire quality of decision-making that plagues all banking systems in all countries.

Scandinavia was rocked by bank failures in the early 1990s; all of Japan's large banks are thought to be technically insolvent at the time of writing, the US small-bank industry, the Savings and Loans institutions, collectively went bust in the late 1980s and France's Credit Lyonnais has gone bust so many times it has picked up the nickname 'Debit Lyonnais'.

In Britain, failures have been concentrated in what one may call 'sort-of banks' rather than mainstream clearers. But the roster of 'sort-of banks' who have gone 'very-much' bust is impressive: London & Counties, Slater Walker, Johnson Matthey Bankers, Bank of Credit and Commerce International, Wallace Smith Trust.

And the rest.

Then there is insurance, an industry whose vulnerability to unforeseen events (such as insolvency) may be thought to cast doubt on its claim to be able to take the worry out of life for the rest of us. From the collapse of Vehicle & General in 1971 through to the disintegration of Independent Insurance thirty years later, British insurers fall apart with appalling regularity, and usually for the same single reason – they underpriced risks in order to grab a bigger piece of the market, confident that premiums could be raised tomorrow, sometime, never . . .

Foreign insurers are little better. In the United States, historically, they have been considerably worse. And we haven't even mentioned Lloyd's of London.

So, given that this brief resume may suggest that there can be few higher-risk occupations than ownership of a bank or insurer, how can it be that these businesses ought by right to be turfed out of the City on the ground of their risk-free status?

This is to confuse two quite separate types of risk. *Owning* a bank or insurer is, indeed, a hazardous affair. But banking and insurance products themselves are *not* risk based.

A bank deposit is not, in theory, at risk. It is a sum of money that the depositor *will* get back, in contrast to an investment, which is a sum of money that the investor *may* get back. There is a deposit protection scheme that insures bank deposits. Money in a bank is money you will get back, one way or another.

The same principle applies to general insurance. Some years ago, Cardiff Central railway station contained a small vending machine in the booking hall out of which, in return for a few coins, the traveller would be dispensed a small ticket, insuring her luggage for the journey to Paddington. Upon arrival at Paddington, assuming bags and baggage were unharmed, the ticket became worthless. This is insurance in a microcosm. It is a service protecting the insured party against something that may happen.

Life *insurance* operates on exactly the same principle. A person's life can be insured for a year. Should the year come to an end and the person be hale and hearty, the life insurance policy will have no value. An insurance policy is not an investment. Not even a life insurance policy. Confusion arises because of the sound-alike industry of life *assurance*. The confusion deepens because the very large insurance groups and the very large assurance groups (life offices, in the jargon) are increasingly one and the same organisations. But assurance is based upon a completely opposite principle from insurance, protecting the assured party not against some that may happen, but against something that will – ageing and death. Assurance is a form of investment, and we will look at it more closely in the chapter covering packaged retail investment products. For now, we need only to bear in mind that an insurance policy is a time-limited contract covering the insured for that time only against a specific happening: a car accident, a house fire, an oil tanker sinking, accidental death or pretty much any of the other misfortunes that can befall the human race.

While we are on the subject, health insurance is not an investment either. Nor is nursing-home insurance, nor redundancy cover. You may think of them as 'a good investment', and you may well be right to do so. But 'investment', in the strict sense of the word, is about risk – that is risk for you, but not necessarily for the large institution with whom you are dealing. Indeed, as we noted earlier, it is a feature of City institutions to try to reap the rewards of risk-taking while enjoying the security of fee-charging. One way of doing this is to let the client rather than the institution take the risk.

It could be that, fired up by films such as *Double Indemnity* and *Fortune is a Woman,* you find the notion of risk-free insurance quite incredible. But the buyer of an insurance policy is taking no risk in the financial-market sense, although the insurance community's renowned ability to reject a claim on the most spurious grounds may be considered a risk of sorts.

A bank deposit is the same sort of transaction. When you walk past the implacable exteriors of the big banks or general insurers, what you see is what you get. They are low risk. Indeed, they are no-risk. Generously, they and their shareholders shoulder all the hazards. You merely reap the benefits, in terms of an interest-free overdraft and an ultra-cheap policy covering what the Americans would call 'fire, auto and theft'.

At least, that is the official version.

The reality is somewhat different. Both the banks and the insurance companies have drunk deep on what one insurance company executive has described as a 'witches' brew of lethal risks'.

Lethal, that is, not only to themselves but also to us.

How? Read on.

'What a wonderful racket!' Banking, twenty-first century-style

Banking is a simple business, really. One attracts deposits at the lowest possible rates and lends those same deposits out at the highest possible rate. Thanks to competition from other banks, both sets of rates are under constant pressure from a new breed of unsentimental, financially-literate consumers who ruthlessly shop around for the best deal. Banks are bastions of the market economy, because they make a market in the most fundamental of all modern commodities – money.

Wrong. Let us try again.

Banks are state-licensed traffickers in a state-manufactured and state-guaranteed product – money. They do not 'lend out deposits'. They create new money. Under the international rules agreed by the Bank for International Settlements at Basle in Switzerland – also known as the Group of Ten central bank governors' forum – banks can lend out £100 for every £8 they take in deposits. How? Because only a small proportion of deposits is ever taken out on any one day, and – more importantly – the loans themselves are deposited, thus forming the basis for new loans far in excess of the amount left with the bank. This process ends eventually, of course, but the BIS believes a ratio of eight 'real' pounds to 100 pretend ones is 'prudent', a definition of the word found in no other walk of life.

Now, this extraordinary money-creation power dates back to Roman times, at the earliest, but in modern times it has been strictly curbed, chiefly by strict Bank of England (hence government) rules putting a lid on the amount of credit a bank could grant. This made sense, give that the vast majority of money in the system – all money other than notes and coins, in fact – was 'debt money'. It existed solely because someone, somewhere had gone into debt.

Furthermore, the Bank told the clearing (i.e. money-creating) banks what rate of interest to charge and kept them under tight control through the operations of the old discount market, which we examined in the chapter covering the Bank of England. But in 1971, this system was turned on its head, and it was decided that, rather than the Bank tell the market what interest rates ought to be, the market would tell the Bank. Meanwhile, credit controls and lending ceilings were removed; henceforth, the banks would take 'commercial' lending decisions and take the consequences.

What could be wrong with that? Well, in fact it did not work out quite that way. What happened instead was that banks lent out as much as they liked, and, when they had lent so much that inflation threatened, they then started to raise their own interest rates, putting pressure in turn on the Bank, which raised its own minimum rate, and so on.

This had the disadvantage of driving some weaker borrowers to the wall. But this was balanced by the fact that it allowed banks to recoup their losses by charging more to the survivors. In short, banks, during the past thirty years, have been allowed to 'book loans' (thus making a profit) and, once this ran out of control, they put up the cost of those loans (booking another profit). As the author and journalist Robin Ramsay out it in a recent book: 'What a wonderful racket! It makes loan-sharking look sophisticated'. *(Prawn Cocktail Party*, Vision, 1998.)

Nor was a hike in interest rates the banks' only weapon in their ceaseless struggle to pass the costs of their own failed risk-taking on to their customers; in the recession of the early 1990s it was estimated that bank charges (especially for small-business customers) had soared by a third as the banks charged ever-increasing amounts for writing rude letters, bouncing cheques, storing people's wills and so forth. One major bank, at the end of 1991, reclassified Anglican churches as 'small businesses' rather than clubs, societies or charities, thus putting them on a higher band of charges.

No, this is not an anti-bank rant. Rather, it is an attempt to look at the mechanisms of the banking system, and to understand that, in many ways, the banks are as much victims as villains. Once the genie of unbridled credit creation was let out of the bottle, the banks could no more control it than could anybody else. With a few short years, bank charges disappeared as banks battled for customers. This development was hailed as a huge victory for the customer, but that was very far from being the truth. In reality, the abolition of charges – on cheques, cash-machine withdrawals and other types of 'activity', in the jargon – swiftly transformed the bank manager from a servant with two masters (the customer and the head office) into a servant with just one, the head office. As bank customers had no economic value by dint simply, of being customers, they would have to be made to 'perform' in financial terms, and that meant that they would have to buy products that cost money, now that the current account had become a profit-free zone.

We look at 'packaged products' in the next chapter. For now, it is worth noting that the largest life assurance (i.e. packaged investment) company in Britain is Barclays Life. That is hardly surprising, given that, by the mid-1990s, the buzz-phrase among the big banks was the vaguely continental-sounding notion of *bancassurance,* a euphemism for the selling to bank customers of non-bank, investment (i.e. risk) products.

However, there was, and is, a much simpler way to make money out of current accounts, which is to persuade their holders to go 'into the red', as it is still known in old-fashioned circles. This, of course, relates directly back to the abovementioned licence allowing the banks to create as much money as they like.

They have been doing so with a vengeance.

In the first quarter of 1988, £13.4 billion was outstanding on credit cards advanced by major British banks. For future reference, they are defined, in no particular order, as Barclays, Royal Bank of Scotland / NatWest, Abbey National, Alliance & Leicester, Bank of Scotland, Bradford & Bingley, Halifax, HSBC, Lloyds TSB and Northern Rock.

By the second quarter of 2001, this had ballooned to £21.6 billion. In June 2001 alone, the amount outstanding had risen by £315 million.

For personal loans, unconnected with house purchase, the figures are even more startling. In the first quarter of 1998, £29.9 billion was outstanding. By the second quarter of 2001, this stood at £43.7 billion. Even the antique overdraft managed to show an increase, from £4.7 billion in the first quarter of 1998 to £5.9 billion by the second quarter of 2001.

Remember, this is all money being created by the banks. Do not be too smug should you have your borrowings firmly under control. As we have seen, when all this new money starts to pump up inflation, it is not only the reckless borrowers who will pay higher interest rates and inventive bank fees. You will pay as well.

On top of packaged products, loans and the invention of new types of hidden charges, there is a fourth method by which the banks can pass on the costs of unbridled lending risk and fierce competition to the customers – branch closures. In 1995, there were 16,809 bank branches in the UK. By 1999, there were 12,026. In the ten years 1991–2001, 150,000 banking jobs were made redundant. This is not a net job loss, because a roughly similar number of posts were created in new bank 'call-centres' – huge hangars to which calls previously dealt with by local branches were routed.

Despite the major bank's insistence that telephone banking was 'what the customer wants', it was noticeable that, at the same time, banks were pouring millions of pounds into buying or building up their 'private banking' businesses – banks for wealthy clients, who could be expected to have several thousand pounds sitting on current account at any one time. These private clients, it seems, did not want telephone banking. On the contrary, they wanted the sort of banks everybody used to enjoy, complete with a branch and a manager.

In parallel with the call-centres was a longer-term drive to get the customers to do as much of the bank clerking as possible. By December 2000, the British Bankers Association reported that of 104.9 million personal accounts held with the major banking groups, 28.2 million could be accessed by telephone and a (largely separate) 6.4 million could be accessed by personal computer via the internet, or via advanced mobile phones. Most of these fell within the 88.3 million total of ordinary accounts, but a significant segment formed part of the 16.6 million deposit accounts, for which a notice period must be given for withdrawals.

The banks also try to spread the risks of credit creation by colonising neighbouring business areas. We have already touched on *bancassurance*. Equally significant is the drive into the mortgage market. At the end of the 1970s, the banks' share of homeloan business was tiny, and tended to be highly specialised. Anyone seeking a mortgage visited a building society. In fact, they would have visited it many times already, because to become eligible for a mortgage one had to have a respectable savings record with the society in question.

All charged much the same rate of interest, and that rate was in fact below what it would have been on the open market. Thus the savings requirement was not only a way of proving the individual's fitness to be entrusted with mortgage debt; it was a method of rationing cheap housing credit.

By 2000, the major British banks had nearly two-thirds of the £360.4 billion market in mortgage lending. In part, this was because most of the larger building societies had become banks themselves: along with those mentioned above as qualifying for 'major bank' status, other 'conversions' have included Birmingham Midshires, Bristol & West, Cheltenham & Gloucester and National & Provincial. The conversion, from mutual ownership to bank status, was, in turn, given its impetus by the banks' invasion of the mortgage market.

Unlike a bank, a mutual society is limited to lending only what it can take in from savers. By the mid-1980s, the unfairness of having the societies competing with credit-creating banks forced legal changes allowing the societies to join the charmed circle if they wished. Given the demutualisation process involved windfall payouts of the societies' assets to savers and borrowers belonging to that society, resistance was not as fierce as one may have expected.

That the current 'members' had never been envisaged by the founders of the building society movement as having the right as 'owners' to sell what was, in effect, to be owned across the generations, was rarely a consideration.

The remaining large societies are, in descending order of size, Nationwide, Britannia, Yorkshire, Portman, Coventry, Skipton, Chelsea, Leeds & Holbeck, West Bromwich and the Derbyshire. They take the bulk of what is left of the homeloan market.

There is one final route by which the banks can seek to escape or pass on the costs of the risks they have taken – merger.

In the ten years to 2001, three of the great names in British banking either disappeared entirely or passed into new ownership: TSB, formerly the Trustee Savings Bank, made an odd but successful blue-collar bedfellow for Lloyds Bank, the first choice of the southern professional classes. Midland was finally subsumed entirely into HSBC, and National Westminster was taken over by Royal Bank of Scotland.

With consolidation came greater opportunities to 'take out costs' – lose staff and branches – and, with luck, to be better able to ride the next downturn in the ever-more volatile credit-creation cycles. Nor did anyone believe that this was anything like the end of the story. 'A big world needs a big bank', declared television advertisements for Barclays in late 2000. It could have been a subliminal message to the competition authorities – hands off, if you want any sort of British banking industry to survive.

A snapshot of the top five banks as at August 2001 is revealing in itself. The ranking, in descending order, is Barclays (with assets of £352 billion), Royal Bank of Scotland / NatWest (£320 billion), Lloyds TSB (£217 billion), Abbey National (£204 billion) and HSBC (£185 billion).

But the running order is altered somewhat should you take out those assets relating to packaged life assurance products and concentrate only on assets relating to traditional banking business: Barclays (£343 billion), Royal Bank of Scotland / NatWest (£309 billion), Abbey National (£185 billion), HSBC (£182 billion) and Lloyds TSB (£166 billion).

The big picture: clearing banks and the City

So how do these colossi fit into the Square Mile?

They may be giants on the home stage, but in the Square Mile they have to jostle with any number of foreign banks for the lucrative business of cross-frontier lending, usually to large industrial and commercial clients, along with national governments and other banks. Ranked by assets, all UK banks have 45 per cent of the total – £1,425 billion – while the foreign banks' assets add up to £1,717 billion.

There are 188 UK-incorporated banks in Britain, of which 111 are British-owned. That's quite a change from the limited selection available on your high street, but these include specialised institutions, many of which are relatively small. The remaining 77 British-incorporated banks are foreign owned.

Then there are 474 banks here which are incorporated outside the UK. Of these 116 are from the European Union and associated European nations and have a physical presence here; another 234 are from the same neck of the woods, but do not have a presence here (although they are authorised to provide cross-frontier services just as if they were), and 124 banks from outside Europe are based here. Finally, 164 foreign banks have 'representative offices' here, allowing them to talk to potential clients but not to transact banking business in the normal sense.

In all, 662 banks are engaged in the UK banking market, of which 481 are foreign. Nowhere else in the world has as large a selection of the international banking community.

Unsurprisingly, perhaps, London is the top centre for cross-frontier lending. Its share of the world market grew from 17 per cent in 1989 to 20 per cent in 2000. By contrast, Japan has 12 per cent, the US and Germany 9 per cent each and France 6 per cent. But much of this share is accounted for by foreign banks based in the City; according to International Financial Services London, only three British banks appear in the top-thirty world league for cross-frontier lending. IFSL points out that banking services, by banks of all nationalities, account for about half of all the City's net overseas earnings. But these earnings are extremely volatile in relation to the markets in which they originate.

In 1997, net banking earnings from the US totalled £650 million; by 1999, that was down to £574 million. In 1997, earnings from France were just £26 million; in 1999 they had shot up to £248 million. Banking services earned £21 million from the Netherlands in 1997, and £178 million in 1999. But while earnings from Switzerland total £450 million in 1997, they had dived to just £139 million by 1999.

It was the same story in Germany (£321 million to £129 million), Belgium and Luxembourg (£39 million to £103 million) and South Africa (£3 million to £101 million). Only Italy stayed reasonably unchanged (£92 million to £124 million) while the share held by 'other countries' shot up from £551 million to £1,224 million.

The total is steady as a heartbeat, with a modest improvement from £2,331 million to £2,929 million. And, of course, exchange rates play their part in moving earnings around the world without anyone lifting a finger.

But the volatility on this scale requires some mighty fancy footwork from the bankers every year. We are back where we were in chapter four on the 'magic money machine', fearing that the City as a whole has made a series of gambles from a precarious overseas asset base and that those gambles have to come good time after time.

Losing even once is not an option

Covered – for what? General insurance

The 2 September 1992 ought to have been a day to go down in history. A gaggle of journalists gathered together by the Institute of Insurance Brokers in the City could hardly believe their ears.

According to the institute, four of Britain's top seventeen general insurance companies were insolvent.

Even by the standards of that extraordinary month – Black / White Wednesday was only a fortnight away – and even by the standards of the slump of the early 1990s, it was a big news story. Four big insurers had breached the Government's 30 per cent 'solvency margin', the safety net ensuring companies are able to meet their liabilities. Soaring claims, insurance frauds, escalating court awards and uneconomic (i.e. low) premiums meant these firms had collectively lost more than half their total shareholders' funds in two years. Worse, sliding stock market prices meant the traditional escape route, of recouping losses on insurance business through returns on investments, was blocked.

Fortunately, Andrew Paddick, head of the institute, and Martin Thornton, an institute legal expert, managed to check the assembled newshounds before they stampeded for the nearest payphones (mobile telephones still being a rarity). The solvency margin, they explained, had become a worthless measure of an insurer's health. Peversely, it could even be a sort of reverse indicator, sending out misleading signals to policyholders.

The margin, as then calculated, was a hangover from the days of the 'tariff', the insurance industry standard that related premiums closely to risk. Thus a young man with a 250cc motor-cycle, paying so much in premiums, would, should he wish to insure a 500cc motor-cycle, pay an increased premium according to the tariff, regardless of which insurer he approached. But in the absence of a tariff, insurers could charge as little or as much as the market would bear. So our man, even were he to hang on to his 250cc motor-cycle, may pay as much as if he had traded up to the 500cc machine. Let us assume this happens, and that his premium doubles despite there being no additional risk involved. Let us further suppose that he grudgingly pays up.

In any normal business. persuading the customer to part with more money for the same product would be a cause of backslapping congratulation all round. But not for the Department of Trade and Industry, then the insurance regulator, back in 1992. All its solvency officials could see was an increased premium. That meant an increased risk. Which in turn ought to mean an increase in the solvency margin.

In fact, by 1992 the DTI was well aware of the shortcomings of the solvency ration, and it has since been completely overhauled. But it does illustrate the huge changes that have come over general insurance in recent years.

During the past two decades the tariff has been dismantled, and the gales of competition have been allowed to blow freely through the general insurance business. The abolition of the tariff – as with the end of mortgage rationing and the scrapping of bank charges – has been routinely hailed as a 'victory for the consumer'. In fact, there is a strong case for suggesting the tariff held down volatility in the insurance industry and enabled the consumer to plan ahead in a way that today's rapid-fire alternation of insurance price wars and steep premium increases make impossible.

At the time of writing, the insurance cycle is turning. This cycle is a wondrous thing, intelligible only to insurance-industry insiders. It bears no relation to economic cycle that governs the rest of us, the ebb and flow of boom and bust.

The cycle has two phases. There is the 'price war', which sees premiums slashed. This continues until one or more senior industry figures declares that the policyholder has 'been living in a fool's paradise', at which point premiums rise.

In the insurance cycle, price wars can break out at the oddest times, as can their opposite, the steep rise in premiums that accompanies a tightening of the cycle. At the time of writing, a two-year tightening is showing signs of coming to an end, with a new price war breaking out.

You may find this strange, given that midsummer 2001 is seeing the peak of a roaring consumer boom, as evidenced by the bank lending figures shown above. In any other industry, rising demand is marked by *rising* prices, not falling ones. But this is insurance, and it plays to its own rules. Propelling the cycle is the fuel that powers the whole insurance industry: capacity.

In contrast to writing a best-seller, or starting a management consultancy, or even setting up as an insurance broker, starting an insurance *company* is not something you can do off the kitchen table 'to see how it goes'. Were you to start issuing policies off your own bat, the FSA would become very excited. Anyone wishing to write a policy needs to demonstrate 'capacity', by which is meant a very large cash reserve just in case all your policies go sour at once. The 'solvency margin' or 'solvency ratio' that we encountered earlier was an attempt to monitor capacity, albeit an imperfect one.

Another key rule of insurance is that premium income is booked to the insurer itself in slices. This makes sense, if you think about it. Should you insure my house for a year for a £500 premium, that £500 is not yours until the year is up. As you do more business, and collect many more lots of £500, most of them – should you be a good underwriter – will be clear profit, once the claims from the ones that are not have been paid.

But at the moment you start business as an insurer, you have none of these retained premiums. If I am your first customer, and my house is burgled in the first week, how are you going to pay me?

Hence the regulators' insistence on capacity. And when premiums are rising, during the tightening phase of the insurance cycle, capacity – in the form of capital investment – becomes more plentiful, as investors are attracted by the profitability of a business in which the customers pay higher premiums year by year.

But, as with the children's game pick-up sticks – in which players try to pull plastic twigs out of a precarious tower without bringing the whole thing crashing down – so the time comes when all this capacity brings the cycle into the down phase, and another price war starts.

Insurance is itself a series of bets, with each policy and its accompanying premium representing the balancing point of a judgment as to its likelihood of becoming the basis of a claim. All these bets fit together, or should do, into the totality of the insurer's position, itself a sort of master-bet. This bet ought to yield a profit at the end of each year.

But this conservative view of the insurance business, the view that gave rise to the previously discussed tariff, was undermined from the 1950s onwards, as once-cautious insurers increasingly invested their spare cash in property and shares rather than government securities. As the value of these assets has inflated, so the insurers have enjoyed a second source of income, one that has helped them through many a crisis.

That said, insurers remain ranked in terms of their income from premiums. The largest is CGNU, the gnomic title of what is a truly polygamous marriage: Commercial Union, General Accident and Norwich Union. Net premium income in 1999 was £4.9 billion. Next is a rather more conventional married couple, Royal & Sun Alliance (£3 billion), followed by Axa, including PPP Healthcare and long-defunct Equity & Law (£2 billion). ZFS, taking in Zurich and Eagle Star is next (£1.5 billion) and the Cornhill, synonymous for years with Test cricket (£0.9 billion).

From the number of mergers contained in this top five, it is clear the insurance business is consolidating almost as quickly as banking, and one of the reasons behind this can be seen at number six in the league table, the telephone insurer Direct Line (£0.7 billion). Founder Peter Wood revolutionised the insurance business in the 1980s, allowing policyholders to cut out the traditional broker and arrange a policy over the telephone. For the established insurers, there was a pressing need to 'take out' costs in order to stay competitive. The 'synergies' (a euphemism for reducing staff) of merging offered a relatively simple way to achieve this.

Another reason can perhaps be found at number eleven on the list – Independent Insurance (£0.4 billion). These figures were compiled before Independent collapsed into insolvency in the early summer of 2001. Inquiries are continuing at the time of writing, but there are suggestions that Independent pitched its premiums too low in order to retain its market share. By merging, the bigger insurers can hope at least to have greater influence over the insurance environment and to be less at its mercy than Independent seems to have been.

Two more excellent reasons for the 'urge to merge' are found at numbers twelve and thirteen respectively, Barclays and Lloyds TSB (both about £0.38 billion). If clearing banks are going to muscle in on general insurance, the insurers need to band together to see them off. They can also, of course, muscle in on banking, as Prudential (number sixteen in the general insurance league with £0.3 billion) is seeking to do with its on-line bank Egg.

The domestic general insurance industry – i.e. policies written for the home market – generated £22 billion in net premium income in 1999, the last year for which accurate figures are available. The UK insurance market generated a further £12.9 billion writing policies for policyholders overseas.

About one third of the total £34.9 billion general business was written in what is called 'the London market', a catch-all phrase for a unique hub of insurance expertise built originally on shipping insurance but now embracing unusual risks of all types.

Yes, I'm afraid so – it is time to look at Lloyd's.

The game of the Names: Lloyd's and the London market

The police presence in Lime Street was kept deliberately low-key as thousands of Lloyd's investors streamed into their annual meeting on 24 June 1992. Outside the once-futuristic Lloyd's building, Upper-Middle Britain had gathered in force as hundreds of penniless 'Names' – the once-wealthy investors who bankrolled the market – vented their fury on anyone thought to represent the Society of Lloyd's. The one-time fruit machine for the well-off had apparently turned into a hole-in-the-wall cash machine that kept swallowing their cards – and keeping their money – again and again and again.

But while the forces of law and order kept their heads down, the media was not so restrained – 'We're ITN. You an angry Name, sir?' – but, to be fair, the Names were less than reluctant to sound off. 'Moderately angry, yes. Where's the camera?' Biros skidded across notebooks as the Names spoke forth. Cash may have been in short supply at Lloyd's that day, but clichés were more forthcoming: 'fiddling while Lloyd's burns'; 'gross mismanagement'; 'new blood needed on the council'. One Name, Alan Price, arrived on a penny-farthing and immediately announced to reporters that he would spend the day begging from passers-by and hoped to raise £10,000.

There were limits, however, to the sort of trouble that could be expected from a well-mannered crowd such as this. Two sporty-looking young men carried a large banner reading 'Lloyd's is bust'. To circumvent the defamation laws, tiny lettering above the slogan added: 'in our opinion'.

As one of the better-known Names, Michael Caine, might have asked had he been present: 'What's it all about?' To which the answer was summed up in two words. Losses. And liability.

Lloyd's had started losing quite spectacular sums of money in 1988 and would continue to do so right through to 1993, after which time it would make some profit, then some loss again. But the *anni horribiles* were 1988–92, during which time the market as a whole managed to burn its way through £7.9 billion.

It was not just the sporty young men who feared Lloyd's was actually insolvent. Many, many others said so too. Prime minister John Major was warned that the world's most famous insurance market was about to go pop. Cash was pouring out of Lloyd's in all directions as the 1980s ended in a spate of disasters: the loss of the Piper Alpha oil platform, the Exxon Valdez oil spill, the 1987 hurricane and a series of serious transport accidents. Again and again, Lloyd's was holding the policies.

This could have been contained, but Lloyd's was bleeding money in quite another direction: asbestos insurance. The market had written millions of pounds' worth of cover in the US related to asbestos sickness claims. It had been barred in the 1950s and 1960s from writing mainstream insurance business in all but two American states, but it was allowed to pick up surplus risks, those the domestic insurers did not wish to touch. Asbestos was the prime example. Claims now poured in as the one-time wonder-material, whose fireproof qualities had given it science-fiction status in the eyes of a generation of schoolboys, left a trail of illness and death in its wake across the industrial world.

Losses were half the equation. Liability was the other. When

Independent Insurance became insolvent in 2001, plenty of people were less than happy but nobody was pursuing Independent shareholders asking for money. Lloyd's was different. It was a market, not a company, and in contrast to company shareholders the Lloyd's Names faced unlimited liability for their share of the losses.

Critics of the 'angry Names' pointed out that they had been quite well aware of this fact when they had joined the market. And that is true enough. But for generations, stretching back to the eighteenth century, the risk was worth it because backing Lloyd's brought a unique privilege – it allowed the same money to be invested twice.

A Name had to 'show' a sum of cash 'free and clear' – i.e. not tied up in a mortgage or similar. That sum was then pledged to whichever underwriting syndicate the Name had joined, and served as part of its 'capacity'. But while the underwriters on that syndicate cheerfully wrote policies on ships, or aeroplanes or pop stars' vocal chords, the Name could reinvest that money, in a bank deposit, for example. So, while the underwriting syndicate was (with luck) making money for the Name, the bank was paying interest – all on the same sum of money.

But when Lloyd's benign ability most years to provide a welcome flow of funds for the meeting of school fees, home extensions and so forth was thrown horribly into reverse, the Names faced ruin. Furthermore, three developments made it most unlikely that the Names would take their ill-fortune on the chin.

The first – ironically, given that the US was the source of so many of Lloyd's losses – was the decision in 1968 to admit non-British and non-Commonwealth Names. US investors joined the market in considerable numbers, and brought with them that same litigious culture that would help push up court awards on asbestos damage.

Second, a new breed of British Name had been recruited during the 1980s as Lloyd's relaxed its once-strict criteria on the ability to 'show' funds 'free and clear'. By the end of the decade, the market was allowing paintings and other works of art to count as part of a

Name's capacity. Meanwhile, the rich who were not already members of the market were clamouring to join in the late-1970s and early-1980s because of the tax breaks on offer to top earners being stung by the highest tax rates. At the same time, Lloyd's was desperate to drum up new members in the United States to compensate for the fact that the pound was dropping against the dollar, limiting the amount of US business the organisation could handle.

But the real recruiting sergeant was the strong rise in property prices in London and the south-east. This meant that very 'ordinary' homeowners could suddenly meet the Lloyd's 'wealth test', designed to deter all but the most affluent. By the end of the 1980s, Lloyd's boasted 34,000 Names. These were not the retired admirals of yesteryear, either in terms of outlook, or their ability to stand the losses should times get tough.

A third development, however, made a confrontation between Lloyd's and the loss-making Names inevitable: scandal. In the early and mid-1980s – in retrospect, the worst possible time – a number of scandals exposed the dark underside of a market whose motto translated as 'utmost good faith'. Market insiders had been running 'baby syndicates' in which they were their own Names, and into which all the best risks were placed. The syndicates backed by outside Names were landed with the poorer risks. Furthermore, conflicts of interest abounded in a market where underwriters (who wrote the policies), members' agents (who shepherded the outside Names around the market) and brokers (who tried to place clients' risk with the underwriters) were able to co-exist under the same corporate umbrella.

These scandals brought reform in their wake, but they also blew a large hole in the moral authority of those who ran Lloyd's. It was not easy for the market's leaders to exhort Names to pay up and play the game when it was quite clear that thousands of Names had been fleeced for years, under the allegedly watchful eye of the market's guardians.

By 1992, on some measures, one-fifth of all Names were engaged in legal action with Lloyds. 'Can't pay; won't pay' became the unlikely battlecry of a genteel but deadly serious 'county' version of the 1990 poll tax revolt.

Lloyd's survived, although in doing so it changed utterly. A settlement offer was made to the Names, part of which involved shifting the truly irredeemable risks into a 'sidecar', leaving the main market 'clean'. Unlimited liability was effectively scrapped as Names were required to take out insurance on their investments, capping any future losses. Corporate underwriters were allowed into Lime Street, ending centuries of tradition. A distress fund was set up to help the worst-hit Names, chaired by Lady Mary Archer.

Business picked up as the recession ended. A gag doing the rounds in the mid-1990s was that the market had gone 'from meltdown to signdown', a reference to the process whereby a broker has to shrink the share of a policy offered to each of a number of underwriters should that policy be oversubscribed; 'signdown' was a symptom of a healthy market. Today, paradoxically, the market's basic structure is much the same as it ever was, although everything else has changed. Underwriters are employed by any one of about 120 syndicates, each with its own speciality: motor, marine, aicraft and so forth. Their capital – their all-important capacity – is provided by Names, who take a share of the syndicate's profits in proportion to their original investment. Individual Names are looked after by a members' agent and corporate Names by a 'Lloyd's adviser'.

On the other side of the syndicate are the 126 Lloyd's accredited broking firms, who bring clients' risks to the syndicate and seek cover. The Lloyd's brokers can be acting directly for the client, if it is large enough (for example, a major shipping line) or, for smaller risks, a local insurance broker may have passed the business on to the Lloyd's-accredited broker.

Strictly by counting heads, one may conclude that individual Names still dominate Lloyd's – there are 2,852 of them, against 894 corporate Names. But there is no doubt where most of the £11 billion-odd capacity has come from. About £9 billion has been put up by companies, and just £2 billion by individuals.

The corporate invasion of Lloyd's has brought the Society

closer to its old rival in the 'London market', the International Underwriting Association of London. This is (after several name changes) the body for all the specialist insurance companies or subsidiaries engaged in Lloyd's-type activities in specialist, international and wholesale insurance. Today, several of its larger members are big players at Lloyd's, and the two bodies are working together on issues such as the introduction of information technology to a market that still tends to get clogged up with paper.

In total, the London market accounts for 19 per cent of world premium income for marine insurance, 28.9 per cent of world aviation premium insurance, and 21.7 per cent of the combined total for both. This puts the City top of the world table; next is the US, with a 15.6 per cent share of the combined total, with Japan at 10.7 per cent. London is also the world centre for reinsurance – the process whereby insurers lay off their risks with someone else. Not surprisingly, three-quarters of the companies in the London market are foreign-owned. But the overall numbers are comparatively small. Domestic UK risks generated £22 billion net premium income in 1999, and overseas risks insured here totalled £12.9 billion. Of that combined £34.9 billion, just £10 billion was insured in the London market.

Ironically, in view of the atrocious publicity, Lloyd's remains a place where a person's word tends to be as good as a contract, at least until the paperwork is finalised. There have been (true) stories of frantic brokers tracking underwriters down to neighbouring pubs on a Friday night and arranging millions of pounds of cover for a ship over the weekend, and of those 'deals' being honoured on rare occasions when the ship in question has hit trouble. Furthermore, Lloyd's has actually separated brokers and underwriters in recent years, at the same time as the Stock Exchange has moved in the opposite direction. Today, Lloyd's has lost its self-governing status and is regulated by the Financial Services Authority. But the years 1988–92 were a vivid illustration of the sort of risks being run by the City's magic money machine, and of what can happen when those risks go wrong.

Gary Hicks, head of public affairs at the giant Dutch credit insurer NCM, warns of an entirely new and unpredictable world risk environment, made up of the economic meltdowns that routinely plague developing countries, natural disasters, trade wars, genetic catastrophes and computer breakdown. He says: 'Taken in isolation, each of these risks is containable. But it is their cumulative effect, the way they impact upon each other, that will create such a new and unpredictable risk environment over the next three years, an environment I have deliberately dramatised as a witches' brew of lethal risks.'

Behind their reassuring facades, the City's banks and insurance companies have drunk deep from that brew.

8

Trust Unlimited Packaged financial products and fund management

'How to broach this subject?' Renault waved his cigarette in the air. 'Rick, has it ever occurred to you to question any aspect of Laszlo's story?

Many times,' answered Rick. 'Ilsa's, too.'

Michael Walsh, *As Time Goes By*
(Warner Books, 1998)

'A stake in the system': the politics of private investment

There is a paradox at the middle of the huge business that is private investment in Britain today. In theory, the private market for financial services is just that – private. There are some decisions that, by their very nature, are taken by one or two people only: marriage, house purchase, children, holiday destination. Investment decisions fit this category like a round peg in a round hole. So that vast industry – £2,265 *billion* under management in the UK for British clients at the end of 1999 – is the product of millions of intensely personal decisions: whether to leave money in unit trusts, whether to top up the pension, and so forth.

And the final outcome of all those little decisions, in the shape of fund management by institutions to whom those people have entrusted their money, owns more than half the shares in issue on the London Stock Exchange.

Which is as it should be, because there is a neat symmetry here. In economic theory, there are many players in the economy: companies, partnerships, banks, co-operatives, trade unions, the self-employed and so forth. But there are two, and only two, ultimate owners of everything in the private (i.e. non-government) sector, and they are individual people and charitable trusts. None of the other actors has any independent existence; each is owned by the only two 'real' private sector players – the individual and the charity.

So, the textbooks were right then? The little guy and the little gal really are on top in the market economy?

Yes, they are – ultimately. But ultimately can be a long way away. In the here and now, these 'owners' of the private sector have entrusted their inheritance to the care of a group of organisations known collectively as 'the institutions'. You will hear, in your wanderings around the City, hushed references to 'the institutions', similar to all that awe-struck talk about 'the Advisers' that we came across in our chapter three look at the equity market. For those old enough to remember when 'institution' was a euphemism for 'mental hospital', all this reverential murmuring is good for a private laugh.

In the City, 'institution' means, effectively, fund manager, and a fund manager is, four times out of five, one of three things: a bank, an investment bank or an insurance company. Thus Barclays is an institution, as is the Prudential. The arm of Barclays that is an institution calls itself 'Barclays Life', a reference to life assurance. Similarly, Prudential, when it has its fund-manager hat on, ceases to be an insurance company and becomes an assurance company. As we saw in the last chapter, life assurance has nothing much to do with life insurance; 'life assurance' means 'personal savings plan'.

So what? Sure, the ordinary person is, rightly, the majority stakeholder in the private sector. But why shouldn't he or she employ a professional to handle the investment decisions?

There's no reason at all. But the paradox is that this essentially private decision has been jollied along by the one economic actor we haven't mentioned yet, the one that is outside the private sector altogether. The government.

That great floating raft of private investment – all £2,265 billion of it – has been conjured into life in its present form by half a century of tax breaks, special allowances and government initiatives. From life premium relief to PEPs, from portable pensions to stakeholder pensions, this apparent triumph for thrift and personal initiative has been shaped and reshaped again and again as successive administrations have brought their own priorities and prejudices to bear on the market for personal investment.

It is no exaggeration to say that the market in 'packaged' financial products as it exists today is largely the outcome of a series of tax exemptions, in that products have been explicitly designed to qualify for whatever is the latest tax relief. Which is only sensible, given that it would be hard to specialise in products attracting tax at the full rate when one's competitors are cheerfully tempting the customer with the ones enjoying tax exemption.

So what are these 'packaged products'? Simply put, they are investment plans sold off the peg, as opposed to investment plans drawn up after consultation with a 'bespoke' adviser such as a stockbroker. They are investments – so you *may* get your money back. They are not savings, where you *will* get your money back. The short-lived Tax Exempt Special Savings Account (Tessa) was not a packaged product, because it was a type of bank account. Mortgages attracting tax relief under a break that lasted from 1963 to 1999 were also not packaged products, they were tax-exempt loans. But the endowment portion of an endowment mortgage is a packaged product.

Pensions are very definitely packaged products – the most important in most people's lives. But a portfolio of shares drawn up over a glass of sherry with your broker and managed by him on your behalf is not a packaged product.

Unit trusts are one of the oldest types of packaged products on the market. Today's individual savings accounts (ISAs) and stakeholder pensions are umbrella names for two key tax breaks beneath which shelter a raft of packaged products designed by institutions to qualify for these breaks.

Not all packaged products sold to the public attract tax relief, for the simple reason that individual consumers ultimately use up their tax allowance, thus any future purchases will face tax at the normal rate. Nor would packaged products cease to exist if all tax reliefs were to vanish overnight. Unit trusts did very well in the earlier part of the last century without any special tax treatment; both they and other packaged products will always be in demand both for their simplicity and for their ability to spread the risk of investment.

To sum up, the vast industry in retail financial services is the product of decades of shifting tax breaks and other incentives from a number of governments. Why did they do it?

The obvious answer is: to encourage saving. But that cannot be the whole answer. Apart from anything else, the Government is itself a player in the savings game, through the gilts market and the National Savings Bank. Furthermore, for much of the post-war period the savings habit was not considered to be a good thing at all times; rather, the balance between savings and consumption was thought to be the pivot upon which the economy could be fine-tuned and full employment maintained.

All right, so it was not to encourage savings as such that brought this thicket of tax incentives into being; perhaps it was, more specifically, to encourage people to provide for their old age? This is closer to the mark. But the true purpose was even more long-term than that. Who better to express it that Sir Edward du Cann, later chairman of the Conservative Party's backbench 1922 Committee and then chairman of the trading group Lonrho? Writing in 1958, he declared that the welfare state had eroded people's sense of personal responsibility:

> We must seek to reverse this trend, to give people the opportunity to accept responsibility and to participate in the management and organisation of British industry. This is the social necessity for encouraging a wider spread of share ownership. To spread wealth; to spread responsibility; to spread power; that is the aim. Every need creates, in time, its own solution. There is a simple answer to all these problems: the unit trust method of investment.

Units trusts had been around for some time and were popular. By pooling the resources of large numbers of small investors, they built up a pot of shares, with each unit representing a slice of the pot as a whole, rather than any of the individual securities in the pot. In the US, they were known as 'mutual funds', and were more popular still.

But Sir Edward was able to launch a unit trust with a difference. Teamed up with another rising star of the Tory party, Peter (now Lord) Walker, he constructed a unit trust that was linked to a life assurance policy. This was to have enormous consequences, because the tax relief on life assurance premiums had never been designed for this sort of thing. Effectively, an assurance policy was a prudential savings scheme in which a life insurance policy was embedded. In the 1950s it was assumed the plan would run its course right up to the death of the 'assured life', at which point the policy would be cashed in and the dead person's dependents provided for. The insurance policy guaranteed a minimum payout regardless of the number of premiums the assured person had managed to pay before his or her demise. The social benefits of such a scheme were unquestionable, hence tax relief was available on the premiums.

Indeed, well into the 1970s ordinary consumers continued to believe life assurance was primarily a form of life insurance. The industry decided they needed re-educating. 'Money if you die – money if you don't', screamed one admirably blunt advertisement. More subtle was the television spot in which a handsome middle-aged woman gazed wistfully from the deck of an ocean liner, her 'thoughts' on the wisdom of having taken out a particular assurance policy spoken in sad voice-over. Then – a hand on her shoulder – she turns and kisses her still-extant husband. He isn't dead at all! They are simply enjoying the copious fruits of a life policy.

Back in 1957, this was all in the future as Sir Edward and Lord Walker launched a new kind of assurance policy, one in which the benefits payable would be explicitly linked to the value of the shares in which the trust would invest. In the words of financial journalist Charles Raw, writing in 1977, 'equity-linked policies often became just a thinly disguised method of securing tax relief on what was no more than direct stock market investment'.

By the 1980s, it had become that – and much more besides. Life-linked packaged products provided far more than a convenient tax shelter for investment; they provided the basis for pretty much the whole long-term savings industry. They also formed the basis of the boom in 'endowment mortgages', effectively a mortgage containing the savings plan by which it would be paid off at the end of the term. In contrast to the standard repayment mortgage – a straightforward loan – endowment mortgages channelled the borrower's monthly payments not into reducing the capital debt but into the endowment plan.

Time was not called on life-assurance premium tax relief until the 1984 Budget. By then, there was an army of upwards of 100,000 salesmen and women all pushing assurance and endowment products. Unemployment was not an option, so they continued pushing them anyway, confident that the next tax break would soon arrive.

It did.

Personal Equity Plans (PEPs) made their debut in the 1986 Budget, with the explicit aim of encouraging share investment. The Treasury had spoken; the packaged-products industry did the rest.

But as PEPs for everyone, including PEP-based mortgages, rolled off the assembly line, far more radical changes were afoot. Prior to 1986, the only way the institutions could pitch mortgages to members of the public was if the member concerned were in no other scheme, either a company scheme or the State Earnings Related Pension Scheme (SERPS). So strict were the rules that even the sharpest practitioner would not even speak to a client about pensions if that client were already 'spoken for'.

In 1986, the Government unveiled a package called, over-optimistically, 'New Beveridge', in order to conjure up warm memories of the father of the welfare state Sir William Beveridge. It had two central aims. One was effectively to begin the winding-down of SERPS, by giving SERPS members big incentives to leave and set up their own private pension, courtesy of the financial services industry. The second was to liberalise the private-pension market in total, giving those in company or public-sector employer schemes the right to 'opt out'.

Depending on whom you believe, this second aim was driven either by the noble desire to make the workforce more mobile and flexible and to increase personal choice, or it followed years of lobbying by the packaged-products institutions who had long been dying to get their hands on the private-pension pot of gold.

Pensions had long carried their own tax breaks quite different from those attaching to life assurance or PEPs. But, once again, the industry responded in full measure to 'New Beveridge'. That sales army went to work, pushing 'portable pensions' for all they were worth. In parallel, PEPs funnelled billions into the equity market, helping the public soak up a raft of huge privatisation issues: British Telecom, British Airways, British Gas, the water services and the electrical power industry.

Meanwhile, endowment mortgages, shorn of their tax breaks but still, as we shall discover, apparently enormously popular, helped millions of people to buy their own homes.

Truly, as the 1980s drew to an end, Sir Edward's dream was coming to fruition, and the public at large was being given what fellow Conservative Lord Cecil Parkinson had described as 'a stake in the system'.

What could possibly go wrong?

Don't mention the M-word: institutions in the dock

The first 'mis-selling' scandal to hit the retail financial industry had nothing whatever to do with pensions and erupted at the turn of the decade in the field of second mortgages. A number of financial advisers had taken big commissions from clients in return for a hybrid product called the 'home-income bond'. This sounded suitably respectable but in fact involved the following: the client would take out a second mortgage on his house, the proceeds of which would then be invested on the stock market. So successful would be the financial adviser's speculations that not only would the new mortgage (and the adviser's fees) be comfortably paid off, but there would be a tidy capital gain for the client.

As house prices crashed in late-1990, home-income clients found themselves stuck in unsellable homes and saddled with an enormous new secured loan. As for the proceeds of all that stock market investment – they were much as one would expect.

While the regulators grappled with home-income bonds, a number of scandals involving financial advisers, both tied and independent, disclosed an aggressive sales culture in which anyone could be sold anything as long as it generated commission for the salesman. This was in flagrant breach of the rules, which required all financial advisers to offer 'best advice' to clients.

As a furious debate about 'best advice' convulsed the assurance / PEPs sector, the hard selling of portable pensions continued unabated. The first official fears that 'New Beveridge' was being promoted in outright defiance of 'best advice' first surfaced inside the Department of Social Security in 1993. Few in Whitehall wanted to know, preferring instead the counter-argument that pensions were 'different', that the clients would know what they were doing and that anyway the whole thing was government-backed, and so quite all right and above board.

Within a year, 'pensions mis-selling' was shaping up to be one of the great scandals of the century. Millions of people had been tempted out of good company schemes into inferior private schemes, courtesy of the packaged products industry. Of course, for most of the time, the same institutions offering the packaged products had also been managing the company schemes out of which the clients had been coaxed. Very few companies manage their own schemes. Banks, investment banks and insurance companies handle 80 per cent of all retail investment funds, with independent institutions, including the Co-op, about 17 per cent.

It was entirely possible that the same institution that managed the company scheme was now advising the pension-fund member to withdraw from that scheme and set up a personal pension with the institution. It was a classic case of 'churning' investment to generate commission, and it was carried out on a huge scale.

Ultimately, the institutions accepted that breaches of the best advice rule had been endemic. Most egregious of all were cases where public-sector employees, entitled to generous index-linked pensions, were 'advised' to give these up in return for much less valuable personal pensions.

By the end of the 1990s, the institutions were facing a total bill for compensating the victims of mis-selling of at least £9 billion. In the wreckage of 'New Beveridge' were to be found the fragments of the institutions' once-solid reputation for integrity, mixed with the sort of dullness one would hope for in providers of long-term investment plans.

But by the end of the 1990s, even the mis-selling scandal looked likely to be dwarfed by a crisis of unimaginable proportions.

The funds were running out of money.

Needle on red: the growing money gap

By midsummer 2001, a black cloud was blotting out the summer skies. It had been growing for at least two years but was now of such a size that it could no longer be ignored. The institutions had placed two very large bets. They had done so using our money. And they had lost, both times.

The first bet was on what is called 'longevity', a polite way of assessing the length of a person's life. The second was on inflation. By losing the first, they were facing much greater liabilities than they had accounted for; their clients were living longer than predicted, thus drawing pensions for longer than expected. By losing the second, they were facing these increasing liabilities with diminished resources. The ebb tide of inflation during the 1990s took the old high investment returns with them. The low inflation era was a low return era.

As we have seen, the institutions provide packaged investment products, so a climate of lower returns would clearly affect the value of all packaged products. This mattered less with shorter-term products, such as the individual savings accounts (ISAs) that replaced PEPs after Labour's 1997 election victory. If the general price level is down, the investor may fret less about a lower overall return when he or she cashes in the plan. Far more serious is the position on longer-term plans that have been specifically set up to pay for something else. Of these, the two most important by far are mortgage endowment plans and pension schemes.

There is, and never was, an explicit guarantee that an endowment plan will, on maturity, be sufficient to pay off the mortgage. But in the 1970s and 1980s there was no need for one. Stock market gains mostly outpaced inflation with ease. Often there was a surplus on the endowment.

In the pensions business, the position was slightly different in that many pensions *did* guarantee a proportion of the pensioner's final salary on retirement. But the fundamental problems were exactly the same. Returns on investments were sliding, and nobody seemed to have very much idea what to do about it.

Either of the two bodyblows – longevity and falling returns – may have been manageable on their own. But coming together, they threaten disaster.

How did it happen?

The longevity problem is simple. Between 1950 and 2000, life expectancy rose by nine years, to 75 for men and nearly 80 for women. Actuaries are employed to ensure the books of any company offering long-term investments will balance; in other words that it has priced its premiums now in a way that will allow it to meet its likely future payments. They perform the same service for general insurance companies, although obviously the time-scales are much shorter.

Actuaries are described as a sort of very superior accountant, but their role is really no different from that of whoever is employed by a bookie to ensure that all his odds are 'rounded out'. For years, the actuarial tables seem to have failed to pick up the ever-increasing life expectancy of the ordinary person. This is not a very impressive performance from the actuarial profession and one cannot but help thinking that a bookie may have done a better job.

At least the concept of the funds being depleted by people living longer and thus costing more is relatively straightforward. More difficult to grasp is the notion that low inflation is *bad* for savings. Surely low inflation is good for savings?

The salient point here is that we are not talking about savings (which do tend to be eroded by high inflation) but about *investment*. And it was a peculiarity of the high-inflation years of the 1970s and early 1980s that inflation was good for share prices and other paper assets. Not 'good' merely in the sense that the value of those assets kept pace with inflation, but that they usually outperformed the inflation rate. Inflation has the effect of silently redistributing wealth from some people and giving it to others. Holders of equities, bullion, fine wines, even vintage sports cars, have tended to benefit as these assets are seen as a hedge against a depreciating paper currency.

Now imagine a senior fund manager today. He will have

started his career in the mid-1970s. Inflation in Britain in 2000 was about two per cent. So it was in 1975 – two per cent *a month,* that is. For 1975 as a whole it touched 25 per cent. In 1981, with unemployment hurtling towards three million, it was still 12 per cent. As recently as 1990, it stood at 11 per cent. Our fund manager has very little experience of managing money in a low inflation environment, where gains can be painfully slow to appear and the effortless rises associated with steadily increasing prices all round are nowhere in sight.

As the crisis struck, it was the non-guaranteed packaged products that first caused alarm. On 26 August 1999, the FSA warned homeowners their endowment plans may not cover their mortgages. Falling rates of inflation and falling interest rates 'could mean that some endowment policies, particularly some "low cost" or "low start" endowments, might no longer be on track to pay out a big enough sum at the end to repay the mortgage in full'.

Exacerbating the problem was the fact that 30 per cent of all mortgages sold were still endowments, fifteen years after the tax advantages had been removed. Critics suggested the generous commission on such mortgages, when compared to traditional homeloans, was the incentive for what amounted to another mis-selling scandal.

Meanwhile, those holding endowment mortgages likely to fail to pay off the homeloan had two choices. They could immediately increase their monthly payments to top up their fund, or they could hope that, on selling the property, they would release enough additional capital value to make up the shortfall.

On pensions, the scale of the potential catastrophe took longer to emerge, largely because of tortuous legal action involving the world's oldest assurer, Equitable Life. The company had miscalculated so badly that it was unable to pay out the returns expected by holders of policies containing a guarantee of future income. Equitable suggested the guarantees be waived in order that all policyholders might share the pain. The holders of guaranteed policies disagreed, and won in court.

In November 2000, the Equitable closed its doors to new business, and by summer 2001 it was teetering on the edge of insolvency as policyholders braved stiff penalty clauses and pulled their money out, convinced that things could only get worse. In all, 900,000 families were affected.

Meanwhile, the pensions managers as a group were coming clean on the scale of the disaster. In August 2001, it was announced that out of Britain's top hundred companies, seventeen were running deficits on their pension schemes. These were final-salary schemes, the sort that guarantee a level of income in retirement.

Worse was to follow. On 16 August 2001, pension consultant William M Mercer warned that millions of workers in so-called 'money purchase' schemes needed to start paying higher contributions immediately – double the current level, in some cases – if they were not to see the value of their pensions halve. Mercer also noted a huge shift by companies towards money purchase schemes, as against final-salary pensions. Both ICI and British Telecom had moved in this direction. Money purchase schemes do not commit the employer to any level of payment to pensioners, and are cheaper to run.

Ironically, some of the biggest financial institutions were putting their own staffs on money purchase schemes: Barclays, Lloyds TSB and Legal & General led the way. Given that these same institutions are responsible for a huge chunk of the pensions industry, it was hardly a vote of confidence.

Yet despite these assorted disasters, the institutions survive and thrive. That £2,265 billion under management is for UK clients only. There is another £592 billion under management for foreign clients, making a grand total of £2,857 billion.

More striking still is the fact that the 'scandal years' of the 1990s saw the amount managed by the average fund manager more than double, to £409 million. And perhaps most startling of all is that the UK fund management industry is expecting to emerge as the European centre of private-pension expertise as continental EU countries shift from generous state-funded pensions to private provision. Ironically, this shift is being driven by the same increase in life expectancy that has holed the private-sector British funds below the waterline.

Meanwhile, packaged products continue to flourish in a magic garden of new tax breaks, reflecting the preoccupations of the Labour government. ISAs and the stakeholder pension dominate the scene at the moment, but are unlikely to be the last attempts to stimulate whatever type of investment is currently thought desirable.

A bigger issue is whether the packaged product market now or ever has involved a proper sharing of risk between the institutions and the investing millions. In the last chapter, we saw how the banks and insurance companies are running very large risks and are forever seeking ways to lay off some of that risk on to their customers. With their 'life office' or 'institution' hats on, they take fund management fees for creating investment products that have an unfortunate tendency to blow up in their customers' faces, whether mis-sold private pensions, mis-managed company pensions or mortgage endowments that will not perform the single task for which they were contracted – to pay off a mortgage.

Until this central issue of risk-sharing is resolved, the institutions' claim to a significant social role in both Britain and Europe will be open to severe doubt.

9

Unreal City
The looking-glass world of derivatives

Suddenly Bond felt the sweat on his palms. Like snow in sunshine his capital had melted. With the covetous deliberations of the winning gambler, Le Chiffre was tapping a light tattoo on the table with his right hand. Bond looked across into the eyes of murky basalt. They held an ironical question. 'Do you want the full treatment?'

Ian Fleming, *Casino Royale*
(Jonathan Cape, 1953)

A zero for a heart: futures and options

Of all the glib catchphrases you are likely to encounter in the Square Mile and its satellite districts, perhaps the most irritating is the chirpy cry of 'two views make a market'. It fills the air whenever a group of off-duty dealers argue about football, or a television programme – or anything. It is irritating because it is not true. Provided a price mechanism is to hand, then one view can 'make a market' all by itself.

Look at it this way. There are two available seats on a London bus, one downstairs and one on the top deck. I am upstairs but prefer to sit downstairs, whereas you are downstairs but wish to enjoy the view from upstairs. We swap. But that isn't a market, that's primitive barter. Had we both wanted the upstairs seat, it would have been a case of first come, first served. Either that, or a fight. But prices allow both of us to want the seat upstairs and, crucially, to work out how much we want it. If it is worth 75p to me and £1 to you, then so be it. I'll take the seat downstairs.

Translate this simple principle to the world of betting odds. Odds are prices, nothing more, nothing less. In the 'two views' scenario, you don't need odds. I think it will rain tomorrow. You are equally certain that it will not. The bet is £1. By tomorrow night, one of us will be £1 down and the other £1 richer. But suppose we both think it will rain tomorrow. With whom do we bet? One answer is to prowl the highways and byways until we find someone who thinks it will not rain tomorrow. Suppose we find this person. We then have to ascertain that his certainty that it will not rain tomorrow is roughly equal to our certainty that it will. Then we have to ensure that he has no objections in principle to gambling – a Wesleyan lay preacher would be little use, no matter how strong his conviction that tomorrow will be dry and sunny.

Finally, having made arrangements to settle up with the chap one way or another tomorrow night, we may just about get to place a bet. The beauty of odds – the beauty, that is, of prices – is that we don't need to do any of this. I would refuse an 'even' bet on tomorrow being dry, because my best guess is that it will not be. But were you to offer me three-to-one – a yard, in gambling parlance – perhaps we could do business. That is because the additional reward I will gain if it doesn't rain tomorrow, set against the smaller loss that I will suffer if it does rain, may compensate for my belief that I will probably lose.

With odds, you don't need someone on the other side of the argument in order to have someone on the other side of the deal. That's the glory of prices: one view can make a market.

By this point you may be wondering why a chapter on derivatives has opened with this simple fare. Surely derivatives are he-man stuff? Cut the baby talk! If so, be patient. All the above is for the benefit of all those convinced they will never understand derivatives; all those who never worked out – no matter how many newspaper articles they read at the time and after – exactly how Nick Leeson's rogue trading shut down Barings Bank in February 1995. Actually, had they been relying on newspaper reports, then their bafflement is understandable; at least half of all financial journalists couldn't get their heads round the Barings debacle either. They tried. But, in the end, it was a lot easier simply to concoct vague references to 'Leeson's wild gambles on Far Eastern markets'.

In fact, derivatives are simple. That doesn't mean derivative products, traded in London and elsewhere, are simple. Far from it. There are derivatives out there so complicated that even the people who put them together don't understand them. The investors to whom they were sold certainly don't. The directors of the banks under whose aegis these derivatives were assembled quite definitely don't. But derivatives themselves are essentially very simple.

We have just looked at prices. Derivatives are prices of prices. They 'derive' from a security or a commodity and represent a bet on future movements of the price of that security or commodity. At bottom, there are only two types of derivatives; two ways of making this bet. There are options and there are futures. Sometimes futures are known as 'forwards' – this description tends to be used about bets that are intended to result in actual delivery of the security or commodity – while 'futures' is used more often to refer to bets made by people with no intention of taking delivery. We shall stick with futures, for the sake of simplicity.

An option is just what it says: the right to buy or sell a financial asset at a given point in the future. A 'call' option is an option to buy; a 'put' option is an option to sell. A futures contract is the obligation to buy or sell a financial asset at a given point in the future.

That's it. That's all there is to it. There are no other types of derivatives. (There are swaps, of course, and we will look at them later, but a swap isn't a derivative.)

Of course, derivatives can be combined and recombined in a kaleidoscopic array to make up the mind-numbingly complex derivatives products that are traded each day. But, ultimately, derivatives come in just two varieties: an option (the *right* to buy or sell), and the futures contract (the *obligation* to buy and sell).

So, studying your lunchtime menu in the local bistro, you notice that entrecote steak is worth £8. Seized with the conviction that entrecote steak will hit £25 in 2010, you buy an option or a future specifying delivery of a piece of steak at £8 on 1 January 2010. If you are right, you will be sitting pretty. Steak bought at £8 will have more than trebled in value. Well done! But were Britain to have been swept by a new beef scare, with the result that steak prices are in free-fall, then you have a problem. If it was an option that you bought, then you can simply let the option expire. If it was a futures contract, then you are staring potentially enormous losses in the face.

So why does anyone ever buy futures? Why not stick to options?

The simple reason is that futures, being riskier, are cheaper. An option comes complete with an 'option premium', effectively the price you pay for knowing that your losses are limited to the money you paid for the contract, premium and all. A futures contract carries no premium, but it is a binding obligation. As one futures broker explained: 'If the price crashes, you can just let your option die. The worst that can happen is that you lose all the money you put down. With futures, you can lose more than all your money'.

Why bother?

Over the years, the conventional explanation for futures and options runs as follows. Out in the fields, a cattle farmer (to stick with our steak analogy) is rearing his beef cattle. He knows (as you do) that steak is currently trading at £8. That price suits him very well – as long as it holds, his herd is economic. But he knows also that the price could fall in the three months between now and selling his cattle at market. Now, suppose he can find someone prepared now to commit themselves to buying all his herd on the basis of £8 per piece of steak, with delivery in three months' time?

On the other side of the country, the company that owns your neighbourhood bistro also has steak prices on its collective mind. Like the farmer, the bistro chain is quite happy with steak at £8. Unlike the farmer, the bistro chain is worried that steak prices will rise over the next three months, rather than fall. A futures contract allows both parties to insulate themselves from the vagaries of the steak market and strike a deal now at a price both can live with.

Now, it is unlikely the farmer and the bistro chain are known to one another. Some sort of market place is needed to connect them. Such a market will clearly attract speculators. But that needn't matter. On the contrary – speculators are the farmer's friend, and the bistro owner's friend as well. How come?

Let's suppose the bistro owner gets cold feet about steak prices on the Monday, while the farmer doesn't feel queasy about steak prices until the Thursday. The bistro owner contacts the futures and options exchange in search of a futures contract for steak at £8 with three-month delivery. Without speculators, the bistro owner would have to camp at the exchange for four days awaiting the farmer's arrival. But he doesn't. A speculator issues a contact for three-month steak at £8 off his own bat – and at his own risk. He doesn't know the farmer is due on Thursday. Nor does he know what will happen to the steak price by the time he can find a farmer to trade with. So he charges the bistro owner a hefty consideration for shouldering the risk. But the bistro owner doesn't care. He doesn't ever need to meet the farmer, or know that he exists. He goes home happy with a three-month steak contract at £8. How the speculator fills the order is not his problem.

So the speculator has oiled the wheels, providing the link

between the farmer and the bistro owner. More than that, he has given both parties a commodity even more valuable than steak – certainty. In the jargon, he has allowed both to 'hedge'. Both can now go about their business without a glance at the steak price, because their own steak commitments have been locked in at £8. The risk of a sudden price movement has been lifted from their shoulders. Oh happy day!

At least, that's the conventional version. For some reason, these narratives always seem to involve homely agricultural products: wheat, cocoa, pork bellies and so forth. And they always – but always – feature hard-grafting farmers, their brows furrowed with anxiety about the outlook for prices, until the joyous moment when they learn about derivatives and all their worries just fade away. Let's suppose for a moment that this standard justification for the derivatives market holds water. US commentator Doug Henwood is unimpressed. In *Wall Street* (Verso, 1997) he draws on research by economist David Newberry and others to take pot shots at the supposed wonders of hedging:

> It's possible that hedging leaves society as a whole worse off that it would be if unhedged ... Newberry offered this example. Compare two arrangements for growing rice, one safe, the other higher-yielding and more profitable but riskier ... Without futures markets, farmers would be less likely to grow the risky rice than they would be if they could sell a portion of the crop forward to speculators. In the second world, supplies would be more volatile than in the first [so] ... in this case, hedging promotes instability.
>
> But even if markets did neutralise price exposure, prices are only part of the story. 'If prices are stabilised,' wrote Newberry, 'but quantities remain unstable, incomes may be less stable than if prices were free to move in response to the quantity changes'.

But aside from all that, there is one more little problem with the official line. It isn't true.

Something like 98 per cent of all futures contracts and a similar percentage of options contracts are entirely speculative. They are not meant to run to delivery. Out in the market are enough equal and opposite 'bets' to cancel each other out. Very, very few of those contracts were even issued by people or institutions intending actually to buy steak at £8 (or whatever), let alone bought by people or institutions who expected to do so. Most of the time, the speculators are not the middlemen in the market – they are the market.

There are, however, two classes of speculators – insiders and outsiders. The professional traders working for the big banks and broking houses, along with smaller operators, form one group – a group that, overall, makes money out of derivatives. Then there are the outsiders, the amateurs, those described by our futures-broking friend thus: 'They are high net worth individuals. That's a euphemism for millionaires, and I don't mean they've got a string of pubs, or something. I mean maybe $1 million to play with'. This group does not make money. 'Ninety per cent of them lose on commodity markets'.

Our broker specialises in handling the affairs of such people from his office in Mayfair. Despite the near-certainty of loss, there is no shortage of clients. He advises such clients, then executes their speculations through a big commodity-broking house in the City. 'I don't tend to contradict clients if they really want to do something. If they think oil is going up and you talk them out of it, then it does go up, then you're the Charlie. I will try to devise, say, three different strategies to allow the client to do what he wants to do. If it goes wrong, I may point out that I did have reservations'.

Sometimes it goes very wrong. 'When a client can't pay what's owed on his account, that is a nightmare situation. Under the rules, we have to make good his losses. When you're talking to him it is basically a scuttle operation – you sweet-talk him because that guy has got to pay up'.

Partly to safeguard against such a crisis, a private-client futures broker such as this is keen on 'asset gathering', the process whereby a client, with perhaps $4.75 million invested in safe securities and

$250,000 'in play' in derivatives gambling will be persuaded to turn over the whole $5 million to the brokerage. The $4.75 million can be allowed to mature quietly, but should the client try to default on derivatives speculations that have turned sour, then it can be seized.

Even without the long odds against making a profit, the private derivatives speculator has to contend also with the possibility that his trades will have been misrecorded. Our man begins his working day reconciling the print-out of the previous day's trades from the City broking house with the deals he recorded as carrying out for his clients. 'They never match. Out of fifty trades a day, maybe forty-five will be correct. Of the five mistakes, four are just typing or a mishearing over the telephone. But once in a while, you get a capital-E error. You said buy and the client wanted to sell, that sort of thing. That could cost $100,000'.

It is a far cry from the world of the insiders, the derivatives professionals. These break down into four broad categories. There are those working for big banking and other financial institutions; those working for industrial or energy groups who trade derivatives full time as part of the parent company's price-hedging strategy; the 'locals' – effectively self-employed traders – and, finally, there are hedge funds. Each of the four categories differs overall in its approach to derivatives, yet the last group, the hedge funds, is quite distinct from the others.

As I discussed in the section covering bonds in chapter three, the phrase 'hedge fund' is entirely misleading. Derivatives can and are used to 'hedge' risk, in a more sophisticated manner than our beef-cattle farmer. Amid the paper blizzard mentioned earlier – the thousands and thousands of contracts that are never intended to run to delivery – genuine commercial and industrial concerns are able to shield themselves against adverse price movements. This is 'hedging'.

But hedge funds do not hedge. On the contrary, they use derivatives as their favoured investment vehicle – full stop. They are not using derivatives to protect some other, mainstream, activity. Derivatives *are* their mainstream activity.

As we saw earlier, 98 per cent of futures and options contracts are 'speculative', in the sense that delivery of the underlying asset never takes place. And perhaps a further 98 per cent of that 98 per cent were never generated with any aim in mind other than speculation. The remaining 3.96 per cent, however, represents either actual contracts for delivery (the minority) and genuine hedging activity.

Many businesses hedge, especially those operating in international markets. Essentially, hedging is an insurance policy. It can apply to any security or commodity for which a derivatives contract exists. Put simply, you have £100 now that you want to exchange in three months' time for US dollars, at the current exchange rate of $1.50 / £1. But the rate may move against you, making your pounds worth less. So you enter a derivatives contract now taking an equal and opposite position to your cash position. You contract to buy the dollars in three months' time at $1.50 / £1. Then you sit back and ignore the currency-market reports for three months, because, whatever happens, you will be taking delivery of $150.

If the exchange rate falls, losses on your 'real' £100 will be cancelled out by gains on the derivatives contract. If the exchange rate rises, gains on your £100 cash will be cancelled out by losses on your derivatives contract. Either way, you will not lose. Nor will you gain, of course. Effectively, the cost of the derivative is the price you are prepared to pay to freeze today's exchange rate for three months.

Hedging, on a very much larger scale, is practised by the whole range of financial, commercial and industrial concerns. A tyre manufacturer will hedge the price of rubber, a food manufacturer will hedge the price of wheat and a power generator would be positively foolhardy not to hedge the price of oil. Those selling or buying goods and services across national frontiers hedge the exchange rate (as in our modest £100 example). Indeed, hedging money itself is probably the largest single hedging activity, from mortgage lenders hedging the risk on their fixed-rate homeloans to large multinationals hedging their earnings around the world.

Indeed, the fixed-rate mortgage is probably the closest most people ever come to 'hedging'. No loss should interest rates rise – and no gain should they fall.

Hedge funds do not hedge against risk. Hedge funds go looking for risk, and buy it up. US author and journalist Roger Lowenstein notes: 'Hedge funds are the equivalent of private clubs on Pall Mall or exclusive Oxbridge colleges; you have to be invited to join. And you have to be extremely rich.' The funds are essentially investment pools for the very wealthy, run by a person or persons with a reputation as a financial genius. George Soros and his Quantum Fund was probably the best-known example, although Quantum – restructured since its days in the limelight – was cautious and conservative in comparison with some of the newer hedge funds.

One such fund was called Long Term Capital Management. There is a scene in a Dashiell Hammett novel in which a private detective finds himself in a sleazy bar. Spotting a sign behind the counter that reads 'Only genuine pre-war Scotch and Canadian whiskies sold here', he passes the time trying to count the number of lies contained in that sentence. With LTCM, you can get to five if you put a hyphen between the 'long' and the 'term'. LTCM was staffed by people who believed that, with the use of complicated mathematical formulae, they had cracked the secret of perpetual profitability on financial markets. This worked well. It worked very well. Right up until the moment that it didn't.

What the formulae had unaccountably failed to predict was the 'Black August' of 1998, when Russia defaulted on its external debt, plunging world markets into turmoil. In September 1998 the New York Federal Reserve Bank learned LTCM was on the verge of collapse, owing nearly $100 billion to those who had backed its hunches. Worse, it had thousands of derivatives contracts outstanding with Wall Street banks, contracts with a face value of $1 trillion. That's right. One thousand, thousand million dollars.

Of course, LTCM was never likely to be asked for this colossal sum directly. It arose because of the special feature of derivatives trading known as gearing (in Britain) or leverage (in the US). Gearing is the ability to buy a derivative while paying only a small portion of the purchase price upfront. Effectively, it means gambling on credit, but that sounds risky and downmarket, while 'gearing' suggests precision financial engineering. This small down payment can vary from one per cent to ten per cent, plus the abovementioned premium for buying an option. Each day the speculator's position is checked by the broking house, and – should the derivatives have lost value – the speculator will need to put enough money down to restore the percentage paid to its original level. In this way it is possible to play in stocks, shares, commodities and currencies for a fraction of what it would cost to buy those assets 'for real' in the cash market. For a relatively small stake, a very large position can be built up, and very large profits made.

Very large losses, as well.

LTCM's behaviour is akin to that of a person who borrows, say, £200 from everyone he knows with the intention of betting the lot on the horses, assuring his creditors he will pay them back out of the winnings. Faced with the prospect of LTCM defaulting on Wall Street, the New York Fed arranged a bail-out, much to the amusement of those who had grown used over the years to Wall Street's strictures on the vital need for a competitive market economy to allow 'lame duck' companies to expire.

This is how hedge funds differ from the other professional players in derivatives markets. The other players speculate as part of their wider roles; the hedge funds are about speculation, and nothing else. Hedge funds are gargantuan, multi-billion dollar versions of our Mayfair man's roster of more modestly-wealthy individuals. But with two important differences. One – the hedge fund clients don't make investment decisions; they let the 'genius' or geniuses running the fund do that for them. Two – they really are in a different wealth league. A few dozen hedge fund clients can bankroll a fund capable of borrowing tens of billions of dollars.

This makes for two big differences in the behaviour of the hedge funds as against the amateur speculator. First, their performance as a rule tends to be better than that of the amateurs. The genius hedge-fund boss may be only a tenth as bright as he thinks he is, but his strike rate in terms of successful 'plays' is rather more impressive than the one in ten enjoyed by the amateurs. Second, even when the hedge fund's speculations turn sour, the vast pool of available cash can disguise the position – for a while, at least – creating a breathing space for the genius-boss to try to turn things around. LTCM was going off track for more than six months before the aghast New York Fed learned the full picture. Other hedge funds have been quietly wound up, with any losses kept confidential, doubtless to spare the blushes of both the 'genius' and his now not-so-rich backers. That sort of leeway is not available to the majority of amateur speculators.

However, even the most generous leeway cannot alter the fact that derivatives are a zero-sum game: for every winner there has to be a loser. This is in contrast to, for example, the stock market, where a rising tide of corporate profits, dividends and market confidence can lift all the players – a positive sum game, in the jargon. Derivatives can be, as we have seen, derived from shares traded on the stock market. They are, however, essentially bets on the performance of those shares, and every betting game requires an equal and opposite loser for every winner. Anyone considering investing in a hedge fund must therefore believe that the fund in question will, most of the time, make mostly correct bets and that the rest of the world will generously lay on an unlimited supply of losers. But remember – it didn't work for LTCM, and they had Nobel Prize-winning economists on board.

Hope, however, springs eternal. LTCM was founded by one John Meriweather. In December 1999, little more than a year after LTCM collapsed, he had raised a quarter of a billion dollars and was running a brand-new hedge fund, JWM Partners.

Given the iron rule of derivatives speculation – every winner needs a loser – it is hardly surprising that the big banks and brokerages have found profitable alternatives to straightforward speculation. The most obvious is to execute derivatives trades for someone else, collecting a fee in the process and shouldering no risk and no responsibility for the outcome of the speculation. The most sought-after clients are the big institutional fund managers, who increasingly use derivatives both to hedge their funds against sudden, adverse price movements and to move the fund quickly in and out of particular assets and markets without incurring the expense and disruption of selling and replacing some or all of the assets currently in the fund. Instead, they buy derivatives based on the assets they wish to flirt with, and leave their original fund unchanged.

You will have noticed that these two reasons for fund-management involvement in derivatives markets are mutually contradictory. The hedging argument suggests a fund manager uses derivatives to prevent price volatility from damaging the value of the fund. It is an essentially cautious stance that could be readily understood by those with their savings or other investments in the fund. But the second argument suggests a fund manager is entitled to gamble on derivatives while at the same time allowing the fund to display all the characteristics of prudence and conservatism. The original securities remain for all the world to see, safely in the fund, while the fund manager is speculating on derivatives, potentially putting the fund at risk. Anyone on the look-out for the next derivatives disaster or rogue-trading scandal could do worse than keep a weather eye on this practice, known by the euphemistic title of 'non-core asset allocation'. Non-core is right enough; whether the allocations prove to be assets or liabilities is open to question.

Not that the banks and brokerages care. A client is a client, and institutional clients are highly prized for the volume of their business and the reliability of their payments.

Another profitable alternative to speculation is market making. Here, the banks and brokerages take derivatives on to their own books and, in the manner of equity market making, they make a 'turn' on the difference between buying and selling prices.

Both trading for others and market making highlight the age-old principle that it is more profitable to run the casino than to play in it. No self-respecting gambling club makes bets itself; it contents itself with clipping the players.

Arbitrage, the third favoured activity of the big derivatives desks, may seem to violate this principle. It involves spotting price differences when an identical derivatives contract is traded on different exchanges; such differences routinely open up for brief periods, and the arbitrageur (or rather, his high-powered computer) can spot them pretty well instantly. The arbitrageur buys the cheaper contract and simultaneously sells the more expensive one, fulfilling the second trade with the contract bought cheaply in the first trade.

It sounds risky, but it ought not to be. This is precisely what Nick Leeson was supposed to be doing during his time at Barings's Singapore derivatives operation. Indeed it is what he was doing, until the last few fatal weeks.

In his early days out east, Leeson had followed a classic, low-risk arbitrage strategy. A futures contract linked to the share prices of Japan's top 225 companies was traded in both Singapore and Osaka. Whenever the prices on the two exchanges diverged, Leeson would buy the cheaper and sell the dearer, making an immediate (if modest) profit. This is classic derivatives arbitrage; not so much gambling as owning a decent computer and knowing how to use it.

Even at the end of 1994, by which time he was hiding losses run up on unauthorised activity, Leeson's depradations amounted to £208 million – a staggering sum, but probably not enough to sink Barings. In the New Year, however, Leeson entirely abandoned matching buy and sell orders and struck out alone, making straightforward bets on the likely performance of the Japanese stock market. Using the 'gearing' we examined earlier, Leeson was able to bet $7 billion that the market would rise. It fell. He then tried to recoup this disastrous position by betting that Japanese interest rates would rise. They didn't. Again, gearing allowed him to run up bets worth more than $21 billion.

These were futures contracts. Remember our friendly private-client broker's warning – that you can lose more than all your money? That was the position facing Leeson and, more to the point, facing his employer, Barings, when the disaster came to light at the end of February 1995. Leeson had bet nearly $30 billion. Of course, he hadn't actually put down more than a sliver of that amount. And, in the event, the losses were capped at closer to $1 billion once the various contracts were closed. But no-one knew that at the time, and the losses were potentially enormous should the Japanese stock market and interest rates have continued to move in the opposite direction to Leeson's wagers.

It was this factor that effectively killed Bank of England attempts to keep Barings afloat. No-one wanted to take on open and unquantifiable futures positions, especially not when they were 'underwater', to use the jargon. Indeed, Leeson's positions were so far underwater that only the late Jacques Cousteau would have been able to find them. But, as we have seen, whatever Leeson thought he was doing, it wasn't arbitrage.

Finally, the banks and brokerages do speculate in derivatives on their own account. Except that they don't call it speculation. Dear me, no. They call it 'position-taking', which has reassuring overtones of thoughtfulness and prudence. The trouble is, that when they stop running the casino and start playing at the tables, the banks seem no less likely to lose money than anybody else. In 1997, NatWest found an £80 million hole in its derivatives operation, and in early-1998 JP Morgan said its fourth-quarter earnings declined by 35 per cent to $271 million with losses 'particularly heavy' in Asian derivatives. Three years earlier, Chemical Bank announced a loss of $70 million because of trading in currency derivatives, and in November 1997 Chase Manhattan was found to have lost up to £125 million on emerging-market debt trades, many of them involving complex derivatives products. Chase's appetite for derivatives was apparently not sated, however; in the second quarter of 2000, the US regulator, the Office of the Comptroller of the Currency, said Chase held derivatives with a notional value of $13,900 billion. And in 1998, the giant Swiss bank UBS announced losses of £439 million on equity derivatives.

At this point, we had better take a look at swaps. They are not derivatives, whatever anyone tells you, but they are closely linked to the derivatives scene – intimately linked in the case of 'swaptions', of which more later.

A swap is, broadly speaking, an agreement between two parties to exchange cashflow, and the most common type of swap involves interest rates. The set-piece example of a swap is that of the building society that is taking in fixed interest payments from its borrowers but has to pay out variable interest payments to its savers. Of course, that is no problem at all should interest rates take a sudden dip, because the society will be harvesting the same amount of income from its mortgage holders and paying out less to its savers. But if rates go the other way, the society has a problem, especially in these days when mortgage rates are often fixed for several years. What the society needs to do is to have the same type of inflow and outflow, either all fixed or all floating. It could round up all its customers – savers and borrowers – and talk them into changing their mortgages and their savings account so that, for example, the savers lock in for five years at a fixed percentage or, conversely, the borrowers agree to give up their fixed mortgages and to let their payments be varied in line with interest rates.

There is an easier way.

The society goes to the swaps market, which is dominated by banks, and finds a friendly bank willing (for a price) to take on the society's floating rate obligations in return for receiving fixed rate payments from the society just as if the society were paying its savers a fixed rate.

Exactly the same principle applies in far more complex swap arrangements involving multinational corporations borrowing and earning in a number of different currencies. Worldwide, the swaps market is colossal: in 1997 the Bank for International Settlements calculated that $17,067 billion of new interest rate swaps was issued. In 1998, according to the Bank of England, daily turnover in the swaps market stood at about $70 billion.

Swaps may not be derivatives, but derivative products can and do involve a swap element. And a 'swaption' is an option conferring the right to enter an interest-rate swap at a future date at a price that has been fixed now. It is an option on a swap.

Closely related to swaps are 'forward rate agreements', or FRAs. These are a sort of giant-scale fixed-rate mortgage, except an

FRA can apply to either a deposit or a loan, with the holder of an FRA having bought the right to pay or receive a fixed rate of interest on a loan or deposit to be made at an agreed future date.

Of the three products we are examining in this chapter, swaps are distinct not only in that they are not derivatives, but in that they are traded only in the 'over-the-counter' market, not on an exchange. Futures and options can be traded either way, although, as we have seen, a future becomes a 'forward' when traded off an exchange.

The two market places are very different, as we shall now discover.

'Over the counter' is another masterly piece of City phrase-making, suggestive of an old-fashioned grocer's shops complete with brass scales and brown paper bags. Nothing could be further removed from the over-the-counter derivatives market in London. This is a professionals-only market dominated by banks, commodities houses and multinational companies, perhaps 250 organisations in all. It is also a bespoke market, in which the parties to a deal can draw up precisely the contract that they want, based on assets of their choice and with terms and conditions to suit themselves.

London dominates over-the-counter derivatives trading worldwide, with 36 per cent of the total market in 1998, according to the Bank for International Settlements, and daily turnover of $171 billion. Over-the-counter derivatives contracts cover oil, bullion, foreign currency, interest rates and equities, but it is interest-rate derivatives that take the lion's share of the action, accounting for 72 per cent of all bargains in 1998. Of those interest-rate contracts, 56 per cent were swaps, 35 per cent FRAs and the remainder interest-rate options. Foreign currency derivatives came second to interest-rate products, with 25 per cent, and commodity and equity derivatives a long way behind, with 3 per cent.

Banks and broking houses accounted for 73 per cent of transactions in 1998, with US banks leading the way. In terms of turnover, 47 per cent of the banks in the over-the-counter market were American in 1998, up from 37 per cent in 1995, followed by

23 per cent British (down from 28 per cent), 12 per cent Swiss (up from 9 per cent), and five per cent Japanese, down from 9 per cent.

Worldwide, the over-the-counter market dwarfs the exchange-based derivatives action, with outstanding over-the-counter contracts totalling $72,000 billion in 1998, about five times the total for the exchanges. Now, $72 trillion is a great deal of money, but remember these are 'notional' values achieved by adding up all the contracts, most of which are designed to cancel each other out. Despite the controversy surrounding derivatives in the late-1990s, the size of the over-the-counter market continued to balloon, with the notional value outstanding increasing worldwide by 52 per cent between 1995 and 1998. The exchanges didn't do too badly either; notional value outstanding there rose 32 per cent.

One of the biggest factors behind the explosion in over-the-counter derivatives trading in recent years is, according to International Financial Services London, 'world-wide volatility in asset prices', against which big players wished to hedge. This may be ironic, if the critics of derivatives – who claim that derivative trading is a prime cause of volatility – are correct.

No such doubts assail the over-the-counter market, however. Indeed, two new-ish derivatives, as yet barely on the radar compared to swaps, FRAs and foreign-currency derivatives, are being promoted on the basis of risk management. The first is the credit derivative, a complex instrument that allows credit risk to be split off from other risks facing a business and then traded. The second, similar, product is the insurance derivative, an attempt to make it possible to sell insurance risk to the big players in the over-the-counter market. This latter product, some claim, will even out the insurance cycle, proving of real benefit to the ordinary homeowner and motorist, currently at the mercy of see-sawing premiums. Let us hope this is the case. In the meantime it is hard not to imagine what fun Nick Leeson could have had with these newcomers to the derivatives scene.

No such exotica are (yet) traded on London's derivatives exchanges, the most important of which is LIFFE, the London International

Financial Futures and Options Exchange. Founded only in 1982, LIFFE has swallowed London's venerable markets in 'soft' (i.e. agricultural) commodities, and has seen off rivals in the options market. It has come a long way from its original role as a market place for trading the then-novel financial futures, and is currently the world's fifth-largest derivatives exchange. In the process, it has shed the floor traders with their distinctive coloured jackets (each signifying a different bank or brokerage) along with the shouting and gesticulating that accompanied their 'open outcry' face-to-face business methods. Today, LIFFE resounds mainly to the hum of computer screens and the click of a mouse. Eventually, all LIFFE derivatives are expected to be traded on screen, including the commodities, currently still bought and sold on the floor.

LIFFE's range of contracts includes short-term interest-rate derivatives; contracts on long-term British and European government securities; derivatives based on the stock markets of Britain, the US, Switzerland, France, Germany and Sweden; and contracts in base metals, oil, gas and agricultural products. Not surprisingly, it accounts for about 75 per cent of all the exchange-based derivatives business in London.

If LIFFE is the young thruster, the London Metal Exchange, founded in 1877, is the greybeard. But unlike LIFFE, the LME is not primarily a derivatives exchange in the modern sense of the word. It trades contracts in seven metals, but the majority of dealing is by industrial and commercial concerns involved in the metals industry seeking to hedge their risks; pure speculation is very much a minority activity. Similarly, the International Petroleum Exchange is much used by oil and gas companies seeking to hedge their price risks. Aluminium is the most traded metal on the LME, followed by copper, while the IPE patriotically flies the flag, trading contracts in Brent crude nearly three times as often as contracts in gas oil. We shall look more closely at all these exchanges in the next chapter; here we are concerned only with their role as market places for derivatives.

Finally, OM – the Swedish market operator – has based its options exchange in London, trading derivatives on Scandinavian company shares and pulp products.

On LIFFE, far and away the biggest slice of total contracts traded is formed by short-term interest rate derivatives – more than 65 per cent. Long-term government stock contracts take 24.3 per cent, with equity contracts at just over 7 per cent and commodities derivatives just over 2 per cent.

How much is it all worth? International Financial Services London has made some estimates. The exchanges have calculated that the value of fees and commissions on their contracts earned from overseas to be £1,350 million. According to IFSL, 'overseas earnings from the over-the-counter market are likely to be at least as large'.

So why does this solid citizen of the financial community, this respectable earner for UK PLC continue to attract controversy and even hostility? It cannot be simply the rogue-trading scandals – there have not been any of those for a while anyway. The most spectacular – the $2 billion lost for Japanese industrial giant Sumitomo by its copper trader Yasuo Hamanaka – was in 1995.

Perhaps part of the problem is the sheer unreality of the pyramid of futures, options, futures on options on swaps on options perched on one small asset, the feeling that this tottering construction is fundamentally unsound.

In *The Crash* (Mandarin, 1988), Mihir Bose put it this way:

> A share, itself a somewhat intangible object, had now acquired all sorts of other intangible barnacles: options, futures, options on futures. Each innovation took us further away from the original purpose of the stock market which was that companies could use it to raise money and investors could trade in company shares expressing their opinion about the company's future. Now the share was merely a device to build a superstructure of gambling.

Not just shares, either. As we saw above, the second biggest slice of business on LIFFE is accounted for by derivatives based on government securities. Doug Henwood, US commentator and author of *Wall Street*, in his critique of the argument that derivatives markets are really all about allowing producers to hedge their risk, points out: 'The sole producer of treasury bonds is the US government, but it has no presence in the futures markets in its paper; the big players are the major financial institutions who trade it. They use futures markets to speculate for their own profit'.

And sometimes for the loss of others. In 1997, former First Boston and Morgan Stanley derivatives trader Frank Partnoy published FIASCO (Profile Books), an exposé concentrating not on rogue traders but rogue salesmen, forcing dangerous, sometimes toxic, derivatives down the throats of ordinary investors who normally ought not to go within a million miles of them. In one passage, Partnoy asks an experienced derivatives salesmen who is actually buying First Boston's derivatives. Is it the hedge funds? '"No way. Are you kidding me?" It was a stupid question. The top hedge funds were much too sophisticated to buy this trade from First Boston. They could place such bets on their own'. Partnoy tries again. Other investment banks? No. Investment funds? No. Commercial banks? No. 'I was running out of choices.'

Finally, the salesman enlightens him: 'He said, "State pension funds and insurance companies". "What?" I was shocked. He just smiled.'

We began with a very simple exploration of the notion of prices, and of derivatives, which are merely prices of prices. We noted that there are in fact only two types of derivatives – options and futures. All very straightforward.

But we end in fearsome complexity. Because there are derivatives so complicated that they are almost impossible to value accurately, and they are sitting on the books of some of the most respected financial institutions in the world.

Let's hope their inventors knew what they were doing.

10

Planet Waves
The foreign exchanges and the commodity markets

The dollar is our currency but it's
your problem

**John Connally,
US Treasury Secretary, 1971**

The trillion-pound jackpot: the foreign currency market

Foreign exchange dealing in London takes place on a scale that beggars the imagination. About $640 billion is traded every working day. Of this huge volume, less than 7 per cent changes hands for the purposes of trade, including tourist exchanges, import-export financing and the purchase of foreign investments. The rest is 'hot money', what former Labour chancellor Denis Healey called 'an "atomic cloud" of footloose funds', roaming the world in search of the best return.

Now, speculation of this size may, you think, reflect the fact that there are, after all, more than 150 sovereign states on the face of the earth, most of which issue their own currencies. All these currencies float against each other, opening up opportunities for speculative betting. Thought of in those terms, the huge scale of the currency market might make sense.

But that is not how it operates. The foreign exchanges do not make up some colourful bazaar in which the Tanzanian shilling can be traded against the Indonesian rupiah. So-called 'cross-rates' – a direct exchange rate from one currency to another – are quoted only for major currencies and some of the monetary units used in the more favoured developing countries. The remainder needs to be exchanged twice – first into a major currency then out again into the currency required, e.g. Tanzanian shillings into sterling and sterling into Swedish kroner.

Indeed, the word 'foreign' is something of a misnomer in 'foreign exchanges', because the currency markets are really about one thing only: the dollar. Two-thirds of world trade is dollar-denominated, and 99 per cent of dollar trades are cleared on the island of Manhattan. Perched on top of this world trading currency is the vast system of speculation that is the foreign exchange market.

85 per cent of London's currency trades involve the dollar. Sterling popped up in just 18 per cent of transactions. Yet London has emerged as the world centre for currency trading. That $640 billion is nearly a third of the $1,900-odd billion total daily turnover in the foreign exchanges. The US takes less than 18 per cent, and Japan just 7.5 per cent.

Although currency interest-rate futures are traded on the London Financial Futures and Options Exchange (LIFFE), the main business of foreign currency trading is essentially bilateral, between two parties known to each other, usually conducted over the telephone. The market itself is unregulated, although the major banks, investment banks and other institutions who account for the bulk of the 'position-taking' (i.e. speculation) are regulated entities. The hedge funds that we met in the chapter on derivatives are not regulated, nor are they likely to be any time soon.

Traditionally, the foreign exchanges were dominated by 'spot' trading, in which traders bought currencies for immediate delivery. Much spot trading still goes on, but derivatives have taken over to a large extent. Without going over the same ground we covered in looking at derivatives, we should note that the two most common exchange-rate derivatives traded in London are forwards (the same as futures, but traded bilaterally, rather than on an exchange) and swaps, which differ from the interest-rate swaps we looked at in that they involve two transactions – one sale or purchase of a foreign currency now and an opposite sale or purchase of the same amount of foreign currency at an agreed date in the future. Swaps, too, are traded bilaterally.

Despite London's dominant role in the foreign currency market, it does not trade currency futures. All trade in these instruments (which are currency forwards traded on an exchange) is conducted mainly in Chicago and Sao Paulo, with smaller markets elsewhere. London is essentially a bilateral currency market, with trading between professionals.

Who are these professionals?

The banks and other institutions, as we have seen, are the big players in terms of effectively making a market in foreign exchange. They do so largely on their own account, although the public is increasingly offered investment funds based on currency dealings, just as they are being offered money-market funds. But while they tend to run ahead of the pack in terms of betting on currency movements, there is a pack of very big beasts just behind them: giant commercial operations, such as BP, Unilever, Rio Tinto and other world-scale businesses that require a constantly changing treasure chest of different currencies in order to oil the wheels of their international activities. They may well need to buy commodities whose price is expressed in another currency: oil and gold are priced in dollars; steel, traditionally, in German marks. While not averse to taking positions themselves, the big beasts tend to do so in order to protect their own assets and revenues, whereas, for a pure speculator, position-taking is a business in its own right.

Any business wishing to invest abroad will need to go to the currency markets, whether that investment be the building of a factory in the Amazon or, less adventurously, the purchase of Brazilian government securities or Brazilian company shares.

Judge and jury? The exchange rate

Currency trading, as with derivatives trading, is a zero-sum game. For every winner, there has to be a loser. I think the dollar is heading up and you are certain it is heading down. You sell me your dollars for pounds now. Only one of us can be right. Of course, my dollars could rise – and your pounds could rise as well. It is possible that we both gain by exactly the same amount. But someone, somewhere, holding another currency, will have had to have lost, possibly the person who sold me the pounds. Exchange rates are merely reference numbers. No two currencies can rise against each other at the same time. If sterling moves up to $2 from $1.50, do we have a weak dollar or a strong pound? Is the rise a response to cheerful investor sentiment about the outlook for the British economy, or has the pound stayed where it was and the dollar collapsed?

To a limited extent it is possible to get some answer from what is called the 'trade-weighted index', or the 'effective sterling exchange rate'. This plots the pound against not one currency but a basket of world currencies, using 100 as the value of sterling in 1990. At the time of writing, sterling is trading at about 104 per cent of its world-wide 1990 value; in mid-2000 it was trading at about 107 per cent.

So, were sterling to be showing weakly on the trade-weighted index but powering ahead against the dollar, it may be justifiable to say that dollar weakness, rather than sterling strength, is behind the impressive-looking sterling performance. Similarly, an all-round good showing on the trade-weighted index may, rightly, suggest that sterling is strengthening in its own right rather than as a result of the misfortunes of others. So assuming the pound is not merely coasting on the back of weakness in other currencies, what are the factors that are supporting its strength?

The first and most important factor is the state of the domestic economy. No country whose goods and services are not in demand will be able to escape exchange-rate weakness for very long. The reason is simple: a country with nothing to sell to the world will find no good reason why anybody should hold its currency. What would be the point, when there is nothing to buy with it?

These goods and services don't have to be physical products, shipped or trucked across a national border. They could take the form of tourists visiting Britain, foreign companies paying for merchant-banking advice in the City, or people overseas down-loading, for a fee, valuable intellectual property over the internet. But they have to exist in some form or another. If half of all Britain's workers were to go on strike for a week, sterling would be sharply marked down, because currency traders would know the demand for pounds was bound to be dented by the absence of so much production, some of which could be traded.

A strong economy, however, on its own – although a pre-condition for a robust, internationally-traded currency – is not sufficient to ensure speculative and other demand for the currency in question. There must also be a steady, predictable supply of that currency, which is another way of saying that inflation must not be allowed to get out of hand. Put simply, if the number of pounds available rises, without there being any corresponding increase in goods and services that those pounds can be spent on, then the price of those pounds will fall.

The exchange rate is essentially a price. And inflation works on the foreign currency markets in exactly the same way as it does in the high street. Should runaway inflation halve the value of the currency, then a £1 packet of fish fingers will cost £2, and $1.50, which used to cost £1, will now cost £2.

Put another way, the pound has been devalued against fish fingers, just as it has been devalued against the dollar.

Inflation leads on to a third key factor supporting (or not) the exchange rate: interest rates. A trader in a white van filling up on British delicacies for resale in Belgium will care little what the outlook for UK interest rates happens to be. He buys pounds simply to execute his trade, then he imports the British goods into Belgium. But any longer-term holder of sterling assets will take a keen interest in interest rate movements. Much foreign currency activity is using the exchanges as a corridor, rather than a destination, buying pounds in order to buy pound-denominated assets, such as British Government gilts. Investors will compute the relative attractions of such a British investment as against an identically sized investment in, say, Japan. To do so they will look at the inflation rate and the rate of interest being offered on the two investments. The rate of interest once the inflation rate has been docked off will give investors the 'real' return, which can then be compared with the rate of return available on the Japanese investment. But it can only be compared through the prism of exchange rates, so the final calculation for our investor is the comparative attraction of the two rates of return once exchange rates have been taken into account – the rate from her currency into pounds and the rate from her currency into yen.

This process is dynamic, not static. If British real interest rates are low, it is likely the currency will be weak, meaning our investor will get more pounds when he changes his own money. If the exchange rate is weak enough, he may get enough pounds to compensate for the low returns, and the British investment may be more attractive than the identical Japanese investment, despite higher real rates of return in Japan. But then, the moment our investor decides to go for Britain and changes his own currency for sterling, that may push up the sterling rate, meaning the *next* investor to make the same calculation will find Japan coming out on top.

Most of the time, a rise in central bank interest rates will strengthen a currency; other short-term rates will fall into line and rise, and overall that country will have immediately become a more attractive prospect for investors. In a sense, the foreign exchanges represent a 24-hour beauty contest, in which the different countries are marked for their attractiveness to investors in a never-ending parade before the judges. But as John Maynard Keynes famously noted when comparing the stock market to a beauty contest, the speculator's role is not to judge which investments he finds attractive, but which investments the rest of the market is likely to find attractive. This constant second-guessing of each other by the speculative players helps to give the foreign exchanges their very considerable volatility.

Sterling is a case in point. In 1987– 88, foreign exchange dealers pushed the pound to three German marks and above. In 1992, the pound could not hold at 2.95 marks. By March 1995, the era of the '10 bob mark' was at hand, with sterling sinking to almost the two-mark level. By 2000, sterling touched 3.43 marks. In the same way, sterling was too weak against the dollar in 1975–76, too strong in 1980–81, chronically weak in 1985, very strong again within a few years.

There is a phrase that states 'foreign exchange markets overshoot'. In other words, they over-react to economic news out of a particular country and either over-sell or over-buy that country's currency. Ultimately, they realise their mistake and promptly over-shoot in the other direction.

The chief tool for judging when a currency is over-sold or over-bought is called 'purchasing power parity'. Using a common basket of goods, and comparing their cost in different countries, it is possible to estimate whether a currency is overvalued or undervalued. First, one tots up the price of the basket in Britain (let us say £10) and in the United States ($15). That suggests the exchange rate ought to be $1.50 / £1. But suppose the foreign currency markets are trading sterling at $1.60. That would suggest a 6.25 per cent overvaluation of the pound.

The trouble with the 'overshoot' argument is that it suggests the currency markets are working to some sort of plan and have simply got their map reading a little awry. They are not working to a plan; their participants are simply trying to make profits. Their only interest in the over or undervaluation of any currency is the fact that it may give them advance warning of changes ahead, thus also giving them the edge over their fellow traders.

One lament you never hear from a currency trader in a City pub when the day's work is done is: 'I made a killing on the euro, but it's all wrong – the purchasing power parity was totally out of line!'

This is a point worth making because, time after time during the past quarter-century, the currency markets have been treated by commentators as some sort of impartial judge and jury on the success or otherwise of British economic policy. Their trading activities, in this version of events, represent 'signals' flashed by the outside world to central bankers and Treasury ministers, and, by using these 'signals', it is possible to steer the economy successfully.

Now it is true that, were the Bank of England to cut interest rates to one per cent and were the Treasury simultaneously to embark on a borrowing binge on the gilt market, the pound would indeed decline very rapidly. But then, one hardly needs the foreign exchanges to tell one that such a course of action is likely to end in tears. From the examples of over and undershooting we examined above, it is hard to place much faith in the currency markets as a wise overseer of economic policy.

The judge and jury theory has been out of fashion since 16 September 1992, when Britain was bounced out of the Exchange Rate Mechanism. According to the 'signals', Britain needed interest rates of upwards of 15 per cent to keep the economy in trim. Once out of the ERM, interest rates declined rapidly into single figures and the economy started to recover. There was no sign of the disaster of which the 'signals' had apparently been warning.

The liberators: White Wednesday and other foreign exchange myths

Still, say what you like about foreign exchange dealers, at least they freed Britain from the ERM. I mean, if it weren't for those young chaps in stripey shirts shouting 'sell sterling!' down the telephone, we would all probably still be paying 15 per cent interest rates and half of us would be living in cardboard city. Hats off to them. Right?

No, not really. This 'liberation' myth is a variation on the mistaken notion that the exchanges have some sort of agenda beyond making money. It is quite true that speculative activity on the foreign exchanges had the effect of pushing sterling out of the ERM – a thoroughly good thing as even the ERM's erstwhile fanatics now grudgingly concede. But it is never a good idea to thank someone for solving a problem he helped to create in the first place, and White Wednesday in September 1992 – also known as 'Black' Wednesday – is a textbook case in point.

From midsummer 1992, the foreign exchanges had been making it clear they wanted a rise in British interest rates as their price for staying in sterling. German interest rates were sky-high in order to hold down the inflation generated by the absorption of East Germany in 1990. Unfortunately, Britain had tied its currency to the German mark.

Foreign exchange dealers were squaring up to the television cameras throughout the late summer, talking of the 'need' for rates to rise above the already-high 11 per cent. As August turned into September, they started warning that one or even two percentage points 'may not be enough'.

On the day itself, interest rates were raised in two stages by four percentage points, to 15 per cent. Now it is quite true that when the second rise failed to give sterling any help, the game was up. But the foreign exchange markets did not keep hitting sterling because they felt sorry for the millions of British people who would lose their homes and their jobs at these levels of interest rates (although it is true that they would have done – even without a prolonged spell of 15 per cent rates after September 1992, the slump of the early-1990s saw one millions jobs lost, along with one million businesses, and 300,000 people lost their homes). The reason they kept hammering the pound was because they judged the government did not have the nerve to keep rates at that cripplingly high level for any prolonged period. Had they felt the rates would hold, there would have been no White Wednesday. Quite the opposite.

September 1992 gave rise to a second myth about the foreign exchanges, which is that 'private capital flows' are now so large that 'no government can stand in their way'. It is quite true that, short of reimposing exchange controls, there is little ministers or central bankers can do to stop people trading in the national currency. But, as we have seen, beneath the huge speculative waves is a bedrock of economic activity. Ultimately, the need to finance purchases and investments in the issuing country will ensure demand for the currency; it would be eccentric indeed were the foreign exchange dealers simply to sell one currency all the time, without regard for underlying demand.

In fact, governments and the foreign exchanges do different jobs. The government sets short-term interest rates. The exchanges react. Of course, they do not always react in the expected manner. But given the crucial role we saw interest rates playing in investment calculations, react they must.

A third myth states that today's vast, speculative foreign exchange market came into being after the 1945–71 Bretton Woods fixed currency system fell apart. That is true only in that the Bretton Woods system entailed heavy disincentives in each member country to be directed against currency speculators. But it is quite misleading to suggest that, politicians having fumbled the management of the currency system, the markets reluctantly stepped into the breach.

In fact, currency speculators and traders existed right through the 1945–71 period, but were tightly circumscribed (by an oddity of the Bretton Woods agreement, speculators based in Tangier and Macao were exempted) both by exchange control and by general official disapproval of their activities. Given the chance to break free, they did not need to be asked twice.

Furthermore, it could be said that they took charge of the currency system having issued a false prospectus. As Bretton Woods creaked and groaned under the pressures of inflation and the escalating costs of US involvement in Indochina, soothing voices urged politicians to go with the flow and let currencies float free. Were they allowed to do so, these voices said, they would actually behave in a much more stable way. Governments were wearing themselves out trying to keep the Bretton Woods system on the road. Better to let it go. Currencies in a free market will find their own level and stay there.

The outcome, however, has been very different, with huge volatility and instability on foreign exchanges, but the prospectus sounded good at the time. Here is one of its most articulate exponents, Enoch Powell, referring to turmoil in the dollar-gold market in April 1968:

> You probably know the story of the man who grabbed a rope while falling down a dark shaft and just managed to hang on to the end of it. Hour after hour he swung there, enduring agonies of fear and exhaustion, screaming for help. At last his fingers could maintain their hold no longer and he fell – three inches ... this week in London the open-market [gold] price was two or three dollars up – yes sir, just two or three dollars.

And on the subject of gold, it is time to turn our attention to a family of assets that were once intimately linked with currency and coinage – commodities.

Limit Down? Commodity markets in London

In little more than a quarter of a century, London's commodity markets have lost a great deal of their old charm and character. No more do fur traders wheel barrows of pelts within a stone's throw of St Paul's Cathedral; the tea auctions have come to an end. In the process, London's commodity markets have merged and consolidated. Firstly, the 'soft' (agricultural) commodities came together as the London Commodities Exchange. Now that exchange is itself part of the London Financial Futures and Options Exchange (LIFFE), which has also absorbed the potato trading that used to be based at the Baltic Exchange. Furthermore, commodities trading today – and for many decades past – overlaps considerably with the world of derivatives that we examined in the previous chapter. Repetition shall therefore be kept to a minimum.

In that spirit, we should begin with one market that involves no futures trading whatever – gold.

Twice a day, the five gold-fixing banks meet at the offices of NM Rothschild and fix the world gold price.

That does not mean that everyone from the miner on the Rand to the New York banker is under any obligation to observe that fixed price. Rather, it is a 'reference' price, the market's best guess at the balancing point of supply and demand.

The five fixing members – Rothschild itself, HSBC, Bank of Nova Scotia, Crédit Suisse First Boston and Deutsche Bank – will have spoken to people around the world before making their judgment. Once the 'fix' is made, it is flashed around the world; many contracts specify the fixed price on a certain day.

The price is expressed in dollars per Troy ounce. At the time of writing, it is $275.75.

No gold futures are traded in London – that is left to other financial centres such as New York. Rather, London is the world's main market for 'spot' trading for gold. Recent figures show nearly 25 million Troy ounces, worth $6.3 billion, were cleared in London every day. This is a bilateral market, with no central exchange; trading takes place over secure telephone lines.

At the heart of the market is the London Bullion Market Association, whose five gold-fixing members are joined by two other gold houses in offering clearing services – Morgan Guaranty Trust and UBS. Then there are 43 ordinary members, permitted to trade in the market. They range from Securicor and the Royal Mint to Lehman Brothers and Citibank.

The Bank of England keeps a fatherly eye on the bullion market and, in particular, its arrangements for storage and delivery. The 'London good delivery bar' – 999 parts fine per 1,000, in bullion-speak – is an international standard.

Excitement hit the market in the late 1960s, and again in January 1980, when roaring inflation, nuclear escalation in Europe and the Iranian hostage crisis propelled the price to $1,000 an ounce. Gold is a traditional safe haven in times of crisis, when paper money threatens to become worthless. It is a tribute to our relatively peaceful times that bullion as an investment has performed very poorly from the mid-1980s onwards, and central banks, including our own, have starting to sell their holdings.

Below the gold market is the market in silver. The spot silver market in London operates very like a smaller version of the gold market. Once a day, three silver banks – HSBC, Deutsche and Bank of Nova Scotia – fix the international silver price. About 119.9 million Troy ounces a day are cleared in the London bullion market, valued at $600 million.

Silver is also traded on the London Metal Exchange (LME), which offers futures and options in the metal as it does in seven others: aluminium, aluminium alloy, copper, lead, nickel, tin and zinc. The LME on Leadenhall Street is the place to be if you like your commodity exchanges to have proper trading floors – the LME's 'ring' is just the ticket, and remains the heart of the market, although electronic screen dealing has been introduced for out-of-hours trades.

It is the world centre for trading base metals other than iron and steel, and oversees a string of 350 warehouses round the world, in eleven different countries, to allow the LME to guarantee delivery on its contracts. In fact, as with most derivatives, the majority of LME contracts, or 'warrants', are cancelled out by other contracts long before they fall due for delivery. Nonetheless, it works on the assumption that every contract will run to delivery and is prepared to deliver itself should a member default.

As with the bullion market, the LME sets reference prices around the world.

LIFFE, by contrast, down at Cannon Bridge, is a rather less romantic outfit. As we saw, it took over potato futures and options from the Baltic Exchange, and trades also derivatives contracts in cocoa, coffee, sugar, wheat and barley. It has set a course to all-screen trading.

The International Petroleum Exchange (IPE) at St Katherine's Dock is right on the river, which has its hazards: on at least one occasion, the IPE was contacted by the captain of a foreign tanker announcing his intention of making a large delivery to the exchange. It has recently shed its mutual status, but a takeover offer from the New York Mercantile Exchange (NYMEX) came to nothing. It is the world's second largest energy exchange (after NYMEX) – daily trading volumes top $1 billion – and its most important contract is Brent crude oil, although both gas oil and natural gas are also traded. Currently trading is floor-based but the future of this has to be in some doubt, given the IPE's management believes ultimately all dealing will go on screen.

London's newest exchange is owned by the Swedish stock market operator OM London. It trades pulp products, but as its parent made a bid in 2000 for the whole of the London Stock Exchange, it may be thinking rather bigger than that in the longer-term.

London's oldest exchange, the Baltic, was founded in 1744. It is one of the world's leading shipbroking markets, with 700 broking companies in London employing 1,600 brokers. London takes half the world market in chartering tankers and up to 40 per cent of the market in chartering bulk dry-goods carriers. For those wishing to buy rather than rent, the Baltic is the world's leading sale and purchase market, with Baltic members buying or selling more than half the world's new and second-hand tonnage. A derivative allowing the shipping industry or its customers to hedge against future movements in freight rates, BIFFEX, is also traded, while many of the large shipbrokers trade over-the-counter freight 'forwards', a market that has grown from nothing in 1992 to £1 billion in 2001.

Strictly speaking, the Baltic is not a commodity exchange. Neither is the London Diamond Bourse at 100 Hatton Garden. Diamonds cannot be traded as commodities because no two are alike, thus tradeable 'contracts' could not be drawn up. There is no diamond equivalent of the 'London good delivery bar' for gold.

For anyone seeking the romance of the old City, however, the bourse is probably the closest they will ever get, with its booths and desks covered in stones, and its members murmuring the odd discreet word as they go about their business.

There is just one problem, however. Security is strict and you will almost certainly not be admitted.

CHAPTER **11**

Ménage à Trois? The professionals get together

Crossing the road to say hello to
you: six shillings
Crossing back across the road when
I realised it was not you: six shillings

**Apocryphal items on
solicitor's bill, 1930s**

Wider still and wider: mega-partnerships are born

Nowhere has the violent reshaping of the City been more evident in
the past twenty years than in the professions: law and accountancy.
It is not simply that the size of partnerships has ballooned, as firms
have merged with both domestic competitors and with opposite

numbers abroad. Once, it was thought quite daring were a solicitor's letterhead to mention an office in Paris, or Washington. Today, the writing paper of the largest firms reads like a gazeteer: Rio, Beijing, Moscow, Berlin, and all points east, west, north and south. Once they confined themselves, at the most, to a modest office block near St Paul's Cathedral. Today, the largest firms occupy vast skyscrapers that resemble air-conditioned versions of Aztec temples.

Once the firms were partnerships. Most still are, but the trend towards limited liability was inexorable in accountancy and was bound sooner or later to affect the legal firms. Now it has. Limited liability partnerships, if not companies, are firmly on the agenda.

Here be monsters. The top City firm is Clifford Chance. It has 932 solicitors on its books and a further 855 personnel elsewhere around the world. You don't go to these bods to do the conveyancing on your house. The next down is Linklaters (721 solicitors in London, 304 more people outside the country), then Allen & Overy (614 solicitors in London, 332 staff overseas), Freshfields (577 solicitors, 373 people abroad) and Lovell White Durrant (473 solicitors in London, 198 overseas employees). Nor does the figure for overseas employees tell the full story, as it includes only people who generate fee income for the firm concerned. Lower down, even the relatively modest SJ Berwin, with 198 solicitors in London, would swallow several dozen small provincial partnerships.

The average defendant on a drink drive charge does not encounter this sort of solicitor. The giant City practices have just one sort of client – giant corporations. They are expanding into fields once considered the province of the merchant banker, helping to put together huge corporate finance and project-finance packages and steering their clients through the minefields of tax, commercial law and international dispute resolution. Total fee income increased by more than half during the 1990s to hit nearly £9 billion by the decade's end. On some measures, the City contains 900 specialist barristers, earning a gross £61 million from overseas clients, and gross overseas earnings by City solicitors' firms is more than £790 million. Only New York rivals London as a legal centre, and New

York is primarily a domestic centre.

Helping all this along is the 'export' status of English law, increasingly specified in international contracts as the medium through which disputes will be resolved. Who better to handle English law than English lawyers?

Inside these mega-partnerships, specialisations can be almost sub-atomic. If you need the top person on patent law as it affects pictures sent over the internet in non-Commonwealth territories, and you can afford to pay, then you can be sure that person is waiting for you.

Similarly, the infusion of professional management into the largest firms has radically changed their ethos. How could it be otherwise, given how difficult it would be to get 500-odd partners around a table?

The same trend towards giantism is evident in accountancy. Indeed, the two professions are increasingly invading each other's territory, with the largest accountants offering legal services and the solicitors more than happy to offer the sort of taxation and capital-market advice that the accountants may once have considered their own preserve.

The biggest accounting practices in the City are headed by a behemoth called PriceWaterhouse Coopers, the constituent parts of which were considered quite large enough when they were Price Waterhouse and Coopers & Lybrand. PWC had fee income of £1.8 billion in 1998–99.

The next down is KPMG, the core of which was Peat Marwick, or just 'Peats'. In 1999–2000, KPMG generated fee income of £1.2 billion.

Third largest is Deloitte & Touche, itself a marriage of Deloitte, Haskins & Sells and Touche Ross – again, they were thought large in their day. Deloittes generated £0.8 billion in fees in 1999–2000.

Two more famous names make up the big five: Ernst & Young made £0.6 billion in the year to June 2000, and Arthur Andersen – now divorced from its management consultancy wing Andersen Consulting (renamed Accenture) – made £0.5 billion in fees in the year ending August 1999.

There is a sharp divide between the big five and the rest. The sixth largest accountant is Grant Thornton whose fee income in the year to June 2000 was just £164 million.

Auditing – the process of checking a company's accounts to ensure they give a 'true and fair' picture – has traditionally provided both the backbone of the profession and the peak to which all City accountants would aspire. Some types of accountants – management accountants and public-sector accountants – are not allowed to perform audit work. The engagement to audit a commercial giant was once the zenith of an accounting career.

Audit remains the largest fee generator, but is increasingly being squeezed from the sides and from below. Regional practices are competing hard, using the latest technology, to win audit work that would previously have gone to a sizeable London firm. The smaller London practices are doing the same. The profession fears computerisation is taking the human factor out of audit and turning it into a commodity product that can be bought off the shelf.

No wonder, then, that the big five are spreading their wings, not only into tax advice – which was always a sister-service to auditing and general accounting – but far more importantly into corporate finance, where they are clashing with the law firms and the investment banks. Taking leading roles in advising on flotations, cross-border takeovers, project finance and mergers is proving a lucrative moneyspinner for the accountants.

Along from corporate finance is the line of work that used to be called 'insolvency' but has been renamed 'business recovery' to give it a more upbeat feel. Huge liquidations such as that of Bank of Credit and Commerce International can put the firm's name (in this case Deloitte) on front pages around the world. And changing insolvency law needs highly specialised advisers to interpret it for their clients. Currently, insolvency accounts for less than 10 per cent of big five income, but this figure is growing steadily.

Fraud investigation is sexy, it can be tied in with insolvency services and it is increasingly in demand as computerisation and other developments have left big companies wide open to embezzlement, computer viruses and other threats.

But the fastest growing non-audit area is management consulting, currently accounting for nearly 25 per cent of big five income. Here the accountants have a clear lead on the solicitors, having been in the game in one way or another since the 1950s, although the solicitors are closing fast. Both are head to head with established management consultancy firms, such as McKinsey and AT Kearney. Both these American consultancies have lucrative operations in London, but rank respectively eighth and thirteenth in terms of revenue. The top five consultancies are all accounting-related in some way: Cap Gemini Ernst & Young, then PWC, then Accenture, Deloitte Consulting DTT and KPMG Consulting.

It is notable that, despite the fact that their divorce is only a few years old, Accenture may soon be looking over its shoulder at Arthur Andersen, its former spouse, whose own consulting business now ranks at number 12.

The growing dependence on consulting is alleged by some to have undesirable side-effects, in that firms may be tempted to 'low ball' their tender for audit work, seeing it as a loss leader for more profitable consulting work. This is turn threatens to produce first a poor audit, because the money will not be available to do a proper job, and second a frame of mind not conducive to asking the management awkward questions about their books, lest they take umbrage and withdraw the consulting contract.

In the US, the Securities and Exchange Commission has taken a very hard line on this; the British authorities have done very little, preferring to sing the praises of international competition in all professional services.

To be fair, Britain is a world leader in accounting and the US is not, so perhaps we see this as an assault on a British 'industry'. But it typifies the way three key issues are being pushed by the City professionals themselves, for their own ends, to the general approval of government.

The first is limited liability, the second is the concept of the 'multidisciplinary firm', in which lawyers, accountants and others will work under one roof, and the third is greater access to international markets. This last issue is on the agenda at the World Trade Organisation, and, while no-one expects any lawyer or accountant from anywhere to be able to set up shop in any country without a by-your-leave, much greater liberalisation is a hot topic.

An endgame is in sight: the creation of a handful of vast firms in the City, going under the banner of 'professional services', offering legal, accounting and consulting to big corporate clients, competing directly with investment banks.

It is not easy to see how this can be in the interests of anyone outside the professionals' magic circle. The potential for conflicts of interest is already evident in the marriage of accountancy and consulting. It would multiply many times over in the proposed ménage à trois with the solicitors.

Who would benefit? Not the small and medium sized business clients, and certainly not private clients. Perhaps not even the big corporations, given that their choice of advisers would gradually diminish. A mating frenzy is brewing in the professions. Someone needs to douse it with a bucket of cold water.

12
Uncertain City
Some tentative conclusions

> Over-regulation is an invisible barrier to invisible exports. We have had an open policy for 2,000 years. London is the greatest souk in Europe.
>
> **Sir Paul Newall, then Lord Mayor of London, quoted in The Guardian, 22 January 1994**

AT the start of this book, I gave one definition of the City and its financial markets: a mechanism for moving money around. On one level, that is perfectly accurate.

Yet at the end of our tour of the Square Mile we can see what an extraordinary mechanism this is, with its hundreds of thousands of employees, huge and complicated salary 'packages' and elaborate equipment. Money is, of course, an important commodity, but so is food and so is water. The movement of food and water is taken extremely seriously by differing groups of professionals, from lorry drivers to environmental health officers, but they appear to achieve it without one hundredth of the palaver that surrounds the financial markets.

I suggested also that the City could be seen as a system of prices, and of people who make prices. To make a price is to take a risk, thus the City is, in one sense, a market place in which risks are traded. Whether these risks end up with the people who took them on, or whether they are passed on to unsuspecting and undeserving third parties is a theme that has run right the way through this book, and it is one that we shall revisit before the end.

More immediately, we have to ask ourselves whether this great money transmission machine has any long-term future. There is no reason why it necessarily should have. Visit the Belgian town of Bruges, famous for providing the location for Baroness Kesteven (then plain Mrs Thatcher) to have a crack at the European Commission in September 1988. It really is a beautiful town, with wonderful buildings, good beer and a strong football team. But this was once one of the most powerful trading centres in Europe.

Not any more it isn't.

We saw earlier how London's supremacy (or, in the present time, its very powerful showing) on the international financial stage has been an extremely patchy affair over the years. It was unchallenged only from about the time of the Panama Canal shares scandal in Paris at the turn of the century until 1919, after which the role was shared on an increasingly unfair basis with an ever-growing baby brother – Wall Street.

It was in abeyance until the explosion of the 'Eurodollar' market in the 1960s, and seemed set to decline again at the start of the 1980s. Since then, it has survived – at an enormous price. There are, as we saw, no sizeable British investment banks left at all. It is possible to argue that ownership doesn't matter. Indeed, this is argued time after time.

But it throws a rather ironic light on the conventional wisdom of the mid-1980s that investment banking – that blend of market making, broking and merchant banking – would prove to be something at which Britain was uniquely skilled. Of course, individual Britons are uniquely skilled at investment banking – or at least as skilled as anybody else. Where we appear to fall down is in actually running these institutions. This in turn is ironic, because it was the 'old City' that supposedly put such a low value on 'admin', an omission that the post-1986 Square Mile would rectify.

Nevertheless, the insouciance with which 'the authorities' (the Bank of England and the Treasury) accepted the hollowing out of the Square Mile was all of a piece with Britain's long-standing commitment to what the DTI calls 'the open world system' – in other words untrammelled free trade. This is all very well, but critics suggest the City is playing cricket while everyone else is playing Gaelic football. France, which allegedly has little talent for investment banking – and, indeed, widespread official hostility to the notion of 'anglo-saxon' shareholder capitalism – maintains several powerful institutions. Germany, which until recently had practically no equity market worth speaking of, currently boasts one investment bank in the City (Dresdner) that has swallowed such once-formidable names as Kleinwort Benson and Grieveson Grant, and another, Deutsche, that owns what was for a brief period in the 1980s Britain's premier merchant bank, Morgan Grenfell, and also one of the five gold-fixing banks, Sharps Pixley.

Faced with this colonisation of the City, the powers that be have concentrated on ensuring that London remains 'the premier place to do business'. If we cannot play at the big tables ourselves, the reasoning runs, we can at least run the most attractive gaming club in the world. Anyone who lived or worked in the City from the time of the Bishopsgate bombing in April 1993 until the end of the 1990s saw this principle in action. Machine-gun toting police officers manned a ring of steel, an anti-terrorist barrier, right round the City. Well, almost right round the City. Its original makeshift checkpoints were placed on the City boundary, but by the time it was made permanent this had been moved in some hundreds of yards to focus the protection on those who really mattered – the financial institutions. The thousands of people living on the Barbican Estate (including the then Lord Chancellor Lord Mackay) were now outside the barrier.

More prosaically, there is a continuous review process under way to ensure that the legal and regulatory structure remains friendly to the City's interests. It is noteworthy that the one issue on which the 1997-2001 Labour government was prepared actually to use Britain's national veto in Brussels was withholding tax on bond trading, a measure seen as damaging to the City bond market. The London art market, meanwhile, lacked the City's clout, and its exemption from what it warned would be a very damaging Euro-tax was sacrificed as part of the process of bolstering Britain's position on the withholding tax.

Similarly, Britain has fought tooth and nail in Brussels against restrictions on takeovers while rolling over on anything on which the City is 'relaxed', which by dint of the specialised nature of most City folk (with their working hats on, at least), means most things. In August 2001, it emerged that the Belgian presidency of the European Union was proposing a massive shift of powers on company law from national to EU level. The Treasury's response when asked about this was that 'the City doesn't have a problem'. Whether the Treasury had 'a problem' seemed almost beside the point; if the City were happy, then so was the government.

This sort of stance assumes the City to be, beyond question, not only a good thing in itself, but also some sort of regulator of Britain's general economic and commercial stance. In large part, this derives from the notion that the Darwinian market in corporate control represented by the equity market – the eternal vigilance of shareholders capable of ousting poor managers at a stroke – is the key instrument for keeping the real economy in trim. This would be dubious anyway, given that France, a country where shareholders are widely regarded as mere 'punters' has a private sector that is, on some measures, 20 per cent more productive than our own.

It becomes frankly unbelievable in light of the evidence that most takeovers destroy value. Not for the previous management (although they obviously do that). Not for the workforce (although that usually happens as well). But for the shareholders themselves, the supposed kings of this particular castle.

In November 1999, accountants KPMG published a detailed report showing that fewer than one in five takeovers produces any value for shareholders in the first year following the merger. The firm played down suggestions that it had tried to pull the report at the last minute because the findings conflicted with its mission to win big-ticket merger and acquisition (M&A) advice business. The research was distinctly unsettling for everyone in M&A, within KPMG and without, particularly as it surfaced so soon after the launch of the world's two largest hostile takeover contests at that time – Vodafone's bid for Mannesmann and Pfizer's assault on fellow drugs group Warner Lambert.

It showed a remarkable lack of analysis by companies when caught up in a bout of takeover frenzy. Although their deals did little if anything for investors – the people who actually own the companies – they were clearly doing a lot for executive egos. Some 82 per cent of those surveyed by KPMG regarded the major deal in which they had been involved as a success. But KPMG found, using its own criteria, that only 17 per cent of mergers added value, while as many as 53 per cent destroyed shareholder value.

This at least blows a large hole in the argument that the City, for all its faults, actually finds the best home for capital. It clearly does not. And remember – 80 per cent of all equities are held on behalf of the population at large. How do those people fare when the experts to whom they have entrusted their life savings – and whom they have effectively bankrolled to play at the big tables – get it so wrong?

The meeting-point between the ordinary person and the City professional is, as we have seen, in the field of packaged products. And we know what happens when the professionals fail badly in their jobs – the product holder is asked to pay more for her endowment plan, or her pension, to make good the shortfall. Needless to say, there is little in the way of pursuit of the market's stars of yesteryear – those who collected huge bonuses for making these erroneous decisions. That, of course, is part of the problem. City rewards are short-term, whereas the damage that can be done emerges only later.

Throughout this book, we come again and again to the question of risk and of its proper apportioning. Too often, the City takes the rewards of risk-taking but passes the consequences to others, who are usually far less able to carry it. Passing the parcel, however, is something of a habit in the new City. In March 1994, traders in gilts marked down sharply the price of British government gilts. They were responding to official data for January that year showing a rise in the rate at which average annual earnings are growing, the first for two years. Fearing wage inflation, the traders marked down gilts in order to make it clear that higher interest rates would be needed to restore confidence in UK economic policy – usually meaning a rise in interest rates for millions of borrowers. Only later did it emerge that the rise was almost entirely due to the enormous bonuses paid in the City during the winter of 1993–94. The markets were chasing their own tail.

This sort of thing is known as 'moral hazard' and the City, in theory at least, disapproves strongly. Furthermore, it is a small example of the charge that the City not only passes risk on to those least able to handle it, but that it actively creates risk that would not otherwise have existed, solely in order to generate the rewards of handling that risk prior to packaging it for consumption by the 'great unwashed'.

This is hotly denied, of course, and the City's apologists do have a point when they insist that 'speculation' and 'gambling' are, contrary to the widespread public misperception, quite different things. A speculator makes prices in risks that would exist anyway – a failed wheat harvest; a fall in currency or share prices; a major insurance claim. Nobody is suggesting these risks would evaporate in the absence of financial speculation. But a gambler makes prices in risks that have either been deliberately created in order to provide a platform for gambling (such as the outcome of major horseraces) or are not really risks at all, such as the final score of a football match. Put simply, wheat harvests fail regardless of any financial superstructure; horses do not normally arrange themselves into a neat line and then charge off across jumps and ditches in a highly competitive manner. And even if they did – so what?

Thus the market in 'risks' has, says the City, a real economic value – and this is true as far as it goes. Yet there is another side to the story. In the summer of 2001, Marconi, formerly the electronics and defence giant GEC, was on the brink of collapse. Its strategy – selling off weapons-related and heavy engineering businesses and concentrating on telecommunications – had gone badly wrong. Many blamed chairman Sir Roger Hurn and chief executive Lord Simpson.

But some had other ideas. Writing in *The Spectator* on 15 September 2001, financial journalist Simon Nixon declared: 'Make no mistake, the City has its fingerprints all over this one.' He explained the big investment banks had strongarmed Marconi into a series of deals (lucrative for the City) that had brought it to its knees.

> The modern investment bank is a highly focused deal machine, unencumbered by any sense of fiduciary duty towards conserving the nation's assets. City banks today employ entire divisions whose sole purpose is to dream up deal ideas to sell to industry. In turn, industry has been obliged to create entire departments simply to listen to these ideas.

At about the same time, there was a vivid illustration of the City's imperviousness to criticism of its inherent conflicts of interest. According to the *Financial Times,* the investment banking arm of HSBC announced on 2 September 2001 it was 'radically restructuring its investment research in a sign that banks are responding to criticism of the quality of equity analysis'. The report added:

> The bank's analysts will be required to publish as many 'sell' recommendations on stocks as 'buys' and HSBC will invest its own money in its best research ideas. The move is in response to criticism that investment banks' analysts are too positive about companies in the hope of generating lucrative corporate finance work.

So far, so good. But elsewhere in the paper, City cynics were reported as scoffing at HSBC's high moral tone, pointing out the bank was not a big player in investment banking, and could thus afford to resist a temptation that had, in truth, never been very great. No serious outfit, it seemed, could afford these sort of scruples. In this reading, HSBC's stance was akin to a second division football club renouncing the evils of multi-million pound player-transfer deals.

The cynics, of course, merely confirmed both their own dishonesty and that of the notion that most City 'analysis' is anything other than corporate advertising designed to help along the Square Mile's time-honoured function of passing risk from the insiders (who have already taken their profits) to outsiders (who will face any losses). Furthermore, the cynics showed that elements in the City can no longer be bothered even to conceal this fact.

It is certainly arguable that the City is spawning a range of products – chiefly but not exclusively derivatives – that generate risk which would otherwise not have existed. There are, for example, derivative products allegedly designed to 'hedge' against liabilities to which no-one could possibly be exposed. Frank Partnoy, whom we met earlier, gives the example of one product relating to the future level of the London Inter-Bank Offered Rate *cubed*. Such products have lost contact entirely with the real economy. They have been designed with one end in mind – to earn large fees for their inventors, who then pass them on to unwitting pension funds or other innocents abroad. The risks against which they supposedly hedge do not exist – it is the product itself that is the sole risk.

Even with regard to more respectable investments, such as shares or bonds, the City seems to have an unnerving habit of being a long way from the scene when, in Partnoy's graphic phrase, the client gets 'blown up'. In some cases, of course, the City institutions missed out on the last ten or twenty per cent rise in the value of a particular security, because that security had been sold on to the general investor. But that is part and parcel of the Square Mile's essentially risk-averse *modus operandi*. Yes, you may miss out on some profit, but you are also cutting your risks. Let someone else have that last giddy surge in a share price or an emerging-market fund; the chances are they will be holding the baby when the iron law of Q – which we looked at earlier – reasserts itself and the aforementioned 'security' crashes back to earth.

This helps to explain why, despite the unimpeachable proposition that all non-government assets are 'ultimately' owned by either private individuals or charitable trusts, the majority of British people have little or no net worth. Of course it could be that the Royal Society for the Prevention of Cruelty to Animals, Hertford College, Oxford, the Archdiocese of Westminster and the rest of the charities have pulled off an enormous sting and are depriving the public of their rightful property. And there is no doubt that many of these charities are enormously wealthy; Britain's richest, the Wellcome Trust, is estimated to be worth £15 billion. But the more likely explanation – given that 80 per cent of one asset-base alone, the value of the London stock market, is held by institutions, largely acting as the agents of ordinary people – is that the little word 'ultimately' means a great deal: those assets often seem (strangely enough) to be past their best by the time they are passed on to their 'ultimate' owners.

This has a secondary side-effect, in that it is very difficult for ordinary people, in particular those saving for a pension, to protect the value of their savings *without* in some way speculating on markets that are – intentionally or not – loaded against them. Right up until the eve of the terrorist outrages in New York and Washington on 11 September 2001, any client of a British financial adviser was urged into the stock market, regardless of the fact the markets had been heading down for sixteen months before the terrorists struck (with little sign of recovery) – and regardless, in some cases, of the fact that the client concerned had specifically asked for advice on any investment forum other than the stock market.

The advisers were not (in the vast majority of cases) dishonest. Their advice reflected the simple fact that it is difficult even to protect the purchasing power of private savings, let alone to share in the general rise in national prosperity, without taking the sort of risks for which most people have little training.

To which the City may well reply – exactly. No-one has devised a better way than the present method by which the ordinary citizen can support industry through his savings and thus have a stake in the ups and downs of the economy as a whole.

This is fair as far as it goes. Through 1999 and early 2000, when the stock market was widely seen as grotesquely overvalued, any client of a British financial adviser was urged to buy shares. Through the remainder of 2000 and the first nine months of 2001, when the market gyrated widly, the recommendation stood – regardless, in some cases, of the fact that the client concerned had specifically asked for advice on any investment forum other than the stock market. But by the middle of 2001 – with some victims of the mis-selling of private pensions still awaiting restitution; with holders of endowment mortgages being asked to pay more than they had ever imagined; with major company pension schemes running out of cash, and with those who had been urged into the stock market facing horrendous losses – the question most likely to be asked is whether the ordinary investor is taking a disproportionately small share of the ups and a correspondingly large share of the downs.

This, perhaps, is the City's Achilles' heel, rather than competition from New York, or the arrival of the euro, or the 'red tape' in which the present British government is accused of strangling the Square Mile's creativity. Lack of public support – or even public hostility – is a far graver threat than any of the above. Wall Street is a giant younger brother with whom the City has learned to live for a century or more. Britain dominated world dollar trading without ever 'joining the dollar', and there is no reason it could not pull off the same trick with the euro. And a sceptic may conclude that – as shown by the quotation that opens this chapter – since the City has traditionally not been closely regulated, has no desire to be closely regulated and will do its best never to be closely regulated – a bracing dose of red tape may be just what it needs.

But for all its sense of being 'a place apart', the City isn't. The Square Mile is one London borough among many, a small corner of a country with 94,549 square miles. Cut the legal, fiscal, economic and other supports with which the British people, through their elected representatives, choose to maintain 'London's position as an international financial centre', and this glittering structure would sag and, eventually, fold up.

Naturally, the City believes this to be unthinkable. But it ought to remember that not so long ago the trade unions held a secure place in the affections of millions as champions of the underdog and responsible social partners. Well into the 1970s, they featured in children's history books alongside women's suffrage and universal education as unquestionably good things in their own right. Within a decade, the public and their representatives had tired of the unions' antics, and they were left beached on the shore as the tide of support ebbed away.

Nothing is certain, of course. The City may change some of its ways and become an uncontroversial national asset. Or it could be that the City will survive without ever resolving the edgy relationship with the rest of the country that first surfaced in the years after the Norman Conquest.

Or perhaps it will expire through factors entirely outside its control – not public hostlity, nor competition, nor any other easily explicable reason.

Perhaps our final (quite literal) port of call ought to be Foynes on the River Shannon in western Ireland. This is a bustling cargo terminal combined with a charming town set a short drive from beautiful scenery. But, between the wars, Foynes was something more – it was the pivot point of international air travel. More than that, it was thought to be the inevitable centre of world aviation. Visit the air musuem and see the huge map, with its routes stretching west to the United States, and east through Europe to India, China and beyond. As with London today, it prided itself on being in the middle of all times zones. Nobody could argue with geography; Foynes was the hub of the global air-travel industry.

What went wrong? In the short term, flying boats 'went wrong' in that the civil jet airliners of the post-war period eliminated the 'clippers' upon which Foynes had built its business. Even so, there is a modern airport, Shannon, not far from Foynes. By rights, surely, this airport ought to have picked up the baton and become the centre of world aviation? It did not, of course. Important though it is to Ireland's west coast, Shannon does not dominate international air travel. It has its hands full trying to dominate Irish air travel.

The reasons for this rapid decline and fall are many, various and, in some cases, unfathomable. Other airports were quicker off the mark; international agreements favoured rivals; technology made possible direct flights from Dublin and London to America.

And so on.

Foynes today is an object lesson in caution against collective arrogance and complacency in any self-appointed 'world centre'. Other than the excellent museum, the defunct flying-boat base's one legacy is the 'Irish coffee', the whiskey-fuelled, sugar-stiff hot drink invented by Foynes bartender Joe Sherridan to welcome shivering passengers and now swigged enthusiastically in suburban grill rooms across Europe and America as a post-prandial treat by diners who have not a clue as to its origins.

Would it matter were the City to go the same way?

On balance, it would. In the short term, there is no functioning alternative in a market economy to the anglo-saxon model of capital markets. Well into the 1990s, the German and Japanese systems of direct investment in industry by long-term holders – chiefly banks – was widely touted as superior to the City 'casino'. That alternative is, at the time of writing, under a cloud, thanks to the serious problems of the Japanese economy and the disappointing German record of the past ten years.

But clouds can lift as quickly as they can descend. Should an alternative free-market model reassert itself, the currently-dormant debate over the City will revive.

In the longer term, too, there is one inescapable reason to wish the Square Mile no ill. For as long as the City remains a system of prices, it will have value. The ability to make a price, however irksome this duty may be to firms who would prefer to charge fat fees, gives the City its worth within the national and international economy, whatever its many shortcomings.

For prices, as John Maynard Keynes once said – in a passionate attack on the notion of wartime rationing – are special. Indeed, as he elaborated: 'They are the essential element of freedom in the system'.

Glossary

ADVISERS: Catch-all phrase for the shoal of professionals surrounding a company whose shares are listed (or are about to be listed) on an exchange. Includes investment bankers, auditors, solicitors and brokers.

AIM: Alternative Investment Market. Latest in a number of 'second divisions' of the Stock Exchange designed to allow smaller companies to raise capital and investors to trade shares in those companies. Predecessors included the Unlisted Securities Market and the Third Market.

ASSURANCE: Financial instrument offering security once an event that *will* happen (ageing or death) takes place. Effectively a long-term savings plan. See Insurance.

AUTHORITIES, THE: 1980s short-hand for the Treasury and the Bank of England. Out of fashion since the Bank was given control of interest rates in 1997.

BALANCE OF PAYMENTS: Extent to which Britain is earning a surplus or deficit on its trade with the rest of the world. Divided into current account (earnings on goods, services and investment income) and the capital account (which reflects the balance of lending or borrowing with overseas creditors or debtors). If the current account is in deficit, the capital account must necessarily be in surplus by an equal and opposite amount, as precisely that amount must have flowed into the country to pay for the excess imports.

BANCASSURANCE: Raffishly continental-sounding term for the rather more prosaic process whereby banks have expanded into the sale of packaged investment products (unit trusts, pensions and so forth) alongside their traditional business of taking deposits and making loans.

BASE RATE: Still the preferred term for what the Bank of England now calls its 'repo' (or repurchase) rate. This is the heartbeat of the City – the rate at which the Bank will effectively bail out the whole system. Previously known as Minimum Lending Rate or Bank Rate.

BID: The price at which a City institution is prepared to buy a security (see Offer).

BILATERAL: One to one financial transactions where both parties are known to each other. Opposite of multilateral trading, the anonymous action of an exchange-based dealing system.

BOND: Either: (a) a security with, usually, a fixed rate of interest and fixed date for the repayment of the capital issued by a company or other borrower; or (b) an IOU issued by a national or municipal government, again usually with a fixed rate of interest and fixed repayment date. In Britain, corporate bonds are known as loan stock and government bonds are known as gilts.

BROKER: A somewhat imprecise term in the stock market these days. Pre-1986, a broker was a member of the Stock Exchange entitled to transact share deals on behalf of clients. Today, it still covers that basic function and is applied to smaller firms who specialise in 'retail' (i.e. individual) clients. It has a second meaning with regard to listed companies (see Advisers). The term 'broker' is used to denote the firm charged with liaising between the company and its shareholders, while 'adviser' refers to the firm charged with liaising between the company and the exchange and other regulatory bodies. Both roles can be performed by the same firm. In the Lloyd's market, 'broker' remains a clearly defined role, that of acting for clients in seeking to place their risks with underwriters. In the world of personal finance, 'broker' is a description used by advisers and salesmen pushing packaged investment products; in this usage, it has no real meaning at all.

CALL OPTION: The right to buy a security at a given date (see Put Option).

CERTIFICATE OF DEPOSIT (CD): Proof of a deposit lodged with a bank that can be traded on the Money Market (see below).

COMMODITY: Any physical item that can be lumped into standardised lots and traded. So-called 'soft' commodities are agricultural products such as cocoa, coffee, wheat, potatoes and pork bellies. Then there are base metals (tin, zinc, copper and similar) and precious metals, such as gold and silver. Diamonds cannot be traded as a commodity because no two stones are alike.

CONVERTIBLE: Phrase attached to both Bonds and Preference Shares (see below) that can be converted, at a future date, into Ordinary Shares (see below).

DEBT MANAGEMENT OFFICE (DMO): Independent Treasury agency that overseas the issue of gilt-edged stock.

DEPOSIT: Money, usually in a bank, that the depositor can expect to get back.

DERIVATIVES: Investment vehicles 'derived' from underlying securities or assets (i.e. shares, bonds, currencies, commodities).

There are two types of derivatives: futures (or 'forwards', if they are traded off an exchange) and options. A Future is an agreement to buy or sell the underlying security at a given price in the future; an Option second is the right to do so. Swaps (see below) are often classed as derivatives, although this is strictly-speaking not the case.

EURODOLLAR / EUROBOND: Nothing to do with the single currency, this is a dated term for currency of any denomination held outside its country of issue (Eurodollar) and then bundled up into loans (Eurobonds) that are made to borrowers also unconnected with the country of issue. The terms are still widely used, although in an era of free capital movement they have little use any more.

FINANCIAL SERVICES AUTHORITY: Chief regulator for all banking, investment and exchange-based activities in the United Kingdom. Has powers of both civil and criminal pursuit against those breaking the rules.

FLOTATION: The process of selling a company's shares on a stock market for the first time. In America, this is known as the Initial Public Offering (IPO).

FORWARDS: See Derivatives.

FUTURES: See Derivatives.

GILTS: British government securities.

HEDGE FUND: Misleadingly-named vehicle, usually based in an offshore tax haven, through which wealthy individuals put up the money with which investment 'gurus' take huge risks in world financial markets.

IPE: International Petroleum Exchange. Trades largely in Brent crude oil.

INSTITUTIONS, THE: Shorthand term for the banks, life assurance companies and pension funds that control huge chunks of the total of the quoted shares on the stock market.

INSURANCE: Financial instrument offering financial security in the event of something that *may* happen actually taking place.

INVESTMENT: Money that the investor may (or may not) get back. See Deposit.

LIBOR: London Inter-Bank Offered Rate. Bedrock interest rate of a number of international currencies calculated in London. Used in a large number of international contracts as an impartial reference point.

LIFFE: London International Financial Futures and Options Market. Trades both financial derivatives and commodities. Pronounced 'Lifer' or 'Life'.

LONDON GOLD FIXING: Twice daily estimate of the balancing price of supply and demand in world bullion markets. Like Libor, it is widely used in contracts.

MONEY MARKET: Bilateral (see above) and informal market, dominated by the banks, in which short-term interest-bearing instruments, usually, maturing in less than twelve months, are traded.

OFFER: The price at which a City institution is prepared to sell a security (see BID).

ORDINARY SHARES: The basic share in a company, known as common stock in the United States. See Preference Shares.

PREFERENCE SHARES: Also known as A-shares, these are a

hybrid of shares and bonds in that their holders rank ahead of ordinary shareholders in the queue for dividends but are not entitled to a vote in the affairs of the company.

PUT OPTION: The right to sell a security at a pre-determined date (see Call Option).

SECURITIES: Umbrella term for most types of investment instruments, including shares and bonds. Notoriously, not very secure.

SETS: Stock Exchange Electronic Trading Service. Computerised order-book clearing system through which the top 200 shares in London are traded.

SWAP: An agreement between two parties to exchange payments due to them, usually interest payments.

UNDERWRITER (1): In the Lloyd's market, the specialist who accepts or rejects risks offered by Brokers (see above) on behalf of clients. Term used more widely to describe the insurance business as a whole.

UNDERWRITER (2): An institution, usually an investment bank, that takes a fee for offering to act as buyer of last resort for shares offered by a company should investors snub them.

WARRANT: Tradeable instrument giving the holder the right to buy a security, traditionally a share, at a given date.

INDEX